THE BOOKMAKER

THE BO

OKMAKER

A MEMOIR OF MONEY, LUCK, AND FAMILY FROM THE UTOPIAN OUTSKIRTS OF NEW YORK CITY

MICHAEL J. AGOVINO

HARPER

An Imprint of HarperCollins Publishers
www.harpercollins.com

This is a work of nonfiction. My mother and father told me stories of their lives and neighborhoods over and over while I was growing up. In recent years, I had them recount these stories, as best they could, in taped interviews, and I have reproduced them as accurately as possible. Names of some individuals have been changed in order to respect their privacy. A scene in the chapter titled "Co-op City, 1988 (Right Downstairs)," was re-created using sworn testimony from eyewitnesses in court records and transcripts obtained from the Bronx County Courthouse.

HarperCollins books may be purchased for educational, business, or sales promotional use. For information, please write: Special Markets Department, HarperCollins Publishers, 10 East 53rd Street, New York, NY 10022.

FIRST EDITION

Designed by Emily Cavett Taff

Library of Congress Cataloging-in-Publication Data is available upon request.

ISBN : 978-0-06-115139-2

08 09 10 11 12 OV/RRD 10 9 8 7 6 5 4 3 2 1

For my father and mother

And why should gambling be worse than any other means of making money—for instance, commerce? It is true that only one out of a hundred wins, but what is that to me?

—Fyodor Dostoyevsky

CONTENTS

PROLOGUE

Yes, at moments like that one forgets all one's former failures!
Why, I had gained this by risking more than life itself, I dared to
risk it, and—there I was again, a man among men.

—Fyodor Dostoyevsky

THE BRONX, 1984

It was Super Bowl Sunday, the only day of the year my mother served dinner in front of the television set. She knew that my father had a vested financial interest in the game and that I was a boy who deeply cared about sports. So she conceded, as she had for many years now: dinner in the living room with the Sony Trinitron. I began to suspect she enjoyed it.

The menu was a concession, too, solely for me this time. Gone was our usual midwinter southern Italian Sunday feast: a homemade ragu over rigatoni, with braciola, sausage, polpette, broccoli rabe on the side or roasted peppers, and a carafe of Valpolicella. No, on this day, my mother, desperate to put meat on my little bones, served up my favorite, determinedly un-Italian: roast beef, roasted potatoes, Boston lettuce, and mountains of green beans sautéed with garlic and olive oil.

My older sister refused to take part. She never would. She always hated two things—red meat and sports. Above all, she hated my father's gambling, the ebb and flow of anxiety that came with it, the screaming matches it provoked between my parents, the dark silences after a bad day at "the office," the absurdity of risking our future on Tampa Bay minus the three and a half or TCU or some horse, maybe Foolish Pleasure.

For my father, gambling and bookmaking were a second job, his clandestine second life. He had been gambling in some form or other since FDR's second term. By the 1980s, it had become his main source of income, his main source of hope and of despair.

On that Super Bowl Sunday in 1984, in our Bronx apartment twenty-two stories above the spindly, *Waiting for Godot* tree sticks, the three of us—my parents and I—watched the Washington Redskins play the Los Angeles Raiders. The Redskins were the defending title-holders and a three-point favorite. My father had wagered heavily on the Raiders. How heavily, I do not know; I knew not to ask. It was my father's business.

Besides the Yankees—the Yankees made him an American, he told me this, more than being born in East Harlem did—he never had favorite teams. Gamblers and bookmakers can't get attached, can't afford to, but he liked the Raiders. Kenny Stabler might have started it; my father had a thing for lefties. And the Raiders were always the bad guys. That helped.

Washington had the self-aggrandizing quarterback Joe Theismann and the impudent receiving corps known as the Smurfs. The Raiders had the stoic Tom Flores and the unfashionable Jim Plunkett—two scions of industrious Chicano laborers who came up the hard way.

In the third quarter, when the game was still a game, there was a play—a very famous play. You remember. Marcus Allen, bright, young stealthy, took a handoff from Plunkett. He ran to the left side of the line of scrimmage, saw it was clogged, spun 180 degrees to the right, got a feeble but well-intentioned block from Plunkett, and turned upfield. For a few interminable seconds, we didn't talk, we didn't chew, we didn't breathe. Our eyes widened, and we watched Marcus Allen run. He kept on running, a silver-and-black streak, away from the pack for seventy-something yards and a touchdown. Roasted potatoes, sautéed green beans, and shouts of joy flew into the air. My sister, eavesdropping, came out of her room, relieved. It was now apparent that the Raiders would win. Her perpetually in-arrears tuition at Clark University would be paid. Outside, a horn honked, someone howled from a windswept terrace. The howl echoed. The Bronx resonated, at least this multiracial, multiethnic, increasingly tensioned corner of the Bronx, an eyesore of gray schematic towers.

It was called Co-op City. I heard it called Nigger City, Shvartze City, Jew Town, Throw-up City, depending.

It was a place no one wanted to be, not anymore. The good intentions covered in graffiti, the rest in puddles of urine in our elevators. A socialist experiment in how we would live, in how we would interact, improve, a product of the Great Society, the biggest housing cooperative in America, some said the world, and maybe it was, brought to you by the unholy troika of Governor Nelson Rockefeller; big labor, communists among them; and Robert Moses, his last big mistake. Thirty-five skyscrapers, soaring, identical, some with views of the World Trade Center, the city's other bookend.

Up here, you could see everything, hear anything, as if you were down there on the street. Sound carried. Especially from boom boxes: At one time it was Stevie Wonder, Earth, Wind & Fire, the O'Jays; later, B.T. Express, the Brothers Johnson; and now Afrika Bambaataa and Mellie Mel.

Our apartment was one of 15,382 units; we were four of sixty thousand people, none of whom were Rockefellers. This was Le Corbusier's vision, tower in the park, put into practice before our eyes, us in the midst of its maquette. Open space, with plenty of green, for children to play, families to blossom. This was rhetoric come to life.

It was front-page news in *The New York Times*, above the fold, in November 1968, and it continued, on and on inside: "Co-op City, a Vast Housing Project Rising in the Northeast Bronx, Is Dedicated." Rockefeller said this: "I think we are on the threshold of a new era in coping with our great urban problems. Today we dedicate a symbol to that era." Co-op City was "a spectacular and heartwarming answer to the problems of American cities." *Newsweek* called it a "Kibbutz in the Bronx." *Time* said it was "relentlessly ugly."

Einstein Loop, Carver Loop, Dreiser Loop, Debs Place, De Kruif Place, Defoe Place, it all looked the same. Was this the ugliest place in America? Or just the weirdest. Or was it ahead of its time, so far ahead, so way, way ahead, that it was backward? It was the biggest; that we knew. That they kept telling us.

"How did we end up here?" my mother said again and again. How did we end up here?

Half of the Bronx was rubble; from that, we were sequestered but we were also sequestered, somehow, from the upper reaches of New York City. We were still the Bronx, we were reminded, in abrupt and subtle ways. But how to get out, how to become more?

The object was to get out of this place. You wouldn't live with urine puddles in your elevators. So why us? Most of our friends, the young families that made it go, that made it healthy and optimistic, had left. Now it was people with nowhere to go. And old people, waiting to die.

And here we were, sixteen years later, tied to this place, a family matured, in our sanctuary on the twenty-second floor, amid the wind, the unrelenting wind, tonight an arctic one, watching a game, a man run, watching a man we never met, save us, to give us opportunity, a way out, a chance, at least, for another experience, as other athletes, great and insignificant, had before. If they and their actions, or nonactions, on the field didn't get us to Westchester, the promised land just north, they got us to Italy, Iberia, Morocco, Britain, the Netherlands, Mexico, the Caribbean, to the Prado, the Tate, the Rijksmuseum, the Louvre. Maybe it wasn't as grand a gesture as Marcus Allen's just now, maybe it was a broken-bat, opposite-field single by Doug Flynn in the bottom of the ninth, just out of the second baseman's reach, or a Sly Williams put-back, late in the fourth, David Overstreet going the distance out of the wishbone on a Saturday afternoon, Rick Upchurch bringing one back at Mile High, during the four o'clock game, that must be Curt Goudy's voice, followed by *Mutual of Omaha's Wild Kingdom*. Whatever it was.

That night, for us, Marcus Allen saved the world. The absurdity.

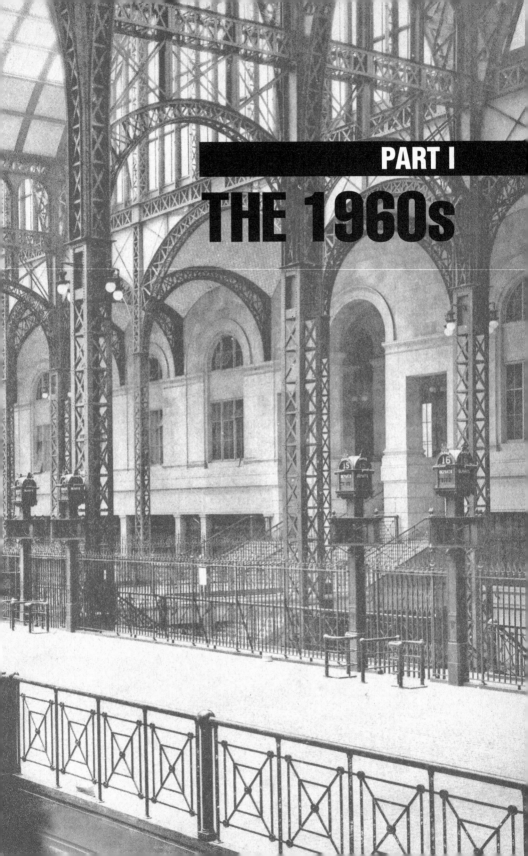

PART I
THE 1960s

I have stood by the fundamental principles which I have always advocated, I have not trimmed. I have not retreated, I do not apologize, and I am not compromising.

—Vito Marcantonio, U.S. congressman, American Labor Party

WASHINGTON, D.C., 1960

He said this: "Holy Christ."

Then this: "It can't be, no. What are the chances?"

He looked again at the number, the three simple digits: *231, if memory serves.*

It was hidden deep in the sports section, in the agate type of the horse-racing results, but you knew where to find it, everyone did. The last three digits to the left of the decibel point of the handle, the race-track's total earnings. It was known as the Brooklyn Number, not to be confused with the New York Number, which, on the street, they called "the Old Way" or "the 3–5–7."

This was illegal but everyone played—street guys, old ladies, working stiffs, cops, nuns. The illegal number was an institution, especially here, in East Harlem. The racket guys ran it; the people, Italians, blacks, Puerto Ricans, played it. *Not the Irish, for some reason, or the Jews—they were gambling crazy, but not for numbers.*

If you won, you were paid, fair and square, $500 to the dollar for a straight bet, $250 for a boxed combination. Each pocket of a neighborhood would have its own number runner. You knew where to find him. If you were a regular, he knew your number by heart. Nice touch.

One more time he looked. It was still there, 231, glaring at him in eight-point type. "Oh, Madon'," he said this time in East Harlem, Neapolitan dialect.

He wasn't a number runner, but when you're from 115th Street—*a hun' fifteenth*—and Second Avenue, you know someone who knows someone who knows a racket guy. That's just how it is. Say the brother-in-law of your second cousin is made. Say you grew up with a kid, a nice kid, a bright kid, pretty good athlete—let's call him Patty or Fish—who made a decision to go a certain way in life, a different way. You don't make moral judgments—that's not your job. They do what they do, you do what you do. *Mind your business.*

Live in East Harlem, things overlap, and you may be called upon—familiar face that you are, no stool pigeon you—to do someone a favor. And so he was asked, by this one guy—*can't even remember his name after all these years, just that goddamn number.* "Ay, Hugo, would you do me a favor," the guy said, didn't ask. "Put in this number for me, will ya: 231, twelve dollars straight."

Hugo says, "Yeah, all right," reluctantly. He's an agreeable guy and takes the twelve dollars. He's thirty-three, has a job, single, without commitments, outgoing, always at the Stadium or the Garden, laying a few bucks, more than a few, on Whitey Ford or some college basketball game. So the day gets away from him. Hugo doesn't see the number runner as he normally would; he doesn't play the number. He forgets. An honest mistake.

But this guy—let's call him just that for now "This Guy," as memory is fickle and selective, and fades—*he's a little smarter than a high-grade moron*, and he knows bad people. Who else plays a number for twelve dollars straight? Who would have such brass ones?

Hugo was in hot water now, six thousand dollars' worth, enough to be made an example of—with one in the back of the head, nice guy, nice family or not, honest mistake maybe. He sought immediate counsel from Tommy, his *cump*—dialect for *compare*, friend, comrade, you know it as *goomba*—who used to work for a number bank himself, one of the bigger ones, and his best friend Bence, irascible, some thought insane, but fiercely loyal. Tommy knew the street and happened to be deft with numbers. He told Hugo—who was also Ugo, Ugolino, Hugh, Hughie, Vincent, from his middle name, Vinny, Vin, or Aggie, from his last name, depending on who was talking, family or friend or foe or something in between, their mood, if they were Italian, Irish, Jewish, black, Puerto Rican, and what the situation was, the provenance being Hugo Vincent—"to invoke." Invoke, meaning mention the name of a made guy. No, better still, physically approach the made guy, explain the situation, say it was an honest mistake, which it was, and This Guy and his people can't touch you. If your life is at risk, now it would be saved.

This shouldn't be a problem. Hugo knows Louie a little bit—let's call him Louie I—and he's a higher-up in Fat Tony's crew. But Louie I is out of town, in Vegas on business. *He was good friends with Sinatra, you know.*

No problem, not a problem, there's always Patty, a close associate to Louie I, and an even closer connection to Hugo. They grew up together and were friends. He was an ex-Marine, Patty, in World War II, blond curly hair when he was young, six feet tall. *How he goes and ends up in this kind of life, I'll never know. You never ask.* But Patty is in jail, doing a short stint—railroaded, of course. This leaves only Joey, Patty's kid brother. Hugo and Joey never got along. Hugo would hate to ask him for a favor, but this was life or death, seriously. So he found Joey and explained. Joey put the palm of his left hand on his forehead, like this: *Madon'.* He had the ribbons at the various number banks checked. No, 231 wasn't played; yes, it was an honest mistake. If he found the number was played, and Hugo was out to keep the money himself, Joey wouldn't have been able to help.

Joey reaches out to This Guy and his people—turns out This Guy's cousin was made—and told them he could vouch for Hugo, that it was a mistake, that the debt would be paid, on the installment plan. If Hugo were dealing with one of the Brooklyn crews, the Sicilians, who knows? *They were real primitive, these Brooklyn Sicilians, believe me when I tell you.*

A deal was brokered. A portion of the winning number was paid up front by Joey and associates, and Hugo would go to a gas station on 108th and First Avenue every other week and pay two hundred dollars to This Guy's people, who would wait there in a car. But Hugo already owed money, to various shylocks, before this mess. He lost badly on the NIT when Lenny Wilkens got hot, then Jerry West for West

Virginia. Now this. The debt was mounting from all directions. He'd already withdrawn the three thousand in his pension fund he'd built up the last ten years. Whatever he could muster up now would have to go to Joey and This Guy.

Bence was always in the street, and as the weeks and months passed he kept hearing things, that the other shylocks wanted their money, and they wanted it now. They didn't care about any deal struck with Joey; they weren't under Joey's jurisdiction. And 231, This Guy? That had nothing to do with them.

"You should lay low for a while," Bence said. Tony, another good friend, told him the same thing, but more directly. "Get out of town, Hugo." Tony wouldn't exaggerate; he was levelheaded, like Tommy, the only one of his friends who went to college, St. Francis. This had to have been serious. So Hugo left. Left his beloved New York, his neighborhood, the people he was from, his job, his real job, everything else, to go to Washington, maybe to save his life, maybe to begin again.

This was before Hugo—Ugo, Ugolino, Hugh, Hughie, Vincent, Vinny, Vin, Aggie—became my father.

Hugo went to his father, expecting a lecture. His father, Michele, was a small, delicate man, stern, even aloof, born the century before, 1889, in Italy's deep south. He didn't speak English, or didn't let on that he did. He was clean, didn't know the ways of the street or of the new world. He worked at the newspaper, first *Corriere della Sera* before it folded then *Il Progresso*, as a linotypist, and did well, provided. In his spare hours, he played a cherrywood clarinet, the same one he played in the Italian Army band from 1909 to 1920. He served in Venice and played that cherrywood clarinet in the Piazza San Marco. He was from a town between Naples, Salerno, and Avellino, a town in the hills, Sarno, and went back home to find a life partner. This would be Eleanora. They honeymooned in Naples.

In Sarno, they manufactured Irish linen, the Irish did, at the turn of the century, but this eventually withered. Now there was no work in southern Italy. The south was bleeding population, from Sicily, Campania, Calabria, Basilicata, Puglia, Molise, to new worlds, Australia, New Zealand, England, Wales, Germany, Switzerland, Uruguay, Venezuela, Argentina, Brazil, Chile, Canada, L'America. Michele would be one of the millions to emigrate. First to Philadelphia for six months, then to New York City, Manhattan, East Harlem, an Italian ghetto, presided over, nurtured, from 116th Street by Vito Marcantonio, the congressman who began as a Republican, gravitated leftward, and ended in the American Labor Party. Even Hugo's junior high school was named Galvani, after the Italian scientist. *You've heard of Galvani? When they use the term* galvanized steel, *it's from his name.*

His father's job at the paper was a good one, with Local 6, the Big 6 union. Even during the Depression, with seven children—three boys, four girls—he quietly provided. When eighteen, twenty relatives gathered for the holidays, he provided. At the beginning of every school year, Hugo's mother would take him to a row of merchants on *a-hun-twenty-first* to the Venetian Jew to buy him and his siblings new underwear and clothes. The Venetian Jew had been a Fascist, *a lot of the Italian Jews were Fascists, believe it or not, we're talkin' the '20s and '30s, until '38*, and was a friend of Hugo's father. They shared Venice.

Michele wasn't an American father; he didn't know these American things, like the two greatest of all, jazz and baseball. The Boys' Club helped raise Hugo, then assimilated him, made him American, taught him things, the pastime, took him to Yankee Stadium for the first time. They had all sorts of sports teams, *you should have seen the athletes.* Hugo was on the boxing team, was pretty good, great left jab, moved well laterally, could take a punch, but couldn't hit. He won his share of fights, though—on points. He was on a couple of the basketball teams, wasn't as good there, but was scrappy on D, made the extra pass, had an acceptable set shot from fifteen feet, would stand there and take the charge. Then he was on the debate team. There he excelled.

Hugo didn't know poverty like the other kids in the 1930s. His father found a way, and for that Hugo was in awe. He only resented Pop for dressing him in short pants, like a little preppy, until he was eight or nine. Among other neighborhood kids, *paisans* or not, this was something to ridicule, and Hugo was pressed to defend himself. He was the fourth child of seven, the only one coming home with stitches or a black eye. The follow-through of a stickball bat to the face, a collision with the makeshift foul pole. His poor mother. There was an emergency room on St. Nicholas and *a hun' twenty-fourth*. He was there six times in eight years. She said in dialect, *"Che succé mo?"*—what happened now? He laughed. Eventually, his mother laughed. *This crazy kid.*

The lecture from his father never came. Not much was exchanged. Disappointment? You can say. Embarrassment? Maybe. Some people are hard to read. But your son is your son. "Go to Washington, to your sister," he told Ugo. He took his son to Pennsylvania Station, and amid its fading Beaux-Arts grandeur, they kissed on the cheek and embraced.

He didn't do much in Washington, Hugo. This was the fall of 1960, an election year, the choices being the status quo with a sinister lean or a youthful leap forward. He didn't like the communist hunter, a man who made others to turn stool pigeon. Hugo was a product of whence he came, a place he loved and even feared, which is why he was here, after all. He despised coercion, bullies, stool pigeons. And he was from the district, for all its bad guys, of Marcantonio, a man who believed in equality, whatever the cost to the state. Marc—they called him Marc on First Avenue—was an orator, and Hugo liked words, and the origin of words, whether in the colors of Neapolitan dialect or in English, especially English now. He loved language, its power, its music, its phrasing. Marc made people like us look good. *But you saw what they did to Marc in Washington.* Nixon himself, *the S.O.B.*, had linked his Democratic opponent for Senate to Marcantonio ten years before. And it worked. Nixon won 59 percent of the vote. Now, there was a good new word for a second-generation Italian to learn: pariah.

So Hugo may not vote for this sneaking bully, but he didn't like the young prince either. Royalty? What royalty? His father was a bootlegger, *who we kiddin'*? Okay, everyone knew that. But he was bankrolling number rackets. The story was told over and over in the neighborhood. It was 1950 or maybe '49, a U.S. warship in Philadelphia harbor, an accident of some kind. It made the front page of the *Daily News*, a number was involved, maybe on the hull of the ship, a three-digit number. Number players are always looking for omens. They have their "dream books" to translate images or symbols into digits. But here was a number, a neat three-digit number, plain and simple for everyone to see, no interpretation necessary. So everyone played it. *And would you believe, the number comes out.* The number banks didn't have enough cash on hand to pay out. Racket or not, you have to pay right away; it's still a business. Frank Costello, the don himself, calls Joe Kennedy, who sends one of his people, by limo, to Rao's, the restaurant, with the cash. *You thought I was making it up, but I read it somewhere, once.*

And his son is running for president? *And we get all the flack?* Hugo wasn't going to take part. He had more on his mind, matters of the personal. How did I wind up here, in exile? What am I going to do with my life? What went wrong? He spent much of the time alone, sometimes at the Lincoln Memorial. Can you gain wisdom through osmosis, he wondered. He liked to read about great men, Greek philosophers, Roman emperors, Russian novelists. There was no one greater than Lincoln. He memorized the Gettysburg Address, succinct, plainspoken, at Stuyvesant High School.

Yeah, he went to Stuyvesant, forgot to say, the best public high school in the city, like his brother before him. You had to take a test to get in. *I got a high mark, believe it or not.* His other friends—Gussy, Nick-a-Nick, Bence—they all went to the local high school, Ben Franklin, well known for basketball, not academics. If you went to Stuyvesant, the few who did from East Harlem, you were a fair-haired boy, even if you didn't have fair hair and never would and, once in certain precincts in this city, would be reminded of that.

At the Boys' Club, he learned baseball; at Stuyvesant he learned

Lincoln—Lincoln as preserver, Lincoln as visionary. If there was never a Lincoln, would his parents still have come to the New-ish World fifty years later? Would they still have had a second chance? Lincoln was what made America great, Hugo thought, not this witch-hunter or rich kid. Besides, they both hated Italians. *You mean, Kennedy and those brothers of his, they weren't calling us dago-guinea bastards*, Harvard or no Harvard? And you know Nixon couldn't stand us, *it's on one of those audiotapes*.

He looked for work in D.C. Hugo was never one to sit still, but he didn't find anything. Opportunity was limited. They didn't know from Stuyvesant down there. Why should they? It was still only high school. He thought about going to Colgate after the war. He swears he got in—swears—but he didn't go. He never came up with a good story, or lie, for not going, only this: *What are you gonna do?*, meaning umbilical attachment? Fear? The potential to fail? Then why not Fordham? *Good school that Fordham*. He always thought highly of the Jesuits, it was close, it would add another dimension, a bit more finesse, something to build on. Why not? There was never a good reason.

In Washington, *down Washington*, Hugo interviewed for two, three, four jobs, through placement offices—what you'd expect without connections, leads, anything. One recruiter sent him to a collection agency, unaware of the irony. *I'm gonna holler at a guy because he can't pay?* Sorry, but I can't, he told them.

He made a friend at one of these job interviews, a guy from Kansas, *he looked like Kansas, nicest guy in the world*, who played pro football for a year, defensive lineman with the Philadelphia Eagles. Life was tough for him. Football was short-lived, over now, and his wife left him.

Besides the face of Kansas and a statue of Lincoln, he made no contacts, nothing else was coming together, no new beginnings, no ideas. He wasn't gambling. This was good, he thought, but it also limited his chance of meeting new customers, creating opportunity, finding new monetary resources. Nothing is gained if nothing is risked—it could be a placard on the desk of your neighborhood financial planner.

But yes, not gambling was good. Right? Isn't that how these things end, by simply stopping, abruptly, traumatically, consciously. Gambler's Anonymous didn't exist and if it had, he wouldn't have gone. *Horseshit*. Problem, what problem? This was economic.

For Hugo, this was the first time since his early twenties that he wasn't gambling. Okay, since high school, but that was different; that was clever games with smart kids. Okay, so it started with crap games off the streets of First Avenue, even before high school, for nickels, dimes, quarters. But let's say it started in high school. What these Stuyvesant boys had was a statistical acumen. *They were Jewish kids, most of them, they were smart*, they not only knew the numbers, but had an eye toward research and tendency.

The name of the game they played, that they gambled on, in freshman year of high school, 1941, and the years that followed, is not known. Maybe it didn't have a name. Let's call it, the way Hugo does, "Six Hits." You'd have to pick three Major Leaguers playing that night, and hope that between them they would get six hits. If they did, you'd win money. You'd pick the .300 hitters—DiMaggio, Williams, Bobby Doerr—but you would also have to know how those hitters matched up against the opposition. This wasn't flipping baseball cards, which they all did in grade school. This took knowledge, preparation. There were variations of this. If you played for seven hits, it would pay higher odds. By junior year, Aggie, that's what the Stuyvesant kids called him, was running the game with his own customers, adjusting the odds to make it more attractive to potential players.

The kids liked him. He knew his baseball, he was similar in disposition and sensibility to them. If they won, he paid, *fair and square.*

He joined the service with these kids, just days after graduation in June 1945. The war was still on. Hugo's eighteenth birthday wasn't until the following month. It was him, another Italian kid, a Spanish kid, and three Jews, two of whom were twins from Hungary and loved the sport of soccer, but had trouble getting anyone interested, even the

immigrants' kids, especially the immigrants' kids. The six of them enlisted together for the Coast Guard.

Michele was an Italian patriot born in 1889, only eighteen years
after the Risorgimento was complete, Venice now part of the unifica-
tion, Rome the new capital. Now all three of his sons were serving this
new country: the oldest in the Navy, from 1940 on, and decorated; the
middle, the first Stuyvesant graduate, in the Air Force, *the cream of*
the crop; and Hugo, the youngest, Ugolino, before he was eighteen.
Michele had served in the Italian Army, as did his three brothers; his
sons would serve for this one.

In the Coast Guard, there was no gambling, *you couldn't fool*
around. After the service, and probably before the service, there was
a blackjack game somewhere on the latitudinal stretch of *a-hun-*
fifteenth, if you knew where to go, knew who to ask—and, remember,
in East Harlem, two degrees of separation. There was always something, somewhere nearby.

But, Hugo asked himself, here in Washington in 1960, with not
much to do: *When did I make my first bet? What led me to people who*
put twelve dollars on a number, what led me to leave, being here? Was
it the kids' craps game? The Six Hits game at Stuyvesant? The black-
jack game when he came home from Camp Pendleton?

No, it was none of that; that was just kids' stuff. *Really, it was.*
This new business, of taking bets, just kind of fell into his lap, at work,
where he made an honest living, helping people at a city job the past
ten years. This new business started with a former FBI agent—*of all*
people.

One thing leads to another. Doesn't it always? Who can even remember, at this point, the first bet, for how much, with whom, against
whom, the players, the teams involved? But you could say the bookmaking started with Freddy. *This guy Freddy, he was a former federal*
agent, an Italian.

Hugo got the city job in 1950, November. After the war, he bounced

around, went to printing school on Twenty-third Street, on the West
Side, to learn to be a linotypist, like his father. This he didn't like.
Then his aunt knew someone who pulled strings to get him something,
a factory job, a plant that made metals, in Long Island City, the afternoon shift. He didn't want it, but he didn't want to show any disrespect to the aunt so he took it. Why show ambition? Be humble.

The factory, it dulls the mind, he thought; how would you even have
the mental energy to read a book when you got home? Two months
later, he left. By now, his father had bought a house in the Bronx, but
Hugo was still in the old neighborhood, *with this one and that one.*
Can you call a room on *a hun tenth* and First a pied-à-terre?

His sister got him a job at B. Altman, the Manhattan department
store on Thirty-fourth and Fifth. He worked for a wholesaler, an Irishman, Mr. Reilly, and sold linen to most of the city's top hotels. Not
the Plaza, but the Waldorf, the Commodore, the Vanderbilt. Mr. Reilly
was older, in his early seventies, and he had a small staff of four or five
people, who didn't much like him. But he treated Hugh—that's what
he called him—well enough, for whatever reason, maybe because this
young man took an interest in linen and its history. He told Mr. Reilly
that there were Irish linen manufacturers in his father's hometown,
outside Naples, and wanted to learn about this. Mr. Reilly said yes, he
had heard of an Irish presence in southern Italy, but more he couldn't
say. He'd try to find out.

Mr. Reilly brought Hugo to business lunches at the Hotel Commodore, on Lexington Avenue, near Grand Central Station. Hugo
saw how people with money, or at least the company's money, maneu-
vered.

He liked it there at Altman's. He got 30 percent off. It felt like a
Catholic store—*Catholics who had money to spend*—and it was tasteful, but from a fashion sense, doughty. Hugo was beginning to develop
a taste for the British look, staid but stylish. He spent a year at Altman,
then went to Saks Fifth Avenue, this time in retail, in the shoe department. Again, 30 percent off, and he liked shoes. But like Altman, Saks
was a dead end.

An older Italian man from the neighborhood, a clean-cut man, told him to look at the civil service newspaper; it had listings for city jobs. He had spent many years in civil service himself, this man, at a municipal union job. So Hugo listened, applied for a clerk's job at the City of New York Department of Welfare, and got it. On November 1, 1950, he started his assignment at a welfare office on 135th Street near the Harlem River. It was near his turf, but different. This was Harlem, not East Harlem. Still, he loved it. He was near the Apollo and just five blocks from the Savoy Ballroom. He went to shows after work, Ellington, Fletcher Henderson. What could be better?

By June 1951, it was on to Sixty-seventh Street between Lex and Third, closer to Third, where he was reassigned to the Non-Residence Welfare Center, second floor. It was next to a little synagogue. The Third Avenue el, which transported him to Stuyvesant, was gone in 1951, but this was a well-trafficked nexus. Newcomers were entering the city, as ever. The city of cities. Puerto Ricans, still some Europeans, blacks still coming from the South, *you familiar with that Jacob Lawrence series? This was a continuation of that.* They would all apply for residency at this office and get assistance from the federal government, all kinds—aid to children, widows, the elderly, and the disabled, at varying degrees. Hugo was good with numbers, and he prepared reports.

It was exciting, all these different people passing through, with their hope and promise, embarking on possibility. He was helping people, he thought, or at least being of help. He liked his immediate unit, mostly Jews, but more and more blacks coming in—Mrs. Blanchard became a lifelong friend, so did Leon, like an older brother almost—a few Irish, a few Italians. *And would you believe it, Fats Waller's widow.*

They got along. Were they all in this together? Maybe, or maybe it was pure coincidence, the whim of diverse personalities who got along. These people shouldn't have gotten along: the blacks were supposed to hate the Jews; the Italians supposedly hated the blacks; the Irish still hated the Italians. But not here, with these people, at this time, in this place, Sixty-seventh and Third, giving new arrivals necessities, a shot.

Hugo knew how the outside world considered city workers: slow, lazy, underqualified, without initiative, creativity, or mobility. Losers. He saw, before his eyes, that this wasn't true. He hated that word now: *losers. Human beings aren't losers, never use that word.* These were people who were discriminated against, the kind corporate America world simply wouldn't hire. If Leon were white, he would have been the vice president of a corporation, *believe me when I tell you.*

He came to love his colleagues. He loved his neighborhood, and his own people, but he liked being around these new groups. They loved him back. They began to love him after the Yankees played the Dodgers, the 1952 World Series, Game One. They all gathered round a television. Jackie, naturally, was their guy. Hugo was all Yankee, since he could remember. It's game time, how he's been looking forward to this. So he lights up a cigar. He's the only white in the room, the rest of his co-workers are black. A woman coughs. Hugo says, "Oh, sorry, I'll put out the cigar." They weren't used to that. *It was 1952, remember.* He was golden after that.

When he left the job, he couldn't tell them why—that, long story short, he was supposed to play a number for This Guy, twelve dollars straight, but didn't, an honest mistake, had already owed a ton of money, and now, just to be safe, he had to get out of town. He only told Leon. But on his last day on the job, they gave him four hundred dollars—they took up a collection, a going-away present. Maybe Leon told them, maybe he didn't. No one embarrassed him. *They didn't ask no questions.*

The Non-Residence Center at the Department of Welfare is where Hugo met Romare Bearden, the artist, in the 1950s. He was a kind, generous man, with a round, cheerful face. Romey, they called him, had been with the department since the 1930s, then entered the service. Through the G.I. Bill, he studied at the Sorbonne and returned to the Department of Welfare. His talents were abundant, but he still had to pay the bills. Hugo hadn't known who he was or what he did at the very beginning. Bearden never put on any airs, no affectation. He was curious, broad-minded, *what an artist should be*. And friendly. Bearden was a case worker, worked in the field, the Gypsy case load. *You read Joe Mitchell, haven't you? Romey took over the Gypsies where the book ends.*

Bearden's partner in the field was Freddy, a Sicilian guy, a former FBI man. When he left the Bureau, he went into social work. Who knows why. *This is '53 or '54.* Freddy had a thing for the ponies. He sensed, from the beginning, Hugo liked to gamble, knew how to gamble, and started giving him bets to place. Hugo thought: Why don't I hold the action for myself, pick up a few bucks, put the money in a draw. If he wins, pay Freddy with Freddy's own money. And Freddy knew it. It was almost a joke.

Then Hugo met Joe T., another social worker, a bright guy, excellent case worker, a black-haired Irishman. He asked Hugo, he must have sensed it, "Do you know where to get those football slips, the ones where you have to hit four out of four against the spread, or five of five, six of six, ten of ten." Innocent enough, child's play really.

But one thing leads to another. A four-dollar daily double at Rockingham Park for Freddy, a take on the football slips, something you and I would play to put a little oomph in a Saturday or Sunday afternoon. Then the two Jewish brothers downstairs, they bet modestly on baseball. They owned a magazine and cigar shop, cops came in, there was a precinct a block away, the silk stocking police precinct. Hugo saw the actress Denise Darcell one day; her agent lived across the street.

Bence thought this was a good move for Hugo, to start gaining a customer base, to be a bookmaker. The bookmaker never loses, he gets his commission, the vig. Bence knew his friend, but he didn't know his friend. He didn't know the extent Hugo lacked discipline, maybe even common business sense.

Would Hugo have booked if people hadn't gotten a sense, a sense that he would know what to do and who to go to, that he knew how to maneuver? That he would pay, that he was ethical? No one wanted to win and not get paid. You could say it was almost flattering that they came to him. But then what?

Did you ever wonder where it would lead, how that one thing would lead to that other thing? Did anyone lend counsel, whisper in your ear, ask you: Where the hell are you headed? Did your father, that day in Penn Station? Did you know where it would lead?

Did the other kids at Stuyvesant, the ones who played Six Hits or whatever that game was called, did they become gamblers? Did they start with Six Hits and become degenerate horse players, or did they bet the Friday Night Fights or just the Dodgers, Jints, Yankees, for fun, a few bucks on the side, while they worked their way up the postwar economic miracle? Don't know, you lost touch with them after the Coast Guard. One you know became a cop. You ran into him at 1 Police Plaza, he recognized you immediately, and when you heard someone call you Aggie, you knew it was one of the Stuyvesant kids. It was good to see him; you hugged.

Instead, you went back to your crowd after the war, to your people, to the old neighborhood, the one that wasn't so old anymore, that was changing and changing fast. You thought all of this over again in Washington, D.C., when you could've fled, took off for something new, something real and tangible, either a place or another way of life.

Instead, the phone rang, or a letter came in the mail, in January of '61, after the inauguration, after four, five months away. It was Gussy.

"Come home," he said. "It's safe now."

EAST HARLEM, 1961

Gussy was the nicest kid in the world, *believe me when I tell you*, a straight arrow. He wasn't involved in any of this. He worked downtown for an insurance company, an adjuster, made an honest living. He was a true and old friend. He was five foot ten, tall for the neighborhood, and was such a good basketball player that he was offered a scholarship to play at the University of Michigan. He turned it down. No good reason. What are you gonna do?

Patty was back, Gussy said. Joey explained to brother Patty, Patty called his boss, Louie I, in Vegas still, and it was settled, for sure this time. Hugo would be safe, from freelance shylocks, from This Guy and his people, whomever. He was under the full protection of Patty and Louie I.

Forget the FBI file, it's wrong. We called him Patty, not Patsy—and the photo is a later photo. He had blond curly hair when he was young. Patty always liked Hugo and Gussy. They grew up together, one block over, played ball. Patty knew Hugo wasn't a tough guy or the best athlete, but he liked his scrappiness. He once told Hugo: "Vin, you remind me of Eddie Stanky." Patty was like Chubby and Gussy, a natural, baseball and basketball. He didn't even look like he came from the neighborhood, Patty. *He looked like he come outta Ohio State, handsome as the day is long* and was a Marine on top of that. The women called him peaches and cream; he could've gone to Hollywood. Patty's wife's family was from Sarno so he was familiar with Hugo's family, knew them as clean-cut. When they got older, and Patty went his way and Hugo his, Patty would ask him and Gussy: "How come you don't come see me no more?"

But you don't moralize with people like this. You don't tell them what they do is beneath you or abhorrent. You laugh it off and say you've been busy, that they should go to one of the NIT doubleheaders sometime or see the Basie band next time they're in town. *And yeah, we'll let you know if we need anything.* It was an open offer. And good thing, because the day came.

I'll say one thing, usually when these people do that kinda thing for you, they put their hooks into you, but Louie never asked anything of me. Neither did Patty.

Back home, the return from exile. A new year, 1961. His family, about all of them now, sisters, brothers, cousins, aunts, uncles, had completed their migration north to the Bronx, where many in East Harlem were heading. But Hugo couldn't stay away from Second, First, and Pleasant avenues. He went to his usual haunts to find out what was going on in the neighborhood, who was doing business with whom, what was what. He would go to Rao's, where he was a regular, two, three times a week, since the war, before celebrities acted as if they found it, as if it were theirs. Wise guys went there but also people like Hugo. His cousin Frank, the undertaker, who ran for State Senate in the Twenty-second District, a few years before, was there every afternoon. After Rao's, he'd go to Lizzie's, the restaurant his friend Tony owned on *a hun sixteenth*.

But before all that, he went to the Club. The Club didn't have an official name, nor was it an official place. It was a storefront with a kitchen and a couple of rooms in the back and upstairs, run by an old man known as the Chief. His real name was Nick. He worked for Jimmy Walker, the former mayor, as an alderman supposedly, part of Tammany Hall. The Chief could cook like you wouldn't believe, a great Italian cook. He took care of the old WWI vets and never took their money. The Chief wasn't involved in anything, just played cards, and if any hoods came in, they behaved in the Club.

Hugo and the Chief hugged. They talked about Joe Fess, poor Joe Fess, how they missed him. He died of leukemia at thirty-one, what a shame. Hugo would call him "my Sicilian friend Joe Fess." They met as teenagers in the Boys' Club, with two brothers, Joey and Louie, let's call him Louie II, another one who went on to the Marines during the war and was decorated. Joe Fess and these two brothers, their people came from San Fratello, almost everyone did on *a-hun-seventh*. Fess's mother spoke an indecipherable Sicilian dialect—who knows what was in there, Moorish, Norman, Greek, Albanian—but she was the nicest lady in the neighborhood.

Hugo didn't remember where the nickname Fess came from anymore, neither did the Chief. All he remembered was how kind he was, clean-cut, a tasteful dresser, he stayed clean even if his uncle was a big racketeer, got a job on the West Side with Color By Deluxe, *you ever see that, at the end of the Hollywood movie credits?* He worked with a bunch of Irish guys who liked to bet, small stuff, he funneled the business to Hugo. What a shame, that young. He would have been a friend for life. He was known from then on as *abunam* Joe Fess, *abunam* a dialect word for "late and beloved." Hugo had visited him at Sloan Kettering. Two years later his mother died of a broken heart.

"Louie and Joey, the two brothers, came by asking about you," Chief said. "They were worried."

"Oh yeah?"

"Yeah. Joey kept talking about how you and him saw Billie Holliday's last concert before she died."

"Yeah," Hugo said. "That was two, three years ago, we went to Carnegie Hall. Place was packed. She died a couple of months later. He married the girl he was with that night."

"What about you, Hugo, maybe you should settle down," Chief said.

"What, you don't want me sleepin' over the Club," Hugo said and laughed.

"Stay all you want, but I think you need to settle down, put this stuff aside."

"That's my plan."

"Smart. Be smart," Chief said. "Like Nick-a-Nick, he spends his money like water. That's no good."

"I know, he's the type of guy, you say Nick-a-Nick, I need your pay-check, and he'll give you his paycheck," Hugo said.

"Your friend Tommy, now there's a smart kid. He was born bright, always good with numbers, can do figures in his head, and see, he goes and uses it to his advantage. He became a number controller. Not a runner, a controller, his own bank. Now he's legit, with his own tax business down Yorkville."

"Yeah, I know, I'm always in touch with Tommy. He's smart as a whip."

"Maybe you should go into business," Chief said.

"Eh," Hugo said, and shrugged. "Tell me, any word about Jimmy and Jake, did they get their shot yet?"

Jimmy and Jake the Baker weren't close friends, just two neigh-borhood kids who both went to Hollywood, *to go give acting a shot.* Jimmy was the cousin of Blackie, another of Hugo's friends. It helped that Jimmy played professional basketball for two or three years. It gave him a stature, a visibility, a credibility, outside the neighborhood.

"No," Chief said. "Haven't heard anything. But ya never know."

Then there were the bosses. Fat Tony was still in charge. His as-sistant, Little Fat, was still the overseer of the agate tape that cranked out the most up-to-the-minute sports scores. Muzz was still the lead bookmaker in all of East Harlem. Muzz, short for Mussolini, because of his big, wide, open forehead, was loud, boisterous, would embar-rass you if you owed him money. But he'd never threaten you. He still ran the craps games *on a hun fifteenth*, in the back garden. He was still paying off the cops not to bother them, and the cops were still on the take. He had the touch, Muzz, whatever he put his finger on.

"What else?"

Fish was being given more and more freedom by Fat Tony, for better or worse. He was becoming his own entity. "Who knows?" Chief said. Hugo also grew up with Fish.

"I have to say, Fish was always a guy I could talk to," Hugo said. "If I called him and said, Fish, you got five hundred dollars, he'd never charge me interest."

"Yeah, he's not a hood that way," Chief said.

"How about the time I saw him smack around two or three cops, I ever tell you that?" Hugo said.

"Yeah, I've heard that story."

"He had 'em."

"Still does."

"And Bence?" Hugo asked, almost in a whisper, as if not wanting to hear the answer.

"Bence is getting worse," Chief said. "You should go talk to him. Or maybe you should cut ties with him."

Bence, how to describe him? Best friend, whip smart, reckless, loyal, psychotic, generous, misfit? He wouldn't tolerate with bullies. Forget if anyone tried to intimidate him or any of his friends. "He's pathologically courageous," Hugo once thought.

But then Bence could turn violent for what looked like no reason, or no good reason. He once strangled a German shepherd who wouldn't stop howling at him. He was a walking, vibrant tragedy.

Hugo and Bence were inseparable since their early teenage years. Bence would debate the older kids about Ben Webster, Coleman Hawkins, and Lester Young, superheroes armed with brass. He'd take blindfold tests, like in *Down Beat* magazine: that was Hawkins soloing in this version, with this bandleader, on this recording. He was mature for his years. When it came to girls, Hugo was seventeen going on twelve; Bence, with the smoldering looks, was seventeen going on thirty.

"Did I ever tell you the story?" Hugo told Chief and years later to anyone else who would listen. "My cousin Neal, he was born with weak insides—he had one lung almost his whole life. Thank God he's still alive. Well anyway, me, Bence, and Tony, this is going back ten years, we went to see the Jim Thorpe movie, Burt Lancaster played Jim Thorpe. We went and see it here, on *a-hun-sixteenth*. I tell Neal to go see, what's his name, the famous Count Basie singer?"

"Jimmy Rushing,"

"Right, Jimmy Rushing, at Stuyvesant Casino, down Second Avenue and Tenth Street. You didn't have to pay a cover charge no more, but they still had great musicians. We get a call, after the movie, I don't remember how it got to us, and they tell us these preppy guys are fighting with Neal's friends. I was terrified. If one of them punched Neal, they'd kill him. So Bence and me and Tony, we get in a car and go down the East River Drive. We're there in no time. It's still going on, these three guys, right out of Harvard or Yale, who the hell knows, with their blazers and all that. I'm trying to calm it down and trying to look after Neal, 'cause with the one lung they would have killed him—he was so frail. Well Bence is punching a guy like this, with these body punches. Then we realize it was a knife, that he's knifing a guy. Tony said to him, 'That's enough!' Bence had a hatred for people like this, he was looking for an excuse. Then I balled him out. I said, 'Whatta you out of your mind?' I don't deal with people who put knives in other people."

"You should have known then," Chief said, shaking his head.

"But balls of a lion."

Bence was dark-skinned, had the face of an angel. He was Hugo's size, five foot six, trim, but a better athlete, *could run like a deer*. He had a loving mother and unusually high IQ.

"So what happened to him?" Chief asked.

"It was the shock treatments," Hugo said. "When he was shipped to Korea, they used kids like him as guinea pigs. They messed him up for life. When Gussy was over there, I wrote to him, 'Don't disobey an order, they're experimenting with shock treatments.' "

Bence wanted an honorable discharge. Instead, he was given Section 8, mentally unfit to serve. Hugo would visit him in the military hospital after the Korean War, in the psychiatric ward, with Joe Fess when Joe Fess was still alive.

He still had that face, and a lively brain, and he met a pretty Jewish girl. A perfect match, except he wasn't Jewish; she couldn't marry him. He never got over it. He met another Jewish girl, not-as-perfect a match, but they got married. It was dysfunctional from the start. He moved *up the Bronx*, and was in and out of hospitals.

"I'm hearin' all kinds of things," Chief said.

"No? What?"

"That he's informing on the local bookmakers up there," Chief said.

"No, Bence wouldn't do that. He's a lot of things, but he's no stool pigeon."

"Maybe not, Hugo, but he's not the same. He's with people now you wouldn't want to associate with. He's only worse off since you left. What's it been four, five months?"

"Yeah, five, six months."

That was the briefing from Chief. Everything was the same, still, but not quite. Not Bence. Hugo should have written about them, this cast, this fraternity of nonconformists, with off-kilter allegiances, kept a journal on the day-to-day. He could've immortalized them on the page, before others would, others from other places, from higher, know-it-all perches, others who would define us.

Hugo wanted to be a writer at one point, thought maybe he could be a writer. He loved writing, especially Dostoyevsky. *He was a gambler, you know that, right?* He was always told he was a good writer, at Stuyvesant, at his job at the Department of Welfare. If there was a letter to be written, they'd ask Hugo to write it. He wrote letters to *The New York Times*, but they were never published. The only thing he ever published was for the UJA newsletter, the United Jewish Appeal, on his friend Chubby.

He didn't go to Stuyvesant, Chubby, but he was smart. He liked to debate; he had socialist leanings and wasn't afraid to voice his opinions. His father was a racketeer but the son wanted no part of it. He got a job working for the city and always stayed in that neighborhood, even after everyone was gone. Chubby wasn't chubby, of course, but reed thin. He looked like Jack Palance, and played competitive fast-pitch softball. *Great athlete, what speed, played the outfield, glided under fly balls like Joe D.* Had a reputation for being one of the best players in the city. When a barnstorming team from Indiana came to town, the Fort Wayne Zollners they were called, Chubby was part of the citywide team invited to challenge them. It was at Jones Beach. He hit two triples.

The two of them would go to movies, one night a feature, another night a documentary. One was on the Holocaust. Chubby was a street-smart Italian, but he was in tears, overcome. Hugo, in the moment, wrote about it; how it affected him and his friend. He told his co-worker Sol, in the department, the next day and showed him what he wrote. Sol asked if he could use the piece for the UJA newsletter, where he contributed. "Sure," Hugo said, "if you think it's good enough." They did.

Other than that, he didn't write. How do you even begin at that stage, without a college degree; who do you contact? He just wrote letters that weren't published. And here, he could've written about this, this place and its people, all around him. But don't air dirty laundry. Remember omerta, *omu*, the Sicilians would say. Keep the stories in the Chief's club, while he's stirring the polpette in the sauce. Stirring and stirring.

Hugo went to Tony's restaurant, on *a hun' sixteenth* and Second, to say hi. Another hug. Tony appeared genuinely happy to see him. He could have not talked to Hugo ever again and that would have been justified. Maybe it was true, maybe Tony was the nicest guy you'll ever want to meet.

A couple of years before, Hugo dropped by the restaurant, as he often did in the '50s. It was a nice place: Tony's father had passed Lizzie's down to him, and his grandfather started off by shucking clams in a cart on the street. Sugar Ray Robinson was a regular at Lizzie's, would drive up in his pink Cadillac. Ray loved the lobster fra'diavolo, *would bring his whole entourage, order it for fifteen people.*

This one night, Tony says, "Hugo, when I close up later, we'll go out, hit a nice place." Tony liked piano bars, with a singer maybe, nice little places. He had an education.

So Hugo watched the Yankee game at the bar. They played the Washington Senators that night. Whitey Ford was pitching. Hugo loved Whitey Ford. Loved him so much he bet two thousand dollars on the game. Never get attached, that was the rule. Whitey was coasting, pitching a shutout through eight. So Hugo needed the Yankees to win by two runs. Baseball was usually bet on odds, but tonight he used the run line, Yankees minus a run, run-and-a-half. Not a big deal: going into the ninth it was 4–0 Yankees. Two up, two down, game won. Then a guy gets on, on an error, then a base-on-balls. *And I start to get nervous. Whitey Ford rarely gives up bases-on-balls.* Next batter, home run; next batter, third out. Yankees win, 4–3, Whitey wins, Hugo loses—two grand. What does he do? He throws a bottle of scotch at the TV—glass and Dewar's everywhere. The restaurant was empty, just a few people, but still. Tony called him into the office and yelled at him: "I'm tryin' to run a business. You're well liked around here, but hold your temper. Control yourself." Tony remained his friend.

Hugo lost more money before. He lost more with a guy named Pat. Not Patty, Patty was made, but Pat. Pat wasn't a close friend, *I wonder what the hell happened to him?* Nice enough guy, from *a hun fourteenth*, and one week he and Hugo, starting with just fifty dollars, caught a hot streak on college basketball. The streak lasted nine days and their combined pot grew to eleven thousand. Hugo actually showed some restraint. "Pat," he said, "why don't we each keep twenty-five hundred each, at least." But Pat, being astute, thought he had a handle on this one game. Wake Forest was playing at home against one of the nearby schools—NC State. Or was it Duke? Maybe Clemson. A pretty good team, whoever it was, since Wake was favored by only a basket. So they put nearly the whole eleven thousand on it, laying the two points.

At the beginning of the second half, Wake is up by eleven, in those days a lock. What a relief. They went to the movies, *if memory serves, it was a French picture*. After the movie, they went to check on the score near Mount Carmel Church, where Little Fat had the scores on the ticker tape. Wake won—but only by a point. They lost.

Hugo cursed. He cursed God, right there in front of Mount Carmel. He began walking, to console himself. This is something he did. He loved walking in the city, block after block, as therapy. After just three blocks, he came across a gumball machine, outside a small grocery store. He made a fist and he put his hand through it.

He had four hundred dollars left and a scar for the rest of his life.

The scar he can show you.

Hugo was back in the city, 1961, and had to find work. *Who came through, but Leon*. Not a *paisan*, but a black man, from his old job at the Department of Welfare. Leon heard from a friend that they needed a night watchman for a construction site, where they were building private houses near the foot of the Whitestone Bridge on the Queens side. Hugo hadn't done anything like it before, but it was steady income, a few bucks, which he needed to pay back his residual debt.

Night watchman. It reminded Hugo of the Rembrandt painting *The Night Watch*, which he'd seen in books. Stuyvesant provided a great education, but it was still only high school. For art and culture, he was on his own, so he tried to teach himself. He'd go to the city's museums, the Met mainly, to look and see. When he met Bearden years before, it had been a revelation. They began chatting politely, first about baseball—Bearden was a pitcher in college, and Hugo loved the act of pitching and pitchers—then about boxing, jazz, swing, Basie and Ellington sure, but Bearden was surprised this Italian knew Jimmie Lunceford, Chu Berry, Coleman Hawkins, Lester Young, Art

Tatum. Weren't the Italians supposed to be the most virulent racists in the city? The most provincial of immigrants? He liked this young kid Hugo, and invited him to his studio. "I make these collages and paintings. Why don't you stop by."

If Hugo knew anything, he knew all things Italian, the bad, the good, and the great. His father told him of Venice, that Venice still looked the way Canaletto and Francesco Guardi painted it. He learned the story of Caravaggio, of his time in Naples, on the run. Now Bearden would rave about Giotto.

Bearden's intellect and warmth sent Hugo to learn still more, so he could hold his own in conversation, to get a real artist's opinion. If he went to see art with anyone, he would go with Vito, a neighborhood friend, a few years younger, who stayed far away from the streets. Vito did some painting and illustrating himself, was a jazz lover, and was trying his hand at writing plays.

After the Italian masters, Hugo liked the Spaniards, then the Flemish, Rubens, Van Dyke, Rembrandt. So when Leon told him "night watchman," Hugo didn't think, "Whitestone Bridge, Queens-side," he thought of *The Night Watch*. And he said, "Sure, I could use the paycheck. Thanks."

The job wasn't out of Rembrandt. It was meaningless, in the graveyard of midnight to seven. He was in a little cabin by himself, with nothing to watch or do. So he would think to himself, or even out loud. Sometimes brass instruments played on the radio.

He thought, again, as he did in Washington for those few months: What to do next? Nothing happened down there, and now he was back. It was time for a clean break. This job was temporary, and not much of a job. It would last six weeks, Leon said, two months tops.

Should I go back to my city job? The city allowed its employees to come back after twelve months and hold on to their past years of service. *But I'd like to start over, doing something new, different.* He spent ten years there, nice years, liked the people, the environment. But why not try something new, like Tommy, who once ran a number bank and now started his own tax business. *Maybe I should do that.*

Hugo had done it before, entrepreneurship, besides taking bets. Three, four years ago, he, Joe Fess, and another guy named Benny, *nice but a little* spustad *this kid, scatterbrained,* opened a bottle club—*do you know what a bottle club is?*—an after-hours place, on Middletown Road in the Bronx. It didn't have a name. Maybe it was known on the street as Hughie's Place. Tony helped them out—he knew that business, taught them the bureaucracy of it, told them to go to such-and-such a lawyer in Midtown, top-shelf lawyer, to get the liquor license. It would be expensive, Tony told them, but you had to get it—it would be worth it. Fess brought in some marble tables, Tony built a bar, Vito, who knew his Canaletto, painted the Grand Canal on the wall, and people came. They all said how nice it was, well-kept, good jukebox, lots of Sinatra, Tony Bennett, Joe Williams. Money was being earned. They were building a good clientele. A lot of East Harlemites who had moved north knew of Fess and Hugo as personable young guys. A famous Washington Redskin, a lineman, would come in and drink there, chat them up, tell funny stories.

But Joe Fess wasn't himself. He wasn't feeling well. He never complained, never said what it was. He didn't know himself, but he wasn't the same, you could see it in his face. Hugo still had his day job at the department, so more of the day-to-day of the place was left to Benny. *And what does Benny go and do?* He starts letting in poseurs, imitation gangsters, looking to prove something. *Kids yeah, but you couldn't control them.*

Hugo yelled at Benny one night, "We can't have this, Ben."

"They spend money, Hugo," Benny yelled back. "We're trying to run a business, not a fucking tearoom."

After six months, they sold the place, to three guys, three scary guys. Bence knew them and brokered the deal. Hugo made a couple of dollars on it—literally a couple of dollars. He never went back to the club again; those new guys spooked him. *They were pathological types, real evil.* He heard no one was going there, no one else liked them either, and they were sorry they ever bought the place, thought they had been taken. Hugo thought this: *I hope I don't run into them.*

That aside, he liked the experience of running a business, so a year later when one of Tony's bartenders came to him—Louie was his name, let's call him Louie III—saying he'd heard good things about him and would he like to partner with him, Hugo said, "Let's give it another shot, as long as I can keep my day job." A racketeer named Tony Hanley would put up some of the money, *an Italian guy, by the way, a Neapolitan, Hanley was just a street name.* Hanley once asked Hugo if he could push out a shylock. "I'm not into that kinda thing, Tony, not at all, that's not my thing." No problem, no pressure, Hanley said, just thought I'd ask. *You could talk with Tony Hanley.* He was rational, a businessman first.

This club again was in the Bronx and again had no name. And again, it went well, they made a few bucks, people liked them. But after six, seven months there was an incident: A guy got stabbed and they were forced to close. Close, not sell.

What the hell am I doin' with this kind of stuff, Hugo thought.

Should I go back to something like that? Hugo would ask himself at the foot of the Whitestone Bridge, at four in the morning. *Maybe I should have stayed in Washington, made it permanent?*

But this was New York, and it was 1961. There was opportunity. He fulfilled his commitment as the nightwatchman—it lasted the full two months. Then he lands at Bache & Company, the brokerage firm on Wall Street. What a chance. How did he get it? Maybe Tommy heard about it, maybe there was an ad in the paper. But they needed help, there was plenty of work, and Hugo was good with numbers, quick, well-dressed, tasteful, and could work a lot of overtime. They liked him.

At Bache, he met a guy named Karl, a brilliant guy, a German-American. Hugo hadn't known any Germans, even if they were just south of East Harlem in Yorkville. There was little interaction between the groups. Karl was pushing marijuana on the side. Hugo didn't go in for marijuana, never went near drugs, he wasn't even a big drinker, but they bonded. When Karl's father died, Hugo said how sorry he was.

"Don't be," Karl said. "No human being should have a German father."

"C'mon, what are you talkin' about," Hugo said. "All our fathers, Italian fathers, Irish fathers, Jewish fathers, they make you think they're angry at you, but they love you, one way or another."

"No, you don't know," Karl said.

More new people. Suddenly, a new world was open. He was earning well, getting back on his feet. Hugo's boss, a distinguished-looking Irishman, who looked like a WASP, pulled him aside. "You do good work here, Hugh," he said. "You're good with numbers, you're quiet, give a nice appearance. I'd like to make a rep out of you. Would you be interested in going to NYU Business School? We would pay for it."

Hugo never aspired to the business world and all that came with it, but wasn't this the way to something new, that way forward he was trying to figure out? So he said, "Sure, that's very kind of you."

"Great," his boss said. "They'll just have to do a background check." And then someone squealed. Someone said that Hugo booked or gambled or did something on the side. Who told? Hugo was convinced it was the custodian at the Non-Residence Center, a drunk. Hugo would run a craps game in the cellar late on Fridays and would give him money to make a sandwich run—plus a few bucks to go with it. He always tipped well; *everyone's gotta eat.*

Hugo played it cool, he let it go. The custodian was a lush, he told himself, and business school, did he really want that? He didn't ask himself, "Why didn't the company come to me, have me give my side of the story." He didn't ask why they would ask a custodian, and a drunken one, much less take his word. They asked the custodian, that's what Hugo told himself.

Soon he left Bache. They said he could stay, doing what he was doing, but who would at that point. Karl left for the same reason. They did a background check and found out he was selling marijuana on the side. But Karl had a degree, an academic record to fall back on.

He went on to an associate professorship at Brooklyn College. Hugo had the City of New York to fall back on—and point spreads.

Exams for the Department of Welfare were coming up again. What timing. It was coming down to the last weeks before Hugo had been gone from the department for one year, the grace period to hold on to your previous years' seniority. He took the test. It was downtown at Seward Park High School on a Saturday morning. He had been "clerk grade two," when he left. The test was for "clerk grade three." He passed, got his old job back, and was reassigned to 271 Church Street, the Family Counseling Unit.

Therapy was in the air, and the city felt it needed to do more than throw money at welfare families. Therapy and professional social work would be a panacea for these families, rehabilitating them and slowly easing them off welfare.

Hugo thought this was a good idea. Therapy, it wasn't for him, he saw it more and more as a substitute religion, especially Freud, but in this context, why not try. He was placed with good people, like at his first job at the department, dedicated social workers, mostly black and Jewish. He was the only Italian. He felt good about being back there. All was not lost.

Downstairs at 271 Church, there was a diner. The department was on the second floor only, with the main office across the street at 250 Church. It was a nice diner, not a greasy spoon, and had cozy booths. It opened early, about six-ish, and closed early, about seven-ish. The owners were Jewish, two brothers-in-law, and one of the wives was the cashier.

There were two waiters, DiLuca and a young Jewish fellow—*what the hell was his name? Sweetheart of a guy.* The working people in the neighborhood would all stop in. It was a friendly place, with good coffee, good scrambled eggs in the morning, and a nice sandwich for lunch. Many of these people liked to gamble and turned to DiLuca and the young Jew, who in turn turned to Hugo, who found himself there just about every day. "Hugo," they said, "can you advise us with this." They just wanted to earn a few extra bucks, like everyone else. Somehow, they knew to ask him, they sensed he would know. Soon, Hugo was getting sixty, seventy, eighty dollars a day in horse business. They were discreet, he was discreet, a cigarette break here, a white envelope there. If a bet was too big—and it usually wasn't, these were just office types betting a five or a ten because they liked a gelding's name—Hugo was still in touch with Muzz, the big bookmaker uptown, with the loud demeanor, big forehead, and bigger clientele. *For some reason, Muzz would always take my business.*

DiLuca and the young Jewish waiter then introduced Hugo to Stan Binsky, who worked upstairs and was in the steel business; Stan then introduced him to Roy, who was a stockbroker; and Roy introduced him to Phil, who owned horses down the Jersey shore. *These weren't knock-around guys, these were businessmen, sophisticated guys.* They all had disposable income and enjoyed a sport that was gaining momentum: professional football, a gambling market with growth potential. One thing leads to another.

BROOKLYN, 1962

I thought he was a tough Jew, Cora said to herself. That was her first impression of Hugo.

Cora was a shy kid from Bushwick, Brooklyn. In the 1940s and '50s Bushwick was close-knit, a community, not only all-Italian, but nearly all-Sicilian, at least the blocks around Knickerbocker and Central avenues. Cora was really Melchiora, named after Melchior, of the Three Kings. She thought this was ridiculous, maybe her parents did too, and soon she was known as Cora. It was that or Mel. Her parents, Lillian and Jimmy, owned a luncheonette on Central Avenue from the early '50s to the mid-'60s.

Cora, when she was small and still Melchiora, watched her mother in the luncheonette closely, examining her every move in the kitchen. While Lilly was doing all the hard work, Jimmy was yucking it up at the cash register with the customers. He was a charmer on the outside, son-of-a-bitch on the inside.

She worked for the Department of Welfare, the Family Counseling Unit, in the Downtown Brooklyn office. It was her first job out of Bushwick High School, which would be the end of her formal education. She liked high school and did well. It opened her up and freed her from the oppressive, humiliating reign of the German nuns in Catholic school. She wasn't good with numbers, but she was good in biology and social studies. College was never discussed seriously. If it came up, her father would say, or yell, "College? What college?" as if he were insulted. That was the beginning and end of it.

She would be twenty in 1962, and she was trying to negotiate the world outside Bushwick. Her parents taught her never to answer back to a relative, an elder, a teacher, or the nuns at Saint Leonard's. So when she encountered a woman at her job who didn't like her, for whatever reason, she didn't say anything. She let it go. This Woman, let's call her that, wasn't in any position of authority, just a functionary, like the rest of them, who yearned for power, to be better, and talk down to people.

Cora didn't interact with This Woman often; she worked on Jay Street in Brooklyn and This Woman worked at the 271 Church Street office, a place where Cora rarely had occasion to go. On one of the days she did, to deliver checks more than likely, This Woman was being loud, belligerent, and self-righteous with a man Cora hadn't seen before. He was in his mid-thirties, black hair with some gray coming in at the temples, a bit thinning in the front, glasses, smartly dressed. Cora thought he must be Jewish. He wasn't having any of This Woman's attitude and cut her off with something along the lines of: "Never mind, sweetheart, just leave it on my desk." Then, under his breath, he said, "What does she take me for, a schnook?"

"Wow," Cora thought, "someone finally stood up to her. He really put her in her place." *A tough Jew.*

He went on his way, never noticed Cora was in the room. When she made the rounds and dropped off the check on his desk, she looked at the name and was surprised. "Oh, he's Italian."

That check, the one she left on Hugo's desk, was owed to someone else, to Peter and Paulie. She didn't know that then.

The Bushwick luncheonette, where so much of Cora's young life revolved, had no name. Maybe by default, Jimmy's, but officially it had no name. Jimmy wasn't even really Jimmy. He was James but before even James he was, apparently, Vincenzo. James was born here in Brooklyn, Flatbush—not on the other side.

His father was Giovanni, or Gianni, his mother Melchiora, though better to call her Nunza. Who would name anyone Melchiora on this side, the other side, wherever? They were from Trapani, in Sicily, the west coast, but Gianni was a carabiniere and worked on the Swiss border. He didn't speak dialect but pure Italian. *He was "questo-quello" not ooh-aah-ehh.* He came across around 1900 with his young wife. They gave their seven American-born children Italian names, but ones that were easily converted to Anglo ones—Andrea became Andrew; Tomaso, Tommy; Rosina, Rosie; Lucia, Lucy; Josephina, *may she rest in peace*, Josie; Eva remained Eva. Vincenzo, for whatever reason, became not Vincent, but James and Jimmy.

Gianni never worked for anyone in this country; he even came to America with money in his pocket. Right away, he opened a small sewing factory in Brooklyn, making novelties for the Five and Dime. As soon as cars were available, he had one. He'd throw big parties in his large East Flatbush house, playing his clarinet, carousing, womanizing. If his wife protested, he'd smack her around. When black-hand poseurs came asking him for money, he bought a shotgun, told them they were thieves, *I ladri*, and shot at them from out of his window. They never came back.

He lost that big house during the Depression. He also lost his daughter Josie, to TB, on an Easter Sunday. *Poor Josie, poor Josie.* But he came back, opened another factory on Bedford Avenue with fifteen women at sewing machines. This time they made novelties for Woolworth's. There was an apartment in the back. That's where the family lived.

In 1941, Vincenzo/James/Jimmy married Lillian. They honeymooned in Manhattan. Only Lillian wasn't Lillian, she was Leria, also of Brooklyn, also with the old-world name. The German nuns at Saint Ambrose, *those fucking German nuns*, called her Emilia. They either couldn't say Leria or didn't like it. But Leria didn't like "Emilia" and became "Lillian," which she shortened to Lilly. *There was always something fluky going on with the names.*

Lilly's mother, Mariette Fidele, came from Marsala, south of Trapani. She did all the work, the hard work with all the chances to fail. Her husband, Antonio, of Trapani, was a sweet man who sat back, let her emigrate by herself, this little woman barely five feet tall, in 1906, or 1904, first to Palermo, then to the new world, New York, settle in, without a word of English, get a job, and find an apartment. Only then did he follow.

She was quiet and strong, and must have lived well in Marsala in the previous century, judging by the things she carried and the stories she told, most of which have been forgotten. Did they really happen? Did they exist? There was supposedly a sea captain on that side of the family. She would tell of how her brothers would dress for church in white linen and her sisters held parasols. She brought her down feather mattresses from Sicily. *It was like sleeping on air.* The pillowcases were crocheted in lace. *You can't buy that stuff today.*

She didn't speak much of Ellis Island, nothing poetic there, not to her, there was work to be done. And two days later she got a job, sewing in a factory. And two weeks after that she had an apartment. And two months after that her husband followed.

She'd say to her children: Don't say too much; don't trust anyone. Cora, her granddaughter, quietly listened.

You hear "luncheonette," "Brooklyn," "1950s." Do they evoke something? A sensibility, a feeling, the Dodgers maybe, or a photograph, if not by Berenice Abbott then someone else, of lesser stature: a storefront with signs in the windows, FRANKFURTERS & KRAUT, 25 CENTS in black and white, with amber edges. But this was not that. It was a different photograph, one not taken or perhaps misplaced. It started with a candy store, and the candy store started with frustration, with Jimmy, born in 1917, unable to serve his country when his country needed him, being on a bus with no other men his age in sight. His brother Andrew, a six-foot Marine, was stationed in Hawaii. He sent back hula skirts for little Cora. *They're still packed away somewhere.* Jimmy was 4F, dizzy spells, but it bothered him, it lingered.

Jimmy was a power press operator for a cosmetics company, Dorset was the name, and pulled in fifty dollars a week. Not much.

He, Lilly, and their little girl lived on 134 Jefferson, on the first floor, in railroad rooms next to the landlords, the Rottolos, whose son Sal looked like an ape, had hair all over, was loud—Cora was afraid of him—but went to medical school. *He goes and becomes a doctor.* The Rottolos approached Jim and Lil: "You've been wonderful tenants, they said, and Cora's never noisy, but Sal needs an office for his new practice and we'd like your apartment. But don't worry, across the street, there's a vacancy at 137 Jefferson with Jenny and Joe. We already sang your praises. And it's boxed rooms, Jimmy, not railroad." *Boxed rooms!*

Jimmy and Lil liked the place immediately. There was a vestibule with a bench, then steps, to the right a sconce, then a parlor. The living room had shelving all around. The bathroom was huge. When you went into the living room, you walked under an archway. They fell in love with it. Jimmy left his fifty-dollar check on the table every week. *As crazy as he was, at least he did that.* Lillian budgeted the money and Jim bought the furniture. *And he had good taste, you have to hand it to him. That desk, I wish I had it today.*

His cousin Tom-a-Lou would stop by for a cocktail, and his brother Andrew would say hi before they'd go to a Friday night movie. Andrew brought Cora storybooks, read half the story that night, and finish it the following Friday.

But Jimmy was tired of fifty dollars a week. The war was over now and TV was pushing the American Dream. He bought into it. Who didn't?

This was Central Avenue in Brooklyn, in the 1940s: Miano's Bakery, which made American cake, Joe Miano made it himself, and across the street Palermo's, which had the Italian cakes, cassatta, cannoli, and those delicious cookies, *they'd melt in your mouth.* There was the pork store, first rate, even if it was owned by northern Italians, the freaks of the neighborhood—*who could understand that dialect of theirs.* Sam had the vegetable store, so did Jack Marsala, and so did Donna Maria, who was widowed in her thirties and wore black from that day on, for the rest of her life. Cora, as a girl, would go there for American cheese sandwiches with iceberg lettuce. The fish store owners were from Marsala, *like us*. Eddie was the shoemaker and for fifty cents you'd get practically a new shoe. The Contis lived behind their pharmacy. It had that smell, not a bad one, but distinctive, maybe the home cooking mixed with the chemicals. The butcher, *what was his name*, was across the street from the Contis. When he cut the meat, there was a conversation, interplay, a relationship. There was no plastic wrap, shrink-wrap, just brown butcher paper. He knew the veal cutlets had to be thin, *paper thin*. That went without saying. It was a working-class neighborhood, but everyone made sure they had enough money for the cotoletta, and everyone made cutlets on the same night. *Was it Thursday?*

And there was a candy store owned by Pete Siddoti. Everyone knew Pete. Jimmy knew Pete; he went in every day, for a paper, cigarettes, to talk. And everyone knew Pete liked the sauce. Just wine, but he had that ruddy nose and by early evening was already liquored up. Once or twice a week he would go to Manhattan and play cards with his friends. They'd play for wine. He had too much one night. He's waiting for the subway back to Brooklyn, he's swaying on the platform, he's looking to see if the train is coming, and he falls in, the train runs over his arm. He loses the arm. He's lucky he's alive. His son Tony tells him, "Pop, you gotta sell the store. How you gonna pour the fountain soda with one arm? How you gonna sort the papers? You have to sell the store."

Jimmy sees the FOR SALE sign. "How much do you want for it, Petey?" he asks. "Five hundred," Pete said. Jim tells Lilly, "What do you think? We could learn, right? I don't want to stay working for fifty a week." The deal was done. Five hundred—or maybe it was seven hundred. His father gave him a little loan. *Or was it his brother?*

By now, we're talking 1951.

Cora was nine years old. Her mother said to her: "After school, you come straight to the store." But Cora was intimidated by the candy store. All these strangers, coming and going, the smell of cardboard, all those dirty pop glasses behind the counter. She hated school, Saint Leonard's, spent every day in fear of those nuns, and now this, people in and out, in and out. But Lilly said, "No, stop, you'll love it. Come, I'll show you, this is how you make an egg cream. You put a little syrup, the Fox's U-Bet, a little milk, very cold, a little seltzer from the fountain, try it, then get one of the long spoons, and stir, see look. *Mmmm*, taste how good."

The egg cream was good, sure, and then Cora made a friend. Next to the candy store was a knitting mill, and Jews bought it, Orthodox Jews. They had two children, a girl and a boy. The girl was Cora's age, the boy younger, and was always studying. They were quiet and so was Cora. They became friends, the girl and Cora in the back of the candy store after school, or Cora in the back of the knitting mill.

The front window of the mill didn't have anything in it, just spools of cotton, so when they lit the candles on Friday night, people in the neighborhood noticed. Lillian told her daughter this: "Don't stare, don't ask questions, don't make her feel uncomfortable. They're Jews, they have a different practice. That's their religion. Never make her feel bad." Cora said, "Yes, okay, I understand. She's quiet and nice to me. I'll be nice back." That was that. Common sense.

But Cora was only one child, and after a few months they moved the sewing mill to a Jewish part of Brooklyn. How could they not feel out of place? They faced Saint Leonard's Church, Saint Joseph's was down the street; on Sunday the church bells. Italians in their immediate neighborhood, down further the Irish, the Germans beyond that. So they left. *Could you blame them?*

Again, a FOR SALE sign. And right next to the candy store. There was space, space and opportunity. Jimmy wanted to buy it. The candy store did well and people got to know him. He could be an SOB: If someone paid in pennies he'd throw them in the air; if someone made a call, reversed the charges, and stayed in the phone booth too long, he'd tap on the glass and say, "Think you can buy a soda pop or something." But then he could charm.

Jimmy bought the space next door; his candy store became a

luncheonette. Lillian went along with it. She would have to do most
of the additional work, but she was sweet and agreeable, even when
Jimmy was at his most petulant.

He consulted with a jobber, who sketched it all out for him: Here
will be your counter; here, the overhead lighting. This will be stainless
steel, this Formica. You'll have your coffee urns here, with one for hot
water, if people want tea. On this side will be your cash register, beside
the door. Facing the counter will be your bain-marie, all stainless steel.
On the bottom you keep your cold cuts, on the top, the compartments,
for your tuna salad, chicken salad, egg salad, sliced tomatoes, lettuce,
bread.

Jimmy picked the colors. *Beautiful, you have to say. He had taste,
that loon.* He picked mauve, a grayish mauve, *what a stunning color,*
for the leather seats and the three booths, with stainless steel poles for
coats and hats. People still wore hats. And in the corner was a jukebox,
you had to have a jukebox. There was Bill Haley and the Comets. The
floor was linoleum. In the front, there were two large bay windows.

Then came the china, the sandwich plates, the sundae glasses,
tulip shaped, the frappe glasses, small dessert dishes for a scoop of ice
cream, the ice-cream soda glasses, then the malted-milk machine, the
spoons, the long spoons.

The companies started coming in. Heinz was the first. Use our
ketchup, they said, use our soups, our chili con carne. Boar's Head, use
our cold cuts. For the grand opening, Dolley Madison did a window
dressing and sent over a model, a beautiful girl, who went in the back
and put on her Dolley Madison costume, with the white wig and pow-
dered cheeks, and handed out free ice cream. This was advertised on
the radio.

On Friday, Lilly made specials, sandwiches, dozens of them, for the
wrought-iron furniture factory down the block. The boss was Russian, his workers all black, *sweet bunch of guys, loyal customers.* "Lil,
what you cookin' up on Friday?" They loved the sausage and peppers

Lilly made, the peppers and eggs, eggplant, *did they go crazy for the eggplant*. She used the best stuff, Joe Miano's bread, the *banuzz'*, the good olive oil, the cans of imported tomatoes. Jimmy charged sixty-five cents a sandwich *and thought what he was getting*.

Good word got around, and they started getting business from the Schlitz Brewery nearby. Cora could see its red smokestacks from her bedroom at 137 Jefferson, and the brew master, Mr. Schmidt, liked them. He'd come the day before and give a breakfast order this long. Lillian would get up at four-thirty, flick on the little overhead lights, set up the containers of coffee, sometimes two dozen, each with its own request: light, no sugar; black, w/sugar; so on. Who wanted a kaiser roll, *oh, those kaiser rolls*, a jelly doughnut, a French cruller. She'd throw in a few packs of cigarettes, Chesterfields, Luckys, Camels.

There were the newspapers, all those newspapers then. Cora's job was to sort the Sunday *New York Times*, all the different sections. She looked at *Il Progresso* and saw pictures of this place Italy. She saw one picture of Sicily, where her grandparents were from. It was of these large lemon trees. It would be a dream to go there, she thought.

It took their whole life, the luncheonette. They weren't even using their apartment on Jefferson Street anymore, but the rooms behind the store instead. Cora was ten, eleven, twelve, sleeping on a canvas cot that was supposed to be temporary. Temporary became permanent. One of the stockrooms became Cora and her newborn sister's bedroom. But they earned. Jimmy bought the Chrysler in '55, *but what life did you have?*

That was the luncheonette, the one without the name, Central Avenue, Bushwick, beginning in 1951, *or was it '52*, with the nice sandwiches, the Dolley Madison ice cream, a phone booth inside, the egg creams, Chesterfields. On Central, between Jefferson Street and Troutman.

Am I adopted or something? He treated Cora like a dog, her own father. He didn't want to look at her, *the lousy son-of-a-bitch*.

Once she got the job, the measly salary from the city—what was it, $102 every other week? Not much in 1961—she gave him fifty dollars every paycheck, still living behind the store, *in that hole back there.*

As soon as she graduated high school, he pressured her to work. "I don't care what you do" were his words. From not letting her go to the movies on Knickerbocker Avenue with a couple of the girls, from never having been on a bus alone, all of a sudden she's supposed to go out in the world and bring home money. She was petrified. No wonder.

When she applied for the city job, her mother went with her. It was in lower Manhattan and Cora hadn't been there before—not alone. A black woman interviewed her and it went well. She told Cora: "We will notify you." This was hard to interpret, but a few weeks later she got a notice in the mail saying she was assigned to a position. Oh, my God, she thought. It was all the way on Church Street, in Manhattan.

She told her friend Ann. Ann was English, a big, heavy girl, lived with her mother. *A good egg.* She was always drinking tea. Cora didn't know from the English, no one did in Bushwick. Everyone said to her, "Whattayou, Irish?" "No," she said, "I'm English." "Oh." Cora told her over tea about her new job, how afraid she was. "Don't worry, Cora, I'll go with you on your first day." But Ann was a late sleeper, she didn't have a job, and she didn't show up. *Where's Ann?*

Cora had to figure it out. She walks to the el, *all the way to Broadway and Myrtle Avenue*, and then she hears someone call her name. "Cora! Wait." It was Ann.

She arrived on time at 250 Church. The men, she noticed, were looking at her, all with glances up and down. They told her she would immediately be sent to the Family Counseling Unit in Downtown Brooklyn. You're going to love it, they said. It will be more convenient for you, closer to home, and you've got Fulton Street right there, you can do your shopping, there are restaurants. So head over there now and check in. Cora said okay, but immediately panicked. Now she had to find her way back.

She went through the downtown streets, looking for the subway. Then she asked. *And you gotta say one thing, New Yorkers help you.*

When she got there, she recognized the area. It was near where her aunts took her to A&S and Schraft's. She was told she would work the dicta-phone, transcribing tapes of interviews between the social workers and welfare recipients. She would put on the earphones, listen, and type. She was a terrible typist, but she loved the job in the beginning. You were hearing everyone's problems, some Cora could relate to, how the social workers perceived those problems, and how they would resolve them, or try to resolve them. Some were referred to psychiatrists, ninety-five dollars for forty-five minutes, something astronomical like that, with the city picking up the tab. One person committed suicide anyway. "Isn't this a waste of money?" she thought, though wouldn't dare say.

After that, she would have to type up the doctor's summation that was then passed on to the commissioner. It had to be letter perfect; if you made a mistake you had to retype it, no erasures, no white out. This kept her up the night before—what if she didn't type fast enough, what if she kept hitting the wrong keys? Would her superiors act like the nuns?

Cora shared a small space with two black women, both older. This was new for her. Bushwick High was a new world compared to Saint Leonard's but even in high school there were hardly any blacks. The two women gave her the cold shoulder. One, Bertha, was from Jamaica, the other, Gladys, from the South; both lived in Brooklyn. *Who is this young white thing? Are we gonna have to take orders from her now?*

In those first days, Cora didn't know what to do during her lunch break. She would end up at Horn & Hardart, not that she liked it, but because it was close. There were homeless men who ate there. She noticed they had food in their beards. She would call her mother from a phone booth, just to kill time. Then she found a place, maybe the third or fourth day, *what was the name of it, with the good coffee and danish?* She'd go in and buy chicken salad on whole wheat, *what the hell was the name of it?* A sandwich and container of coffee you'd get for $1.50 and it was good food.

She began to make friends. A nice Jewish woman, maybe a lesbian—Cora hadn't known any lesbians, unless some of those nuns were—told her, "Watch out for those two blacks you work with, they're going to scapegoat you." Cora didn't know what *scapegoat* meant, but she thought she would take the first step. She was the new kid, so when she went for her chicken salad sandwich, she'd bring back a few danish, *and that place made such good danish.* She'd say to Bertha and Gladys, "Here, let's have some cake, we can all share it." They liked that, *maybe this white girl ain't so bad.* By the second week, they were giving her gossip on the other departments. The Jewish woman, who may or may not have been a lesbian, was referred to by Gladys as "that Jew dyke bitch." Gladys didn't like much of anyone, white, black, it didn't matter. She told Cora, "You see how you and me go out and buy some cake or cookies, do you see Bertha doing that? You know why: These West Indians are cheap. They're tighter than a chicken's ass. They don't give you nothin'."

Cora remembered that line forever. She'd told her mother. Her father loved one. *Tighter than a chicken's ass—ha!* Then when Bertha was alone with Cora, she'd say: "I'm Jamaican. I was educated under the British system. I'm a higher class than the ones here, like Gladys."

Oh my God, Cora said to her mother, can you believe the things they say about each other. "Just keep your mouth shut," her mother said, "and be nice to everyone." She did, and she was, and soon she was their confidante.

Gladys told Cora, "I want what I want, when I want it," that she was having an affair and would chat up the same man's wife as if she were the woman's best friend.

When Bertha got divorced, she had three or four male friends, or would you call them clients, who would come to her house on a semi-regular basis. They gave her a little money. She referred to them only by nickname, and seemed most fond of someone she called "Fine Voice."

"I've got bills to pay," she told Cora. What good is $102 every other week?

———————

What did she have to fear at this new job, her first job, this new world, these new people? Nothing, she thought. Why had she been so paralyzed by fear?

The social workers took a liking to her, too. They began taking her to lunch. They made her feel good about herself. It went beyond name-calling and gossip, who was a bitch, who was a snake, who you shouldn't trust. They asked her what she thought about things, what her opinion was. Mr. Weiner said to her, "You should really be in college. What are you doing here?"

His children were her age, late teens, early twenties, and were away studying. His colleagues' children were in college, local, community, something, anything, but studying, developing, furthering their prospects.

So when he asked, at lunch at The Cozy, where they all ate manicotti, "What are you doing here, on the dictaphone?" even as a kind of endorsement, as encouragement, as a hint maybe, what could she say? That it was never an option, that her father would never have it, ever, that no one in her family had gone to college, none of her friends, that to be fair she wasn't sure if she even wanted it herself. That, yeah, public high school was more open, more engaging than Catholic school but she would still daydream. That she was so quiet, none of her teachers knew she was there, even the one she liked, Mrs. Shiftman, the English teacher who taught Shakespeare with such purpose and command Cora still remembered the "Tomorrow and tomorrow and tomorrow" soliloquy, *creeps in this petty pace from day to day*. That Mrs. Shiftman was enamored not with Cora but instead with Enzo Marino, just off the boat, very bright, but a little shit, *you know those Italians when they just come over, how they're peacocks*, a math whiz and good with Shakespeare. Good in math and English, it didn't seem fair.

Instead, Cora didn't answer. *Signifying nothing.*

This was it, Cora couldn't take it anymore. She had started to date, and Jimmy told her to be back at ten, and when he said ten, he meant earlier. She knew this because the one time she did come in at ten, he knocked her into a wall and a piece of her tooth broke off. It had to stop. Being ignored or belittled is one thing, but this was something else. Soon after, Jimmy—who can remember the reason? he was always losing it—hit Lilly, maybe the nicest person alive, and Cora intervened, to defend her mother. So he smacked Cora and said get the hell out of here, all of you.

They were scared. He wasn't drunk, he never drank, he was just an occasional psycho case. Lilly took the little money she had and with her two daughters walked out. It was ten-thirty, eleven at night. *Where are we gonna go now, at this hour?* They spotted a taxi, so they went to Lilly's family, to Island Park.

Lilly had a brother and two sisters, none were married, and they lived with their mother, Mariette Fidele. She was old now, and when Lilly got there, she was the only one home. Sal, Kittie, and Angie had gone out for Chinese. When they got home, they asked what was going on. Lillian told them. *That son-of-a—yeah of course, you stay here.* It was a spacious house on Long Island, where many of the Italians from Brooklyn were migrating, and they all squeezed in.

Three days later, Lilly called Jimmy; it wasn't even Jimmy calling Lilly.

He said, "What are you, crazy? Come home."

"Cora's not coming back," Lilly said.

"Well, you come home, never mind. I'll come pick you up."

Lilly's family told her she should stay, that they should all stay, the girls too, but Lilly went back, with the little one. She had to get back to the luncheonette. Who else was going to run it?

Cora remained. She wouldn't go home.

THE PLAZA HOTEL, 1964

We went and see a movie. The first must have been in late 1962 then. Soon after Hugo told off That Woman and impressed Cora from afar, an introduction was made by one of the social workers. Dinner and a movie, like anyone else. The dinner was at Isle of Capri on Third Avenue, *it's still there, you're kidding?* It rained that night, it poured. Cora bought a brown crepe dress with an orange beaded necklace for the date. She was a nervous wreck. She had no umbrella, *how stupid*, and when the dress got wet it shriveled and bunched up. When she got to the restaurant, she apologized. He said, "Well if you wear good clothes, these things don't happen." Something along those lines. She didn't like that. She paid, at the time, $30 for it.

She said, "This is a good dress." He said, "Oh, okay," maybe apologized. As the night went on, and the dress began to dry and reclaim its form, she said to him, "You see."

When it was time to order, she was still nervous, too nervous too eat. She ordered the veal Milanese, with escarole on the side, and began to settle down. The movie was *Boys' Night Out* with Kim Novak and Tony Randall, a comedy. Hugo didn't seem to know where else to take her. She wasn't enjoying the movie, and when she turned around to look at her date, he had fallen asleep. She thought he didn't look the type for Hollywood comedies. Maybe he thought he was doing her a favor, coming down to her level. She wasn't impressed.

Cora said she had to get back home by ten o'clock. He thought she had another boyfriend; he didn't know the father she had. They agreed to another date, despite the comment about the dress and the movie. There were things she liked about him: He was intelligent, could carry a conversation, was a smart dresser. He didn't seem cheap, not at all, he was chivalrous, but with an edge, something street-smart about him, not a neighborhood *gooch*. And he was funny. He used those Neapolitan dialect words—guttural, awful sounds that were hilarious somehow—to emphasize a point or convey a notion all his own. Like when he told her about the service, when he enlisted right after he graduated from Stuyvesant, how disorienting it all was. He said: "What did I know? I was seventeen *ga-ga-zot*."

It was the second date, or maybe the third by now, and they went back to Isle of Capri. This time she was more relaxed. She ends up ordering two desserts. It was tiramisu, or panna cotta, one of them, something with custard that she hadn't tried, that wasn't offered at her Bushwick bakeries, Palermo's or Miano's, and after the first she whispered to Hugo, "Do you mind if I have another?" "Sure, go ahead," he said. He liked indulging. He waved over the waiter, and said, "Another please and two demitasse to go with that."

Then he said, "There's this good movie I want to see. Would you? It's from Italy." "Sure," she said. And she liked it very much. It was *The Four Days of Naples*. "That's where my family is from," he said.

He started introducing her to these films. She took to them. That's all they went to see in the coming months. *Il Gatopardo*, "there's Sicily again," she thought; *8½*, "oh that Marcello"; *Contempt*, "that really is Capri." They talked about all the places they'd like to go. Hugo told her about Satyajit Ray, that he was from India, that wasn't it funny how Italians also used that as a last name, that they'd have to see his next movie when it came out. And Kurosawa. *These guys are heavyweights.*

They'd go to Greenwich Village, where she'd never been. She couldn't believe it, those tiny winding streets, the little cafés, the outdoor art show around the park, *that's where I bought those two little paintings, and those two over there.* They went to Teddy's, *nice place, politicians went there,* in TriBeCa. Was it even TriBeCa then?

By '63, her emancipation from Bushwick, from her father, was nearly complete. She was living in Island Park. She'd take the LIRR to Penn Station. She loved Penn Station, it was open and it soared. She'd run down the stairs, then up, as fast as she could. It felt like the center of the world, far, far away from Knickerbocker Avenue. After dinner or the movie, Hugo would take her all the way home, first to Penn Station, then to her door in Island Park, then back to Manhattan, East Harlem, where he would still spend some nights. No sense in going all the way up to his parents' house in the Bronx, where he lived officially. No, it was too late. He'd wake the Chief, and sleep at the Club. He still loved his old neighborhood, couldn't be away for too long, even if it was changing.

Soon he was allowed to stay over at the Island Park house on weekends, in the guestroom. Cora's grandmother and aunts liked Hugo. He was gentlemanly, and always brought cake or pastry when he'd visit, never empty-handed. In return, they were generous with him, always served the best food, the best ingredients. Hugo got along with her uncle Sal, the man of the house since Cora's grandfather died. Sal might have been short, very short, but was a guy's guy, liked the fights, a good cigar, played a number. How could you not like Sal? Sal was why they were all here, in this nice little house, on the South Shore, overlooking the water.

Uncle Sal was short—not even, short wasn't the word exactly. *He was like Danny DeVito, like that.* When he was a kid, or a teenager, he came home early one afternoon to the apartment they rented on Park Avenue, in Brooklyn, and found everyone, his parents and sisters, on the floor, unconscious. This must have been the 1930s. They had a coal stove; right away, he knew. He opened the windows and dragged them out into the street. He saved their lives. They used to talk about that, over and over. "For the grace of God he came home early that day. Another ten minutes they would have been dead." *It's not funny.*

Soon, he got a job. He was sharp, Sal, he should've been in college, his sister Kittie, too—she was good with numbers. He lands a job with a Jewish couple, the Hellers, *they barely escaped the Holocaust*, they lost everyone, their family, everything. They were well into middle age already but started this factory, just the two of them, and they needed a helper. They saw Sal, they saw his size, and they were full of compassion, *you have to say the Jews had compassion*, and they hired him. It was the three of them in the little factory. *They made, you know those . . . no, how would you know?*—they made gold tassels that tied around bottles of liquor, Four Roses bourbon and Schenley whiskey, *who knows who drank that stuff?* Not the Hellers and not Uncle Sal, but people did, the Irish and the Germans maybe. The Hellers got rich, and they loved Sal. He was a giver, they sensed, not a taker.

He worked hard for them. When Mr. Heller died, his wife called in Sal. He thought, this was it, he'd be out of a job now. "No," she said, "I want you to run the business. I have no one else. I trust you, my husband always trusted you." Sal took over, everything on the up-and-up. Soon after, Mrs. Heller passed away. Then his doorbell rings: "Salvatore?" "Yes?" "I'm an attorney for the Hellers. May I come in? There's been a will."

They left him the business, their brownstone on Pulaski Street, and who knows what else. He didn't tell Lilly; he and his sisters never trusted Jimmy. All Lilly knew was that "Sally inherited the business and the brownstone."

Pulaski Street was all Jewish, professional Jews. The Hellers' doctor, Dr. Lake, Lakovitz was the real name, lived next door and became their family doctor. It was a beautiful home, but Sal and his sisters decided to redecorate it, top to bottom. *I wanna tell you, that was a home.* High ceilings, grand bedrooms, chandeliers, a library. When they hosted New Year's Eve, it was Cora's favorite day of the year, party hats, kazoos, streamers, wall-to-wall food, drink, cookies, cake, pastries. And presents. This was her Christmas Eve, better. Her mother was the only one of the four siblings who married, Cora the only niece or grandchild for ten years, until her sister was born. They spoiled her without her knowing it.

As warm and homey as the brownstone was, they moved on. The Jews were leaving the neighborhood; they decided to follow. In 1958, Sal sold the brownstone and moved to Island Park to have a house built, with a view. It was Kittie who mentioned the place to her brother. Two of her co-workers, a Jewish couple, kept saying, "Island Park, Island Park, you have to see Island Park. We know people there. It's like little Venice." There were a lot of Jews there, some lace-curtain Irish, a few Italians. Sal and his sisters moved into this contemporary red thing in the middle of the block. It wasn't a house for them, *it totally was not a house for them*, coming from that beautiful brownstone. Sure there was the water, but they weren't even swimmers, they didn't own a boat, they didn't fish. *No sooner do they move in, not even a few months, it starts to rain.* There was some kind of a storm, Reynolds Channel is right there, and his sister Angie almost drowns trying to walk home. *It's not funny.* No one from her family could swim.

But they were there because everyone else was moving, because one followed the other, because they thought they could see things changing. They wouldn't say, or didn't know, it was out of fear of the future, better to keep things as they were. The future was on Long Island, everyone said. They didn't know from Westchester or New Jersey. And Sal saw an opening. If more Italians come here, they'll need the good food. He bought a storefront, like Jimmy, but instead of a luncheonette made a deli. From Long Beach, Atlantic Beach, Lido Beach they came to Sal for the veal cutlets, the cheeses, the cold cuts. Angie worked for him, then on weekends, Kittie. They did well, but it was all work, nonstop.

Jimmy watched and listened. In the late '50s, he would drive out there with Lilly and the girls on Sundays—he closed the luncheonette in the early afternoon. He was going to use that Chrysler, dammit, and he wanted to see what was out there on Long Island. He would start to scout it, take the long way back, looking for something, something better, for down the road.

With Cora, Hugo was vague. He told her that he had a little side job to pick up a few extra dollars, that he helped out a friend, something about gambling but not using that word. No, he took bets for this friend, something about "sheets," "commission."

When they were several dates into the courtship, that's what they called it, "courting," deep into the French and Italian New Waves by now, they went back to Isle of Capri again, their favorite place. Hugo runs into someone, he was always running into people. "Hey, Vinny, howya doin'?" or "Hugo, what's the good word?" or "Hughie, where you been hiding?" or "Ugo, che se dice?" but this time he froze. In walks someone from Uptown, one of the guys that collected the money from the gas station, three years before. *A bad hombre if there ever was one.*

He comes over to the table, gives Hugo a big hello. "How's everything?" he asked.

Hugo can't remember his name, Rino was the other guy, is all that he remembers. "Yeah, good, good. Everything's good."

"You still around Pleasant Avenue?"

"Yeah, not as much, my family is up the Bronx, but I'm still in touch with a few guys, yeah."

"I haven't seen you in a couple of years, since that thing. Remind me again, you ended up straightening it out, right?"

"Yeah, yeah, more or less. Everything's good. I still go up and see the Chief. How 'bout you?"

"I'm good, I'm in the jewelry business now."

"Oh really? That's good."

He offered to pay for the meal. Hugo said, "Thank you, but I just paid. I appreciate it though."

Could've been worse, Hugo thought, but Cora wanted to know more.

"Why did he offer to pay for our dinner?" she asked.

"Oh, he was just someone from the old neighborhood. I don't

even remember his name. His friend was a fella named Rino, but his, I forgot."

Later, over coffee, he said more: "Yeah, I was in a little trouble, a couple of years ago. I had to go to Washington, but it was nothing really bad, you know."

Soon after, Hugo heard from the Chief that they found the same guy dead, in the trunk of a car, outside LaGuardia Airport. Turns out he was fooling around with a made guy's wife. And he was never in the jewelry business.

The more Cora met his friends, the more she didn't like them. Only Vito she liked. He was intelligent, well-spoken, not a tough guy, a bit of a dreamer, unrealistic, but he was still young, why not dream of being a writer, a critic, an artist. Hugo spoke of the rest of them as if they were out of Homer, even if he was losing touch with them. They were getting married, leaving East Harlem, scattering, self-destructing.

Self-destructing, that was Bence.

Cora was drawing Hugo away from his old group. She was doing him a favor. He knew it; he knew it was for the best. He was improving her. And she was improving him. No one remembers the details, but Hugo finally introduced Bence to Cora. "He's been a great friend to me," Hugo said. The encounter didn't last long, and Bence didn't say much. Cora hadn't met anyone like him before. To her, he seemed unstable, possibly criminal, no one she would ever want to spend time with. "What's so great about him?" she said.

It was starting to sink in: Maybe she's right? Before Hugo proposed to her, he had the ring made by a guy named Anthony, who came highly recommended from Uptown. Hugo said to Bence, this was ridiculous but true, "I just won six hundred dollars. Can you do me a favor and pick up the ring?" Bence takes the money and spends it all, gambles it, women, who knows? It was the only time Hugo yelled at him—he was willing to do battle at this point. He knew Bence was dangerous, but he said to him, he yelled, "The one time I meet a girl I want to marry and you do that? You fuck around with six hundred dollars? You couldn't ask me for two hundred dollars? I'd give you the shirt off my back—that's what you do?"

He doesn't remember what Bence said. It didn't matter what he said.

Hugo had to borrow the money to get the ring.

Hugo and Cora were married in 1964, November, Thanksgiving Day. It was her aunt Kittie's idea: Not everyone gets married on weekdays, elites get married on weekdays. Why not be bold, why can't people like us strive?

The Plaza was Hugo's idea; Cora fell for it. Who wouldn't? The Plaza was always the Plaza, even in those days, especially in those days. This was two years before the Black and White Ball, Truman Capote. Regular people could go there, ethnics with strange names like Melchiora, Leria, Salvatore, from the boroughs. It wasn't closed off in that way.

They had looked at other places, the Essex House, that was nice, but Cora loved the Plaza. When they saw the rooms it felt like being in someone's mansion. There were fireplaces. She said, "This is what I like."

Cocktail hour in the Blue Room and dinner in the Gold Room. Cora didn't want any loud music or dancing—she couldn't dance, neither could he. They just had violins. *You saw the wedding album, didn't you?* It was small, there were fifty people. They wanted to keep it intimate. And there was a rift, at the last minute, so there were no-shows. This was an Italian family, two Italian families, and someone would be slighted, someone always was. It was Uncle Sal and her aunts, who Cora lived with for a full year in Island Park, escaping her father.

The slight was over who would walk her down the aisle. Cora had reconciled with her father. She went back home to Brooklyn, in early 1964. Only because she had to. Her mother was sick, and she had to help get her through that—it was her mother. She reached a kind of peace, a fragile one, with her father. He would send her off. Uncle Sal and the aunts didn't want to hear that. They were offended—Sal should walk her down the aisle. But they were also conflicted, guilt-ridden; it was their sister who was sick, they could've been helping, too. *You know, all this back-and-forth, this primitive mentality.* She really couldn't wait to get away from all of them, *to be honest.*

Hugo's family, bigger and vast, they were all there, the inner circle at least. They seemed a little more normal.

It was a happy day, a triumphant Thanksgiving, it's all there on the Super 8 film, quick take after quick take. The camera's shaky, *who's holding it anyway?* Look at everyone, they look so young. It overlooked Central Park South. Bence? He wasn't there. Hugo wanted him there; he let it go, the thing about the ring, the six hundred dollars. How do you let something like that go? But he did. He said to Bence, "Please come, I want you there." Bence said, "I got no clothes, no suit. I got no money."

"I'll lend you one of my suits," Hugo said. "Don't worry about the money." It didn't matter what he said.

The next morning, Cora and Hugo had breakfast in the Edwardian Room.

CENTRAL PARK, 1969

Karen and Russell were the first friends, friends who had nothing to do with old neighborhoods and old ways, who were not from New York, friends who were new, with different perspectives, different backgrounds, different goals. These were the American friends. *They came from Indiana.*

They were neighbors first, friends later. This was in the northeast Bronx, on Bruckner Boulevard, a well-kept, twelve-story apartment building, tall in this placid district of two-family houses. The building was managed by a middle-aged German couple, Germans from Germany. The last name ended with two Ns, *who can remember the first names?* They called them Mr. and Mrs. anyway.

"These krauts keep the building nice." Jimmy said that when he first came to visit his daughter and his new son-in-law soon after the wedding. He laughed after he said this. He loved saying the word *krauts,* the way they did in World War II movies, and he drew out the K for as long as he could. *These Kkkkrauts.*

He still had the luncheonette but moved to Long Island, way out in Smithtown, in Suffolk County, bought a house with a big yard, a weeping willow tree, a driveway, and a Saint Bernard. To him, the Bronx was an unreal place, unknown, not bad, not good, just "Why?"

The building was only about ten years old when they moved in and overlooked the New England Thruway, I-95, and beyond that Pelham Bay Park. Beyond that was City Island, even if you couldn't see it. There was a sitting room in the lobby, down two steps, up two steps.

The building managers, the Germans from Germany, kept a Scotch-pine Christmas tree there. They were big on Christmas.

Cora and Hugo moved in to their one-bedroom during Christmas season, 1964, so the tree, the lights, stood out. It had plain white lights—tasteful. When the season changed to spring, they would go up to the roof solarium. It had a wrought-iron table and chairs with a view of the highway and the park. They'd sit up there and Hugo would sing old standards, ditties about stars, "Stardust," "Stella by Starlight," "Star Eyes," "Stars Fell on Alabama." He wasn't much of a singer but they laughed.

There were well-spoken, well-dressed professional tenants in the building, quiet, all heading to Manhattan to work in the morning on the number 6 subway, Hugo and Cora among them. Two Irish sisters lived with their mother down the hall. There was a woman who worked at the Parpenet Gallery, an Anglo, articulate, you'd see her sometimes up on the roof, she used to go in her one-piece bathing suit, with a big picture hat. *She was dramatic, that one.* Another couple, they were teachers, had a cleaning woman come once a week, just for a one-bedroom. They ended up buying a home in Pelham Manor; they had money. *They rang our bell to say good-bye.*

Hugo and Cora's original neighbors were the Barones, an old-fashioned Italian couple, sweet, you couldn't have asked for nicer, but familiar. For the first year, the second year, the third year, '65, '66, '67. The '60s were only on TV. The Barones liked the place, they had a terrace, they had a view, but they used to complain about the noise from the thruway, that constant whir of those trailers, especially the trailers, at two, three, four in the morning, it never stopped.

Then Karen and Russell came. They sounded like the perfect couple. Those two names had such a ring—Karen and Russell—like a movie. They came from Paris, not that they were French, but because Russell studied at the Sorbonne, theoretical physics. There were no theoretical physicists in East Harlem or Bushwick.

Karen was expecting and they wanted their first child to be born in the United States so they came home. They were Midwesterners,

Indiana was their real home, but Russell said this: "New York is the place to be." Three weeks before Karen was due, they arrived in New York, in the Bronx. They didn't know where else to go. They didn't know what the Bronx was or what it meant—only that they needed an apartment. And this little section of the Bronx, it wasn't Paris, but it had some of the small enchantments of Paris, only in Italian: butcher shops with sawdust on the floors; pork-only stores; dairy-only stores; bakeries that only did sweets, and what pretty sweets; bakeries that only made bread, and *mmmm* what a smell. To them it seemed international. And it was near a subway stop. At least it wasn't Indiana.

Right away, Russell had to go out West for a high-paying job he landed upon arriving. It was for a large, famous bank, something having to do with computers. Right place at the right time. His wife, Karen, was all alone in a new city, far from the city, with the newborn. When Cora saw Karen with the baby carriage, she made small talk, the way new mothers do. Cora had her first in 1966, in April, a daughter, and the second, me, two years later, in March, four weeks after the launch of the Tet Offensive, two weeks before My Lai, a month before the King assassination, three months before Bobby's.

They got along from the start. *She was educated, I wasn't, but she was a very nice girl, very sensitive.* Karen was a clinical psychologist, the thing to be then, if you weren't a theoretical physicist working for a large, famous bank doing something with computers.

Cora and Hugo had her over soon, took her out, got a babysitter for the three kids, and took her to the movies. They took her to see *Medium Cool*, about what happened the year before, in 1968. They were disturbed by it, Karen especially, *what kind of world are we bringing our kids into?* The actor reminded my mother of her cousin, the junky, who she hadn't seen since she was a little girl. The character wasn't a junky, it was just a feeling she got, that voice of Robert Forster.

When Karen's mother came to visit from Indiana, she felt relieved that her daughter found some new friends, Cora and Hugo, who seemed to have a good sense of this overwhelming city. When Russell called from out West, she told him about these very nice neighbors, that they'd been very helpful, that they took her out and they invited her in. "When he comes back," she said to Cora and Hugo, "you must meet Russell."

Cora hadn't liked Russell when she first ran into him in the elevator, and she told him as much later, something about the baby carriages and him not holding the door. *Jesus Christ*, she thought, *we hold doors for one another, you WASP son-of-a-bitch*. When she got upstairs, she told Hugo, "This Kraut, I don't know what he is, who's living next door, if I ever see him again I'm going to slam the door in his face." Hugo said, "Take it easy, calm down."

But Karen was sweet, she had those round glasses that the hippies wore and was crazy about Cora's little girl. Russell was nice-looking, young, he looked like Jim Bouton, *do you remember Jim Bouton?* exactly like Jim Bouton, and he was wearing a mock-turtleneck with this camel-hair jacket, like they were wearing, with the silky hair swept to the side. And when he returned from out West, despite the door-slamming incident, a friendship was born.

They went everywhere together. They'd go to movies, go out to eat in Manhattan every Saturday night. Russell was earning well, Hugo juggling as always but he was gaining more bookmaking business, so there was money to spend. Cora and Hugo showed Karen and Russell New York City and they appreciated it.

It was Karen and Russell who suggested they all go to El Faro. They'd read about this little Spanish place in the West Village and said, "Let us make a suggestion this time. Why don't we all go?" They waited outside on Horatio Street, in the freezing cold, for two hours, and finally got in, sat at a corner table, ordered this thing paella for the first time, and there it came to the table, in those steaming hot crocks, with sangria. Wouldn't it be nice to go to Spain? Yes, they all agreed, but what about Franco? Was it ethical, moral, to go while Franco was still alive?

A few nights, Hugo and Russell went out on their own, probably to see the Knicks at the new Garden, and when they came back Cora made beignets. "Wow, this is the way to live," Russell said, "we go out, go to a game, come back, and have hot French beignets and coffee waiting." He had a PhD, and probably some paycheck, but he was still a chauvinist, Cora thought. Was he that different from the neighborhood guys?

Cora and Karen would take walks in Pelham Bay Park, with the kids, even in the autumn with jackets—fall foliage in the Bronx—then along the pebbly shore. *I think I still have the pictures.* Then they'd go to the A&P together.

They had picnics, birthday picnics, for one of their girls. There was one in Central Park. It was a hot day, it must have been the summer of '69. The park was nice, *not as nice as when we were courting, when we would take those long walks, by the pond, when it was safe,* but still okay. Cora was wearing khaki pants, tight and flared at the bottom, and a shirt, more or less the same color, with strings at the top. She remembers only because they were on a blanket, they had just eaten, and she unsnapped the top button on her pants, discreetly, she thought, and someone, just some guy walking by, said, "Undo it, the whole thing." Jesus, she didn't think anyone was looking. She was embarrassed and just ignored it. No one else heard. Hugo, Russell, the kids, Karen were loud among themselves.

There was another picnic, this one was at the state park, not Robert Moses, *what's that other one,* Sunken Meadow, near where Cora's parents lived now. Lilly got upset when she found out. She said to Cora, "You were right here and you didn't come visit?" She said, "Ma, I wasn't going to come with them, with their kids. They don't control their kids like we do. As it is, they broke my Asian teapot. They don't believe in disciplining the children, these educated types."

At Sunken Meadow, it was mostly Puerto Rican, and the Puerto Ricans were having a ball. They had their lounge chairs, with balloons and streamers marking their space, big radios, music, coolers with soda and cerveza, plenty of ice, and most of all food, grilling pork, chicken, hamburgers, steaks. Russell goes and brings some tinfoil for the fire and a pack of franks, and on the side maybe a bag of potato chips, not even sauerkraut or relish or a pickle. He hadn't tasted a pickle before he came to New York, he once told Cora. She thought he was joking, in that wry, Midwestern way, *ironic, you know*. How could he, this brilliant guy, PhD and all, not have had a pickle? Then he said, "No, I'm serious, I grew up never eating anything green."

But when they got a flat on the L.I.E. on the way back, Russell knew exactly what to do, right away, *one, two, three, by himself*. Cora thought, he hadn't eaten a pickle but he could change a tire like that. That's something Hugo couldn't do. He could negotiate his way out of an unusually difficult financial fix, but he couldn't change a tire. He couldn't even drive. He never learned, so entrusted he was in his city, in its systems, in its healing power.

Sunken Meadow, so it wasn't the best day out, it didn't look as fun as the Puerto Ricans, but that was just one afternoon. And they had a good time just talking. It was one day of a wonderful friendship, something unexpected and new.

And then Karen and Russell had a big announcement: They were moving, to Morningside Heights, near Columbia University. They liked those old buildings. Karen told Cora that they went through hell to get it, *they were put through the mill*, the fact that they had two kids in a building that was made up of all professionals didn't help, but they had good references, they had to sign something that said their children wouldn't play musical instruments, they had to get lawyers involved, everything in black and white. Cora thought, "All this for an apartment?" She didn't know it was like that.

Then Karen—open, forthcoming, as usual—surprised Cora again. She told her, "We had to put down fifteen." Cora thought, *That's good they have fifteen hundred dollars in the bank*; it was more than she had. *We didn't have a pot to pee in*. Yeah, she and Hugo could see *Medium Cool, Two or Three Things I Know About Her, Red Desert, The Battle of Algiers, Persona, Belle de Jour, Faces,* have a dinner at El Faro's, Isle of Capri, the Monk's Inn was another place, for the duck à l'orange, but Hugo didn't have much else, even at thirty-six. Cora probably had more than he did. Her mother bought her a partial trousseau, the bed linens, the towels, but Cora bought her own wedding gown, eight hundred dollars right there, her own dishes, glasses, all the rest was out of her own pocket. *He had nothing. He had to borrow money for my engagement ring.* There was a small problem getting the second kid, the boy, out of the hospital the year before, New York Hospital, a money issue. Hugo didn't have enough to get his infant out, but it was their mistake, the bank's. He held on to the slip all these years, he still laughs about it, *let me show it to you,* how the bank put the decimal in the wrong place, something like a $525 deposit became $5.25, that bank on *you know when you go to Ferrara's, near there, on Lower Broadway?*

So Cora said to Karen, "Fifteen hundred, that's a good start."

"No," Karen said, nonchalantly, "fifteen thousand."

Cora almost fainted. *I almost fainted.* That sounded like an unreal amount to her.

When Hugo came home from work, she told him, first the bad news, that they were moving, and then that they had FIFTEEN THOUSAND to put down. "Can you believe that! They're just kids."

"Well, he's got a PhD," Hugo said. "He studied at the Sorbonne. He got a job with the bank as soon as he got back, they sent him away for six weeks. He must make a fortune."

Truth was, Hugo had gotten his own job offer. He was approached. He hadn't told his wife this. He had gone to see Anthony, the one who made the ring, to say hi, and Anthony told him that Rino was asking about him and wanted to see him, something about an opportunity. Hugo took the number down. He shouldn't have, but he didn't want to disrespect anyone, *you know these people are not normal.* Rino was friendly, as friendly as he knew how to be. He told Hugo he was impressed with the way he paid the debt all those years ago with that number. "You're honest," Rino said. He wanted to open a restaurant, an upscale place, and he wanted Hugo to run it—*$950 a week he promised me, would you believe it?* That's 50Gs a year, *and back* *then*? Hugo's salary from the department was nothing, not compared to that. But Hugo knew what he was dealing with; he wasn't stupid. This guy Rino had a kind of depravity to him. So he held his breath, and said, "Rino, I don't want that life, the late nights, the flashy guys, these women. I just got married, I wanna go have a coupla kids, I want to tuck them in at night." He understood, Rino, he said that was a good enough reason. He wasn't stupid, either.

Hugo asked Cora, "Why Morningside Heights, do you think? Why are they moving there?"

"Why?" Cora answered. "To them, this is working class, with uneducated people, too ethnic. He's out in the world, and I guess when he tells people where he lives, Pelham Bay, Bruckner Boulevard, the Bronx, they must say, 'What the hell are you doing there? You're a PhD, your wife is educated.' "

"You're imagining things," Hugo said. "They don't think like that."

"No?" she said.

After the move, they invited Cora, Hugo, and the two kids. When Cora saw their apartment, she thought, "My God, if you paid me I wouldn't live here." The neighborhood felt ominous, despite the university, and the buildings were very old, which is what Karen and Russell liked about them. The apartment had a terrace. Not a real terrace, maybe you could put two pots of flowers out there; you couldn't even stand on it. But it had French doors.

How depressing, Cora thought, coming from a new apartment on Bruckner Boulevard, where they had parquet floors and all, going to this old thing. On Morningside Heights, the floors creaked. That reminded Karen and Russell of Paris.

It was across the street from the Columbia president's apartment. *Could that be? Or was it the dean's?* Still, either way.

Russell picked us up in his Peugeot. He drove to Bruckner, took us to the new place, and drove us back home.

Cora said, "Gee Russell, I feel like we're inconveniencing you."

"No, no, no," he said, "we want to be with you."

He did it once, twice, a third time. One of those times was Christmas 1969. "We want you to spend Christmas with us," Russell said.

They had a beautiful tree, with those high ceilings, *you know those old buildings*. They weren't Catholic, they were something, Protestant, but not Episcopalian or Presbyterian, nothing like that, *but something God forsaken*—was it the Assembly of God? They didn't practice anything really, but what a nice tree, there in the corner, by the French doors.

Karen made a beef fondue with a frozen vegetable. She tried. Russell brought home chocolate-covered gingerbread from a German bakery in Yorkville, and that was nice. Cora kept her eyes out for chocolate-covered gingerbread after that. The last movie they saw together was *They Shoot Horses, Don't They?*

Cora and Hugo would have to move, too. The German supers were gone, and the building wasn't as well kept. And what happened to her Christmas lights she kept in the storage space in the basement? They were gone. The new next-door neighbors, let's say they weren't Karen and Russell. Their names, don't know. Cora never met them. She heard them, but never met them. She met the girl's mother, an Italian woman, at the A&P, just by chance, waiting on the checkout line, making small talk.

"Yeah, I'm buying some groceries for my daughter," a woman told Cora. "She just got married."

"That's nice," Cora said. "Where will they be living?"

"Right here around the corner on Bruckner."

"You're kidding, that's where I live," Cora said.

The older woman gave her the number of the building.

"That's my building," Cora said. "What a coincidence." The woman said her daughter would be in 7E. "We'll be neighbors then," Cora said. "I'm 7D."

Forget it. They came back from their honeymoon, these new neighbors, these newlyweds, and they didn't stop fighting. *I thought he was going to kill her*. The marriage didn't even last a month. He was beating the hell out of her, you could hear it. Pots and pans being thrown, objects clanging, others shattering, her squealing, him screaming. "YOUR MOTHER, I DON'T WANT HER IN THIS FUCKIN' HOUSE. NOT IN THIS HOUSE." You could hear this word for word in 7D.

The last straw was this: They were fighting with such purpose, he opened the door. Cora heard this and looked through the peephole. She saw him lift his wife and throw her toward the elevator, through the air. Cora couldn't even tell what they looked like. *He looked like a big galoot*; her, it was harder to tell—she was in midflight.

Cora said to Hugo, "Oh God, I hope they move, he's going to kill her."

"Let's mind our business," he told her. The new bride didn't come home for a couple of days, and when she did it was with men, maybe those were her brothers. They were yelling at the husband, "DON'T YOU PUT YOUR HANDS ON HER, WE'LL MURDER YOU, YOU SON OF A BITCH." All this was going on in the hallway, Cora again watching through the peephole. The husband said to her brothers, or whoever these men were, "GET OUT, I'LL KILL ALL OF YOUS."

Soon, they were gone, her and him. *Good riddance*. Who wants that living next to you. Cora heard their door a last time, and went to the peephole. It was the woman's mother, the one who seemed nice enough on line at the A&P, moving things out. She looked embarrassed, *I could hear her tut-tutting*, she was shaking her head as if, "God, what the neighbors must be thinking." But Cora didn't open the door; *I would never embarrass her*. What could you say anyway?

Every Saturday night, parties, *till two, three, four in the morning*. The newest neighbors were black, professional and well dressed, like many of the other tenants, and they couldn't care less what you thought of them.

After Karen and Russell left, Hugo and Cora knew they had to move. The one-bedroom was unbearable now with a three-year-old and a one-year-old crawling around. These next months wouldn't be any easier.

Hugo had been working with blacks since he joined the department in 1950; he was a regular guest at their annual functions. Cora worked closely with them. It wasn't "there goes the neighborhood," they were moving soon anyway, an application was in, but "how about some thoughtfulness?"

It was hard to say what was worse, the music, the thudding bass turned up, the repetitive backbeat, the same monotonous song, over and over and over, or the pot smoke? Hugo couldn't hear the music that well; his hearing had continued to dull over the years since the service. If he had been able to hear it all, he would've raged, not even out of their disrespect, but because he considered the music, to him it was all rock music, junk, no matter who was producing it. He had nothing in common with youth culture, white or black. Here he was singing Sinatra and Nat Cole on the roof, to his new bride, or humming Ben Webster solos.

Cora was fifteen years younger; she did like the music—some of it. She liked the Beatles. Who didn't her age? By the late '60s, they'd argue: She said the Beatles changed the world; he said it was ephemera, all that they created, that it wouldn't hold up.

She got a kick out of Hugo's friend Louie, still another Louie, Louie IV. Louie was Italian but she thought he looked like James Brown, they had the same haircut and he'd do those little dance steps and spins that James Brown did; he'd do splits in tight pants. He was hilarious. So that song, the one these new neighbors played over and over, couldn't have been James Brown, she would have remembered. Let's say it was Sly Stone, "Thank You Falettinme Be Mice Elf Agin."

As inconsiderate as the music was, the pot smoke was worse. The music was only on Saturday nights, when they had their parties, the parties that would spill out onto their terrace, *okay fine, it was their terrace*, but also into the hallway; the marijuana you could smell anytime, afternoons, weekday evenings. It would waft into 7D. Cora thought, "What is this, we have kids in the apartment, I don't want this smell." But she didn't want to knock on the door, she didn't want to provoke.

Hugo thought about it. He knew his people, the New York Italian, had a thing with blacks, not all Italians, some. Why, he didn't know. It bothered him, embarrassed him. We should be better than that, *especially after what we were called—guinea, dago, wop*. Nigger, tizzone, coon, moulinyan, he'd hear these words in the street. Not in his house, not Gussy or Chubby. Even Bence, who would back down from no one, black or white, sometimes he'd encourage the confrontation, wouldn't use those kinds of words. Other neighborhood guys would, as a reflex. He could see, from Stuyvesant, the Service, the other neighborhoods around the city, that other white groups were racist, all white groups were racist, they just didn't wear it on their sleeves the way his people did. Instead, they moved, where there were no black faces.

Hugo remembered this, he always remembered something: It was 1935, in the summer, he was almost eight, born a month before Sacco and Vanzetti were put to death for treason in 1927, and he was given money by the older kids, nickels, dimes, to buy a couple of new softballs. They played on concrete, sometimes all day, so after a couple of weeks the covering might get ripped or mushy. He headed toward Davega, a sporting goods store, on 125th near Madison. Close, but far; Harlem, but not East Harlem. Earlier in the year there had been a race riot in Harlem, not with blacks and Italians, but with storekeepers and cops on the one hand, local black residents on the other. It was bad, all over the papers. Suddenly little Hugo, with the two softballs, is surrounded by a bunch of black kids. He was scared. If you're surrounded, you're surrounded. An older black kid, maybe seventeen, eighteen, appears in front of Hugo. He asked the little white kid: "Where you live?"

"*A hun' fifteenth* and Second," Ugolino answered.

He took Hugo by the shoulder, pushed through the kids, and hailed a taxi, even gave the driver a quarter, which would have been enough, or close to it. It's an anecdote, and only that, but it stuck. *How can you forget these things?*

So about the music, the James Brown or the Sly Stone, the pot smoke, Hugo said, "Let it go, we'll be out of here soon."

Cora wanted Westchester, she always wanted Westchester. She didn't want city living anymore. She wanted a house and backyard, with good schools, with neighbors of means, streets that were quiet and safe, an investment in the future, an investment in her children, so they wouldn't have to know Bushwick or East Harlem or the Bronx. It wouldn't be Long Island—that was Brooklyn East, same nonsense; it was where her father lived. It would be Westchester, with commuter rails, quaint main streets, Lord & Taylor, and good schools—did she mention that. No Catholic schools like she had, nothing Brooklyn, nothing Italian, except the food, the movies, and the art.

But they didn't have a pot to pee in, they didn't have fifteen, hundred or thousand, to put down. Hugo, he seemed to have a way with money. If he didn't have any now, and he didn't, he might have some tomorrow. Westchester would have to wait.

Now we would have to settle for Utopia.

PART II
THE 1970s

Moral certainty is always a sign of cultural inferiority. The more uncivilized the man, the surer he is that he knows precisely what is right and what is wrong.

—H. L. Mencken

FREEDOMLAND, 1970

This is a land of promise. A new start, a new beginning, a tabula rasa, a future, a salvation. And here come the people, by the thousands, the tens of thousands. What was once an amusement park, one of sun-dappled afternoons, catchy jingles, laughing children, and candy, so much candy, kinds you'd never seen before, will now be something else, a place to nurture, to teach, to point the way forward.

Out of nothing, something. Nothing gutted, no one displaced, no neighborhoods skewered, no lives stunted. From a flat plain where a determined wind blew through abandoned, rusted bits of American history, now a canyon is rising. Towers, one after the other, built on this marsh. Don't say no, don't protest, what can you protest? Just watch. It's not even done yet. Is it even half done? There are still dirt roads and scaffolding. Some of it is still a blueprint.

Look at the moving vans, Allied trucks everywhere, station wagons with partial lives bundled just so on rooftops. Thick brown paper with masking tape lines everything, the lobbies, the elevators, the long hallways, listen to how they echo. And cardboard and Styrofoam and bubble wrap and stickers, crumpled now, that say "Handle with Care." Nothing's finished yet, but don't worry, everything is on the way, more supermarkets, more playgrounds, more buses, the schools, wait until you see the schools. Just be patient.

Welcome to Co-op City, our new home.

When you told so-and-so, anyone, in 1970 that you were moving to Co-op City, they said this: "So you're moving to Freedomland." Or this: "Oh, where Freedomland used to be." You couldn't make that up, the name Freedomland.

They, like you, knew the history. Before this vast expanse of marsh was what it is now, or was set to become, the largest housing complex, some said project, in the world, it was the largest amusement park in the world, bigger than Disneyland.

It was tucked away in the uppermost reaches of the city, set off by I-95, the Hutchinson River Parkway, and the wilds of Pelham Bay Park. The money came from developer William Zeckendorf, sixty-five million dollars. C. V. Wood Jr., Disneyland's architect, designed it. Pat Boone was at the ribbon-cutting ceremony, June 19, 1960, the day Mayor Robert Wagner declared Freedomland Day, an official city proclamation.

Seven American flags towered over the entrance. The park was in the shape of the United States, somehow, roughly. That was the idea: rides on replica Mississippi riverboats; a reenactment of the 1906 San Francisco earthquake; Mohawk Indians, real ones they said, giving canoe rides; Little Old New York; the Northwest fur-trappers ride; the Battle of the Blue and the Gray; Appomattox Court House, Lee, himself, there before you, on hand surrendering to Grant; a German beer garden beside the Great Lakes, re-created in twenty-million-gallon replica; a buccaneer ship in "New Orleans"; you could put out the Chicago Fire of 1871, the kids loved that one. Tony Bennett, Smokey Robinson, Little Stevie Wonder performed here. Paul Anka sang the theme song, played over and over on WCBS Radio.

It was wholesome. It may have been 1960, '61, '62, but it was still the 1950s. Hugo never went, why would he? Besides, he was going to see New Orleans, the real New Orleans, one of these days. It was where Armstrong was born; this alone was worthy of pilgrimage. But everyone else went to Freedomland—except Cora. *I was in Brooklyn, why would I go to a stupid thing like that?*

Hugo's friend Louie, Louie IV, the one who danced like James

Brown, went to Freedomland, took his two little kids, spent his whole paycheck there.

All kinds of people came, in swarms, thousands, tens of thousands, from all over the Northeast. They stopped traffic, the New York State Thruway was shut down. But then the next year, and the year after that, and the year after that, they came less, no longer in swarms, no longer to be the first—their kids wanted something new.

Traffic, who wanted to sit through it? Had anyone thought this through? And parking, where did you park, anyway? Then Robert Moses, the Power Broker himself, who thought big, who dominated a century, who imperiously made the city his own, developed the World's Fair. This didn't bring only America and its blink-of-an-eye two hundred years of history to reality, it brought the whole world, its past and its future. It was global and interstellar. And Flushing was accessible—because this indomitable man Moses made it so. His bridges and parkways made it so. Those were his bridges, his parkways, that he conceived, created, executed. He followed through; if he didn't, who would? New York wouldn't be what it was if it weren't for this bold, arrogant doer. People from Indiana, by way of the Sorbonne, wouldn't proclaim, "New York is the place to be" if it weren't for this man.

More and more went to the World's Fair. This is what was new. For that, Cora and Hugo made the trip. Sure they liked it; it made them want to travel, to see the world, not just a pavilion.

By 1964, Freedomland was no more. What now? What to do with this massive stretch of land in the outermost of the northernmost borough, a place the American Institute of Architects called "the middle of nowhere"? What else—turn it into the largest housing development in the world. So thought the United Housing Foundation—*we need affordable housing!*—with Moses behind them, his grip waning. This would be his final exclamation point, or ellipses. Was he guilt-ridden, "that bastard Moses"? Had he a conscience after all? What of those displaced people, his own people? Might this be for them? Neighborhoods tarred over, families displaced in the name of the almighty auto-mobile, buildings, lives, pasts, personal histories imploded and made over into bleak function. Maybe this would lessen the force of his cur-riculum vitae, that or accentuate it: Build up, way up, where nothing had been before, just a failed bit of kitsch, desolate now and melan-choly.

The governor, Nelson Rockefeller, our own Rocky, who kept Moses at arm's length, linked up for this one; the city needed it, everyone said, and on February 9, 1965, it was announced at City Hall by governor and mayor. On June 11, the Board of Estimate unanimously approved the application; a month later, the RiverBay Corporation purchased the site from the National Development Corporation for sixteen mil-lion dollars. The United Housing Foundation, a nonprofit group made up of a coalition of forty labor unions (the Amalgamated Clothing Union was the largest) and the country's leading developer of coopera-tive housing communities, would be the overseer.

The UHF began in 1951. It was led by Abraham Kazan and built de-velopment after development in New York City. They were well known around here: East River Houses; Seward Park Houses; Electchester; Rochdale Village. If Moses, larger than life, the city, the century itself, was glib and coarse in the rejiggering of neighborhoods—uncaring, unfeeling, *that bastard*—Kazan and the UHF apparatchik meant well. *They were good people, these people.* They wanted good, affordable housing for their flock, union workers. Could you argue? But they wanted more than housing: They wanted—no, expected—coopera-tion; they wanted organization, interaction; they wanted you to fur-ther this vision of theirs. You're on board, right?

Even UHF's designated architect, Herman Jessor, born in Ukraine, was an avowed Socialist. Co-op City would be almost three times the size of his next largest project, Rochdale Village. The buildings were designed so there would be cross ventilation—"for tired workers." And who doesn't enjoy a nice, gentle breeze?

So they went up, and up and up, the massive buildings of this new city, with startling speed, urgency, you might say. Ruin the Bronx? This was going to save the Bronx, save the city. This was going to save mankind itself.

But how do you build skyscrapers, dozens of them, on marshland? You don't question Moses, catalyst and executor. No big deal: We'll just need a two-year dredging operation that produces five million cubic yards of sand. Problem solved, now begin. Build, he said.

It would become this: 305 acres with thirty-five high-rise buildings (between twenty-four and thirty-three stories) in three different designs, "the tower," "the triple core," and "the chevron"; seven two-level town house clusters, in identical design, scattered around the complex (some with semiprivate backyards); in total 15,382 apartments; eight identical four-story parking-garage blocks for ten thousand cars; shopping centers and community centers; four schools, also identical, with a fifth, the massive Harry S. Truman High School, as the educational park's centerpiece.

Where did these street names come from? Einstein Loop; Cooper Place, *James Fenimore? Gary?*; Carver Loop; Donizetti Place. De Kruif Place—*after whom, a bacteriologist?*—was next to Defoe Place next to Dreiser Loop next to Debs Place.

Most important, there would be up to sixty thousand people. This was Le Corbusier's screechingly maligned "tower in the park" idea, sans the Euro glam, stripped to its most ascetic. Le Corbusier, the visionary who wanted to level central Paris and build blocks. He gave the Herman Jessors an intellectual ballast. Could you even call it "architecture"?

The money for this idea, for this experiment, came from New York State, the Limited Profit Housing Law, created in 1955 by Manhattan state senator MacNeil Mitchell and Brooklyn assemblyman Alfred Lama. You've heard of Mitchell-Lama legislation, affordable housing for the middle income; they were the Mitchell and the Lama.

Between May 1966 and the end of 1973, Co-op City was built and opened in stages. The first tenants moved into Building 1 by December 1968. As soon as Building 6 was finished, we moved in, in April 1970. I'm two now. The first thing I did was look up, all the way up.

Here we are, here we were, the Allied vans, the cars double-parked, triple-parked, if there were paved roads, if there were paved sidewalks, the cardboard, the brown paper, the masking tape, the people, suddenly all these people. My mother said: "This is a menagerie."

How did we end up here? How did anyone end up here? Look at this, the front page of *The New York Times*, November 25, 1968, above the fold, "Vast Co-op City Is Dedicated in the Bronx." Look at the photo, Governor Rocky, Moses, and Herman Badillo, the young Bronx borough president. If you hadn't heard about Co-op City before, you did now. The article is long, it jumps to page 43. The jump headline is different: "Co-op City, a Vast Housing Project Rising in the Northeast Bronx, Is Dedicated."

"Project." Project? Who said anything about a project? You mean we're moving into a project? That's a dirty word. Who wants to live in a project, even a grandiose project, one that's going to save the world? There's more in *The Times* that day, three articles: "A Singularly New York Product: Co-op City, Monumental In Size, Minimal In Planning." It begins, "It's hard to grasp the size, importance, and impact of Co-op City." It cites the precise planning of postwar communities in Britain and Scandinavia, which was absent in this new, oversized New York version. Sweden, then, we weren't.

Ah, and this, on why whites will be fleeing to Co-op City in the first place: "Housing specialists say that the biggest factor is fear, and in New York today many whites are afraid of Negroes and Puerto Ricans."

Nelson Rockefeller says this: "I think we are on the threshold of a new era in coping with our great urban problems. Today we dedicate a symbol to that era." He calls Co-op City "a spectacular and heartwarming answer to the problems of American cities." Moses, even now at eighty, knows it all. He ridicules critics who "haggle over inconsequential elements like aesthetic design."

After that, page 1 of *The New York Times*, above the fold, it's everywhere; everyone has an opinion. *Time* magazine follows up, in January 1969, just weeks after Co-op City opened its doors to the first handful of tenants. Co-op City, they write, is "shaping up as an eminently depressing place to live. . . . It is relentlessly ugly. Its buildings are overbearing bullies of concrete and brick. Its layout dreary and unimaginative. . . . The saddest thing about Co-op City is that its bleak environment was achieved at great public cost." The article is titled, "The Lessons of Co-op City." Lessons? We didn't even move in yet. Lessons?

It's a good dollar-for-dollar value, that's what people kept saying. Those voices, that's all Cora kept hearing about this place, from friends, relatives, acquaintances. It's a good dollar-for-dollar value, okay, but is there anyplace else to go? The search was narrow, the options limited. Cora looked in Country Club, that's in the Bronx if you can believe it, in the east, by the water. Some woman and her father had a two-family house and they were renting out the ground floor. The woman said, "My father is nervous about this house. You don't have any big pieces of furniture, do you? Cora said to herself, "Oh, boy, it's one of these proprietary Italians. Forget it. Who needs it?"

It was the Irish girl down the hall at the Bruckner Boulevard apartment, with the sister and the elderly mother, who said, "Yeah, I know all about Co-op City. It's going to be the next big thing, we've been thinking about it. I'll drive you there, we'll take a look. It's only five minutes down the road, not even." So she drove us there, before there was a there there; it was still a construction site. You couldn't see the apartments, you had to go down to the office in Manhattan. They gave you the application and the blueprints, and you had to select your apartment from that.

The town houses looked nice from the artist's rendition. Jessor didn't design them. There was an eleventh-hour panic that this was going to look like the ugliest place on earth so a new architect was brought in to soften the edges. Cora said to Hugo, "Let's go for one of the town houses, at least. I don't want to live in one of those big ugly buildings, with elevators, with the babies, at least in the town house it looks like we'll have a little ground in the front." *And him? No, no, no, it's extra money.*

In the newspapers, the advertisement showed the three-bedroom, tower-building layout—ours. That's what we applied for. It was settled. Despite the reservations—Cora's, *Time* magazine's, *The New York Times'*—it was $172 a month, utilities included. Where are you going to get that? Hugo was a union man, buttoned up, not blue-collar, no hard hat, but still believed in unions. For him, Marcantonio still loomed, all these decades later. He said, "There'll be good people in this place." *And dollar for dollar. . . .* The median income would be $7,000, the working-class utopia, the utopia of utopias, with a progressive racial and ethnic makeup: 75 percent Jewish; 20 percent "Negro" and Puerto Rican; 5 percent Irish and Italian. We were part of that last 2.5 percent.

We would be moving into a blueprint. My mother stayed up every night going over the floor plan, studying it, running her finger over it, trying to envision the space, what led to what, the foyer to the kitchen, this hallway to that bedroom. What the best way to the supermarket was, to cross at this corner here or the middle of the block, or will that be dangerous, with those buses coming and going?

She read the *Co-op City Times*, a community newspaper we would have. It wasn't yet a newspaper, it wasn't yet a community, but more like a pamphlet. It would come in the mail, at our Bruckner Boulevard address, glossy, maybe four pages in the beginning. In the Q&A section, people asked, "What will our cabinets look like? Is it going to be wood?" *It's going to be laminated, not wood, but it's going to look like wood, no handles.* What are the appliances going to be? *You'll have a beautiful gas range and a Westinghouse refrigerator.* And what about this, what about that? People were dying to know.

They went again, my parents, after the application was approved, again with the Irish girl down the hall, again in her car, again to get some kind of picture. Building 1 was open by now, a massive chevron monolith. Cora thought it was foreboding, all this concrete. It turned her off. She got nauseous. *It gave me the willies, to be honest with you.*

The Irish girl was outgoing. At the time, she was the only one on the floor to confront the pot-smoking, Sly Stone–blasting black neighbors who moved into Karen and Russell's apartment. "Hey, you mind piping down, there. We have an old woman in the house." So when she saw a little Jewish woman in this new Co-op City, outside Building 1, she approached her immediately and said, "I'm interested in getting an apartment, and my friends here already signed up for one."

Cora said, "Yes, we'll be in the tower, but I'm very nervous, I don't know what the apartment will look like."

The Jewish woman said, "Come in, darling, come in."

It was very nice of her. She was so proud. She said it once or twice more: *Come up, darling, come in.* Then she said, "But it's not finished."

"How do you like living here?" Cora asked.

The little Jewish woman said, "It's a beautiful building. We have friends already, so many friends. It's a very nice place. It's going to be a wonderful place to live."

She opened the door; she had a one-bedroom. *God, was the furniture tacky.* But okay, so she didn't have money, so what? She was proud, and she was open. She bragged about the parquet floors. Cora, Hugo, and the Irish girl thanked her, said good luck, maybe we'll see you, we probably will see you. "Oh, you're such a sweetheart," she said to Cora. "Don't worry, you're going to love it here."

Cora said to Hugo, "I still don't think this is going to be for me; I don't like this at all, it's making my stomach turn."

The Irish neighbor interjected, "Oh, your apartment isn't going to look like that, you're going to have three bedrooms." *Like you know these types, they always have to put in their two cents?*

When Cora and Hugo would meet her in the hall or by the elevator, still at Bruckner, she'd say, "So, Co-op City—you getting ready?"

"I don't know if it's the right thing," Cora said. "I have two small children. I don't think high-rises are a place to raise little children, going up and down elevators."

So she turns around and says, "Well, you're not the only ones with small children."

Hugo kind of went, "Ha, ha," he kind of gloated. *And I resented that. I wanted to say to her, Who the hell are you?*

In the end, the Irish girl and her sister never moved to Co-op City. *You know these people, the kind who think, "It's good for you, it's wonderful for you. Don't think you're better than you are."*

If the lace-curtain Irish weren't going to move there, the Manhattan liberal from the Upper West Side or wherever weren't either. But they would write about it; it was interesting, as a concept. It was good for people like us, but not them. We read this in *Newsweek*, in 1970, "Kibbutz in the Bronx" it was called, and said that on the two-year anniversary tenants were going about "their task with much the same kind of pioneering gusto that marked the Israeli kibbutzim." And "This kind of civil involvement has also helped dampen some of the nasty racial tensions that were building up between the predominantly Jewish cooperative and the largely black and Puerto Rican low-income housing areas adjacent to it."

Did any of *Time*'s or *Newsweek*'s or *The New York Times*' editors or writers move to Co-op City? It was a good story, idea, experiment, this new project, but was it a good way to live, day in, day out? Were you going to raise *your* kids here? Stupid question. *Don't think you're better than you are.*

When we finally moved in, my mother said, "Okay, we're in." She was glad at that point, relieved that the long, drawn-out mental move, into nothingness, into a blueprint, was over. She thought, "Well, this is it, we're here, and we'll see. If we don't like it, we'll move." *That's what he told me that time, if we don't like it we'll move.*

At least it was new, that was nice. You could still smell the fresh paint. Out the window, standing on the balcony, you could see it now, the development, the concept, taking shape. Our building, Building 6, was a "tower" building, like 7 and 8 right there, the largest at thirty-three stories, all gray concrete. The "triple core," like buildings 4 and 5, were gray or maroon, and the "chevron," 1, 2, and 3, gray or a kind of peach color. All three were more like noncolors; peach, maroon, that's generous. Straight down below, those were town houses. They weren't as nice as the artist's rendering, but still looked more private somehow. More like a house.

There were twelve apartments on each floor of our building, which was divided into four separate sections—three apartments per section. At the end of the hall was the three-bedroom apartment, with terrace, this is what we had, and to each side was a two-bedroom and a one-bedroom apartment. Two incinerators for the garbage, two stairwells, and two elevators. Floors 18–33 had their own elevators, express as they were known, without irony; floors 2–18 had two of their own elevators that ran "local." In the basement, there was a large laundry room, and, for your convenience, a milk machine. They thought of everything. And there was more to come.

My mother flipped through the welcoming guidebook. She read this, by Harold Ostroff, the executive vice president of the UHF, in a letter to tenants, to us: "Co-op City was not built in a day. It will take time for things to 'settle down.' But every experienced Co-operator will tell you it's worth the wait and worry. Good things don't come easily, but, by working together in the spirit of friendship, we expect Co-op City to be, before too long, a shining example of what people can do together in a housing Co-operative community. . . . May you and your family have many years of happy life in them. And share in the many benefits of co-operation."

Who's he kidding, she thought. *But all right, we're here now, I'll keep my mouth shut, I'll give it a chance.*

So she didn't say anything when she saw this letter in the *Co-op City Times* the next month, by a black woman: "To think that Co-op City is a utopia, free from the prejudices and ills of our society, is certainly foolish."

Or two months after that, in August, when it ran a story on a rash of break-ins but said, "In the best interest of the community, the methods of the break-ins will not be disclosed." Or later in the month, the report of all of the abandoned cars in Co-op City, set on fire in the outlying dead-ends and bushes. What that looked like, automobile carcasses right by the entrance to the New England Thruway, for all the visitors to see. That would be their first impression.

It was all dizzying those first days. Jews, so many Jews, Sephardim, Ashkenazim. Half the Grand Concourse was here. They told you how the Ashkenazim looked down on the Sephardim, how the Sephardim were dark and yeah maybe tough, but low, and how the German Jews looked down on all of them, us included, how Robert Moses was a German Jew. There were Irish and Italians, just a few, and no longer at one another's throats; blacks, three families on our floor—where else in America in 1970?; Puerto Ricans; old people, very old people; young people, teenagers, kids, babies; middle class, working class, lower class; the educated; the uneducated. Was this meant to be? Were we all meant to be together? One on top of the other, building after building? Where else could you get a Sephardic Jew, an Irish Catholic, a Jamaican, a black American from Pittsburgh by way of Alabama, an East Harlem Italian, and an Indian family from New Delhi in the same building, maybe on the same floor? Was there anyplace like this? Should there be a place like this? Was this a step up or a step down? Or was it lateral? Was it the past, passé before its time, or was it the future?

It was left to us, the children of Moses.

WESTCHESTER, 1972

I hated it, I absolutely hated it. My mother hated Co-op City, she absolutely hated it. She couldn't keep quiet about it for much longer.

Karen, of Karen and Russell, came over once, for lunch in '70 or '71, and my mother said, "You see what I mean? It's this big concrete jungle. I feel out of place." Karen said, "Yes, I can see what you mean." She didn't want to knock it; she was from the Midwest and was discreet.

Russell was interested in Co-op City because he was curious about everything, and this was on the front page of *The New York Times*, above the fold. So when we invited Karen, Russell, and their two young daughters for Christmas, Eve and Day, to spend the night, they said, you bet—maybe literally said, "You bet."

Christmas for us usually meant going to Smithtown, to my mother's parents' house, Jimmy and Lilly. But my mother didn't want to deal with her father. He was always picking on someone, something, usually something inconsequential—"the chair's too close to the wall, goddammit!"—flying off the handle. And then we'd have to hear him ridicule Co-op City.

When he visited us, *Oh, God, forget it. You can imagine, right?* He was there once, no twice, then he refused to come. The first time he said, "Jesus Christ, where did he take his bride, to a factory? These are factories, it all looks the same. I'm going in circles over here, what the hell is he—what the hell are you moving into? You're raising a family, for cryin' out loud."

Her father was all for ownership; invest in a home, he said. And not only him.

Upstairs, he admitted the apartment was nice. He stood on the terrace overlooking all this, and he said, this time quietly, not to provoke, "But you're gonna raise the kids here?"

Her mother, my grandmother, sunny and ebullient, was claustrophobic, and when the elevator door closed, she said, "Oh my God, get me out of here." Even she said, "Cora, be careful with the kids, the door closes and you're in this box." At least the elevator at Bruckner had the round window.

This Christmas, '70 or '71, my mother decided she didn't want to contend with her father. Hugo wasn't confrontational, he always saw the bright side, but her father knew how to antagonize, especially about Co-op City, *even if the nutcase was right this time.* This Christmas would be with Karen and Russell.

On Christmas Eve, my mother made lasagna. Her lasagna could have been out of a magazine. Russell went berserk, *he was absolutely going berserk.* She said, "Russell could you go for another piece?" and he said, "Yeah, just slice it right down the middle—I'll eat the whole thing."

My parents gave them their bedroom, and their two girls my sister's room. The next day, the apartment suddenly felt small with eight people. Russell said he wanted to go out with the kids, he wanted to see some of this Co-op City. When he came back, he didn't say anything. Did he see something, the carcass of a car, a puddle of urine in the elevator—had that started yet? Did he hear something? That was the last time we saw them. *To them, this is working class.*

Or was it the neighbors, did he see the neighbors?

Neighbors, there were so many of them. Twelve apartments on our floor alone, at least thirty-five people. They were such a mixed bag, it was hard to call them anything—but none of them went to the Sorbonne. We would learn about them in those first days, weeks, months, years, more or less, waiting for the elevators.

Our immediate neighbors, in the one-bedroom, were an elderly

Jewish couple. There were many elderly among the new tenants. What a mix: geriatrics, or close to it, and down all the halls of all the towers, little children, the kind who made noise, made a mess of things, made playing fields of the long echoing corridors, vexing the aged.

The other immediate neighbor, in the two-bedroom, was a family of four, like us: the Kings. They were black, from the South Bronx.

My mother first saw the matriarch of the King family through the peephole. She had a handkerchief wrapped around her head, was of ample build, and appeared to be a few years older than herself. This woman looked street, there was no other way to describe it. To a girl from provincial Brooklyn—no, for virtually any white person in 1970—this was something new, and possibly alarming. Where have we moved, what have we done?

Her name was Beverly, Bee, from Georgia, and her husband, Ricardo, also of ample build, was from Saint Thomas. They had twin sons, as identical as twins could be, who were inseparable and named Ricardo and Richard, which added to the confusion.

Ricardo was happy-go-lucky, even if he was often out of work. Most of the time he was a porter at Kennedy Airport, and worked afternoons and evenings. No matter where you'd see him, often bounding around with what looked like a cane or walking stick, he'd say in his slight Caribbean accent, "Hey Mikey, how's school, how's you Mamma? How's your Daddy?" Beverly worked the graveyard shift cleaning bedpans at New York Hospital; she was more introverted, had more edge.

She hated Co-op City, one minute blaming something, everything on black people, her own, the next blaming something, everything on whites or these "damn Jews." But she had a kind, generous side, sometimes making us sweet potato or pecan pies and gossiping with my mother for hours. She was a protective mother—could you blame her? Her sons, once they reached high school, had an intimidating air, even if they were gentle giants. She'd tell my mother, over and over, "All my sons have to do is be in the wrong place at the wrong time." And she was right, they would get blamed, arrested, hurt, something.

Down the other end of the hall were the DiBernardos, one of the few Italian families in the building. Diane DiBernardo was out of a movie, cigarette dangling out of her mouth, regaling my mother with stories of how her husband, Frank—of high, raspy voice, the quietest neighbor on our floor—would beat the living hell out of her before they moved to Co-op City. She repeated these stories over and over: How Frank threw her down the stairs; how he knocked her teeth out; how he kicked her in the stomach when she was pregnant. She told these stories in slow, hyperbolic delivery—"And so what does he do to me, this son-of-a-bitch I'm married to, he kicks me in my stomach after I'm knocked up, this piece of shit"—that when they were retold, by my mother to us, or by Beverly to my mother and then to us, had a perverse comic edge to them. *No, it couldn't be, not Frank, is she making this up? She's going for a sick laugh.*

Across from them was an old Irish couple. They had their own famous battles, which we, and everyone else, could hear while waiting for the elevators or while throwing out the garbage down the incinerator chute. My father would do their taxes every year and knew they had some money stashed away. But the old husband, Archie, didn't spend a penny of it. He was embittered that his son married, and had children, with a black woman, whom he would divorce. He spent many of his days in a complete drunken stupor. That or beating his wife, Colleen. In this case, unlike the DiBernardos, whom they lived next door to, Colleen would fight back, often pounding her smaller husband into eventual submission.

Next to them, in one of the other three bedrooms, was another older couple, a black couple. We basically knew them as "Lefty and his wife." Lefty was a very happy man. Small, a bit hunched over, he was always in a hat. He, too, liked his drink, and we'd hear from other neighbors how they had to carry him to his door. *No, not Lefty, I don't believe that.* "Lefty's Wife" was heavyset, also endlessly cheerful, a churchgoer. No matter what day of the week or hour of the day, she seemed to be in Sunday best, with a hat.

There were the Millers on the other side, a middle-aged Jewish couple, who seemed to have more money, in a nouveau-riche way, than anyone on our floor or most others in Co-op City. They had a place in Florida, two Caddies, season tickets to the Giants, and the wife had two furs. The husband would start his sentences off with: "Lemme tell ya somethin'."

The Abramses, besides the Millers, were a nice family with two kids, a boy and a girl, but several years older than my sister and I. When the older son was applying for colleges, my mother asked where he wanted to go. "Yale," he said. My mother said, "There's no way that kid's getting into Yale." She was right; he ended up at a local school, I forget which. But after that we ended up referring to him as "Yale." As in: "I saw Yale today, you wouldn't believe it, he's getting married."

One more over from them was a sweet, old, learned Jewish man, Mr. Lipman, who used to play the mandolin, in a quiet part under our building. He survived the Holocaust and one day threw himself out the window.

On the other end of the hall was a black man who had a '70s-gangster lean to him, hat tilted to the side, lamb-chop sideburns, goatee, and toothpick. He always said: "You stay in school now, ya hear?"

There were two other families on our floor. Them I don't remember. Were they even there?

It had been solitary at the beginning. Solitary one moment, then swarming the next, everyone trying too hard to be friends. It was stifling. It took my mother twenty minutes to get down to the lobby to check the mail, another twenty minutes to get back up. Movers used one of the elevators, the other was left for us. You didn't know who you were going to meet in the lobby; some of them you didn't want to meet.

She'd wait for my father to come home from work and say, "Sorry but I can't live here." He couldn't have cared less. He had his routine down already: get up early, very early, go down, get on the bus, get off at Pelham Bay, take the subway, go to work. He was picking up his gambling business. He even ran numbers for two months as favor to a black man he worked with.

This was a place to hang his hat. As long as he could get to and from work, get upstairs, see his two kids, and the dinner was made, a beautiful dinner, and he could get on the phones, field the calls, he didn't care. The only thing that worried him was that on our terrace, there was an open space in the corner. It wasn't completely closed off, and he feared me or my sister, little squirts, could slip through and fall twenty-two floors to our death. He had it partially closed off. Besides that, he was content.

He had seen in one of the tabloids that Rino, who he paid the 231 debt to and who approached him to run the restaurant for $950 a week, was picked up by the feds for a drug operation. Not only him but a few of his family members. My father was happy that he stayed clear of him, and that way of life, happy to tuck in his kids, happy to be just where he was. *Anyway, where were we?*

My mother was interacting with Co-op City, trying to make sense of this strange place, day to day. She would look down from her bedroom window and see they were making a sandbox, and surrounding that, they were building these steps. She'd watch from the window and say, "What are they doing down there?" There was still all this construction. We were confined to one area, where the first few buildings were. Walking paths weren't complete.

She tried to hide out in the apartment, *but you kids had to have air, what were you, two and four when we moved in?* So she would bring us downstairs, me in the stroller. She would sit on one of these steps and my sister would play on a piece of circular concrete. I would walk around in circles. And we were alone. My mother thought, "How lonely is this?" At Bruckner we had Karen and Russell, other neighbors, you could walk around the neighborhood, it was on a human scale.

Soon, a larger sand garden was built, with monkey bars and slides, with a pine forest. My mother brought us there. Then people realized that the sand was breeding disease, kids were getting impetigo. The Jews started to complain: *What is this, you keep the same kids in the same sand, there's bacteria.* It's good someone spoke up; I might have gotten impetigo. My mother stopped taking us to the sand garden.

But it was better being alone than sized up, judged, maybe looked down on.

In the beginning, my sister made a little friend in kindergarten. The girl's mother invited my sister over to play after school. To reciprocate, my mother invited the girl to our house—that's what we called it, house, not apartment.

After the play date, the girl's mother went into my sister's room to pick up her daughter. *The room was beautifully decorated, if you remember, it was like a showplace, everyone admired it. It was a Walter's Wicker bedroom set.* The mother walked into the bedroom, she took her kid, and we never saw her again. Was it our last name, that when she came to the door she saw our name wasn't Jewish? My mother looked Jewish, was assumed to be Jewish—old ladies around the building already began greeting her with *Shabbat Shalom* on Friday afternoons. When she said to these old ladies, "Thank you, but I'm not Jewish, I'm Sicilian," they still said *Shabbat Shalom* next time they saw her, the next week or the next month.

Was my sister's bedroom nicer than the other girl's room? Was it too much to compete with? Was it too nice or not nice enough? Were we supposed to be in construction? The little girl wasn't among the first-grade class. They moved. Already. *Who needed them?*

Which is why Sara was the first friend. She seemed natural. My mother met her in the lobby, waiting for the elevator—what else? All these people were buzzing around, and she looked at my mother and me and said something like, "He's cute, how old is he?"

"Two and a half," my mother said.

"Oh really, so is my son. What floor are you on?"

"Twenty-two."

"I'm on twenty-four," she said. "Do you like it so far?"

"I don't," my mother said. "How do you feel about it?"

"Well, it's all right. It's a pretty good deal. Why don't you come over, the boys look like they'll get along."

She may have invited us right then and there. My mother went in and the friendship took hold, like that. *The two of you were playing very nicely, quietly.* We could see our own kitchen window from their apartment. And vice versa. My mother had seen her husband from the window, two flights up, diagonally across. Everything was open, everyone was still moving in, the blinds weren't on the windows yet. My mother thought this man looked big and tough, like no one she would want to know. He was the opposite. He was big, bigger than my father, but gentle. He was a New York City high school teacher, like his wife. They were Jewish, Sara and Max Cohn. They said to my mother, "Very nice to meet you, we'll have to get together."

My mother felt very comfortable with them. It made her feel better.

A little better, but one nice couple and a playmate for me, my first best friend, couldn't save her from this concrete monster. So she would wait for my father to get home, and she would hound him. *It was terrible what I did*, but there was no getting through to him. She had to be assertive. She would yell: "I had to wait twenty goddamn minutes for an elevator, and I'm surrounded by all these people, it's like being in high school. It's like they never grew up, and I didn't behave that way in high school. It's cliquey. The people are clones. I'm not a clone. I was never a clone. They follow, I don't like to follow. I hate this place." She did this every night until finally he got disgusted. "Then go look for a house," he said.

She did just that. She did her research, and she found a house, a nice house, in Mount Vernon, off Route 22, in Westchester County. Not the bad part of Mount Vernon, the good part. Sedate, wide streets, lawns that came to the road, very quiet, very mature, built, someone told her, in the 1920s and '30s by an Englishman with the best materials, slate, stucco, stone. It was a block from Bronxville, where they flew the American flag outside the front door. *I thought if they ever changed the zoning, and it became part of Bronxville, the property value sky-rockets, you're a millionaire.*

The owner was an old woman in a chair. We could have moved in just the way it was. It had gables and turrets, an English country house, three bedrooms, enclosed screen-in porch, you could eat in there, you didn't have to worry about mosquitoes. There was a small backyard, beautifully manicured, with day lilies, very easy to take care of. The woman only wanted $42,990. All the house needed was a rewiring, which would have been another $2,000.

My father showed no real interest. *If his parents never moved, he would still be in East Harlem, he would have never left.* He didn't know, he procrastinated, he wasn't sure. We never made a bid, and the owner passed away. The house was left to her nephew, who was older, married, and lived in Massachusetts. *What did they care about Mount Vernon, they were on the New Hampshire border, beautiful.* More procrastinating, and someone else grabbed it, right out of our hands, and that was that. *What that would be worth today.*

After it fell through, my mother said: "Well, at least let's go to Italy."

ITALY, 1973

The dream started in Queens, where else, southeast Queens, the airport, John F. Kennedy. *Kids, we're going to Idlewild.*

It was one thing to be going to Italy, that by itself seemed not real somehow, but to leave like this, in such style, the Eero Saarinen building, was something else. *Why not us?* All those sensual parabolas, the vaults, the pods, the sunken lounge, swooping banisters, the streaming light of late afternoon, all that delectable modernism, the white and red logo, Trans World Airlines.

My aunts drove us, my father's sisters. It was sunny that afternoon of departure. It was early July. They gave my sister a bouquet of lollipops, and me they bought a TWA flight bag in the terminal. This bag, in bright red, was my immediate, trusted friend, slung around my chest. More than a friend, a substitute security blanket. My regular blanky, once powder blue like Linus's and now gray, with holes, I couldn't bring on the plane. *You're not a baby anymore.* I was five, and I was going on an airplane, with all these people, dressed fancy.

It was our first trip together, the four of us. My mother thought, "I'm really on my way. I can't believe it. I used to see those Italian newspapers at my parents' store, the pictures, those lemon trees, and now I'm going."

My father was going to his father's land, of Garibaldi, Cavour, and before them, Pirandello, Dante, Michelangelo, Raphael, the pope, and before them Augustus, Trajan, Seneca.

The movies they'd seen, before dinner at Isle of Capri: Christ himself flying over Rome, via helicopter, dangling. Soon we would be there.

We would be there only if the plane, the white one I was watching out of the window, the biggest thing I'd ever seen, would get off the ground. It looked like a monster, close up. It frightened me. "That won't be able to fly," I said to my mother. "It's too big." She said, "Yes it will, honey, it's safe, don't worry. It's a 747. See that row of windows there? That's the upstairs, it has an upstairs. It's like being in a house."

"How do you get upstairs?"

"There's a winding staircase, maybe we'll see it."

"Will we be upstairs, in that bump, on top of the plane?" I asked.

"No," she said, "that's first class, but the plane is big enough that you won't feel anything."

"It won't rock?"

"No, it won't rock," she said.

Still, I was petrified. I sat next to my father, the window seat. I held on to my flight bag for dear life. I put the shoulder strap in my mouth. I bit down and grinded my teeth on the plastic. *There's no way this can fly.*

And we just waited, watching all these people file in, *this is taking forever.* Suddenly, to my left, where the window was, a leg, a calf and foot, appeared, extended onto my armrest. What should I do? It was old this leg, dried, wrinkled, and bony. The foot was the same, but it didn't smell. There was something horrifying about this. I grabbed my father by the arm, and with the plastic strap of my flight bag in my mouth, pointed at this ossified leg sticking out, possibly on its last voyage. My father drew me close to him. He might have said, Go to sleep. Which I did, before take-off, hugging my flight bag against me. When I woke up, the leg was gone. "We're on autopilot," my mother leaned back and said. "Look out the window." We were beyond the clouds.

Milano-Centrale. The destination was Verona, but for now, even the Milan central station was its own five-act play. We watched from a small marble table. It was noon, our train was late, we were starving. We ordered little pizzas. *They were prewrapped, but it was still better than the junk you get here.* We stared up at the high, high ceilings; there was art on the ceilings. We looked to the sides. There were Italian men, standing in a semicircle, with their sport coats draped over their shoulders, like Marcello, *they still do that here?*, smoking cigarettes. There were small bands of gypsies that would gather out of nowhere. My mother took out the movie camera, the Super 8. *Look, quick, the men in the semicircle with the hand gestures, maybe cursing the gypsies.* People drank espresso, usually standing up, in three quick rhythmic sips. Then, the announcement, *attenzione, attenzione*, the train to Verona had arrived, finally, departing from *binario numero*, whichever it was.

My mother was back in Bushwick High. Of all places, back there. This is Verona, La Casa Giulietta, and she's thinking of her English teacher, Mrs. Shiftman, the spinster, well not exactly a spinster, the old math teacher married her, and how she explained to these Brooklyn kids iambic pentameter. She remembered how Mrs. Shiftman didn't know who she was, just that boy in her class, that *ginzo*. God, now she was sounding like her father. Jimmy loved that word, *ginzo*. He loved all the ethnic slurs, even the ones directed at his own people, at him.

I never asked, but I understood *ginzo*, unlike *dago* and *guinea* and *wop*, to mean an Italian from the other side, and one who emigrated later, in the '50s or '60s. That kid Mrs. Shiftman liked, yeah he was a *ginzo*, smart as a whip, but a *ginzo*, not because he was from Italy, but because he had that strut, those smarts, not just of the books, which he had, both in math, as Mrs. Shiftman's husband would tell her at home, and in this foreign language, this foreign literature, but in how to play a role, in how to manipulate those enthralled with the role. Like Mrs. Shiftman.

But c'mon, Mom, forget Brooklyn for now, Bushwick High, did she even teach Romeo and Juliet, *or just* Macbeth *and* Hamlet? *This is Verona, how is it?*

It was so exciting, she couldn't sleep that first night. The hotel was called the Il Due Torri, the two towers. It was an elegant little place, like a museum, with antiques and artifacts in each room. Garibaldi stayed here, they said. And that enchanting courtyard. *I wonder if it's still there.* We can check, that we can check.

That first night, back to that first night, we were all out cold, from staying up all day, but my mother couldn't sleep. It wasn't even jet lag; she was wired from disbelief. *I can't believe I'm here.* This was stupid, she'll tell you, but she put a towel over the lamp, to dim the light so we could sleep, and she could read, absorb all this.

The next morning she noticed that the bulb burned a hole through the towel. She should have known better, but she wasn't thinking straight. When we checked out, the concierge knew. *Don't you think he asked us to pay for it. I thought that was so creepy. These Veronese.*

There was a little restaurant. We stopped in. Already we were hungry. We sat outside. The restaurateur was young and gentlemanly, spoke English, with a thick accent, and wanted to chat. It was quiet, we were the only ones there. Turns out he was Sicilian, so was his wife, and he told us of his time in America. It's hard to remember the details, but he was working in the commissary at Harvard University. He'd only been there a few months but had gotten to know some people. Everyone was nice. When Christmas came, being an Italian, coming from where he comes, it's custom to take people in for a holiday, *feed you and all of that.*

But Massachusetts is not Italy and not Sicily, that's for sure, and he said, "I'm all alone here, they all knew me, they knew I was alone in a strange country, nobody offered me a Christmas Eve dinner or said come stay with us. I was left alone."

He reiterated that story. He would never forget it all his life. He was still bitter about it. We said that it was different in America, things were different there, and we apologized on their behalf. Those *stronzi.* New York was better, we said, people there were kind, *molto gentile.*

The train from Verona to Venice is what, a half hour? It took forever. When are we going to get there, when are we going to see water? Gondolas? The wait was unbearable. And then: *Oh, God, we're here.* My mother's aunt, Kitty, it was always her dream to go to Venice, but she died before she could. And even if she lived, would she have gone? Or would she have stayed in Island Park, with the family, always with the family. When the train pulled in, and we walked down those steps and saw the Grand Canal, glistening, for the first time, the *vaporetto* waiting, my mother thought of her aunt. My father thought of his father, playing the cherrywood clarinet.

But wait, the luggage. It's crowded, there's people everywhere, some leaving, sad, others arriving, exhilarated. There's confusion, this is Italy, where do you go, where do you look, the *vaporetto* is waiting, ready to leave, but everyone is staring at the canal, already getting cameras out, posing, here come the sunglasses, you'll want to look good, this is Italy, you have to have sunglasses, even if it were December. But it's July and hot and bright, and wait, where's that guy with our luggage, with the wheelbarrow, we're going to lose him, make sure the *vaporetto* doesn't leave without us.

Now we get off, and the thin man with our luggage is off, fast, wheeling our luggage at an impossible speed through all these slow people, these narrow streets, not even streets, alleys. Don't lose sight of him, whatever you do. But they have it down, my father said. They're professionals. They know what they're doing, where they're going.

The hotel was forgettable. To stay on the Piazza San Marco or the Grand Canal was beyond our means. This was between the Piazza and the Rialto Bridge, on the third floor, noisy, with a restaurant right downstairs, nothing like the Il Due Torri, but who cares, this is Venice. *Kids, we're in Venice, look all around you, take it all in.*

What else in Venice? What was not to like. It really did look like a Canaletto painting. *We bought those two porcelain pieces in Venice,* the violinist and the piano player. We kept it behind glass, in the secretary in Co-op City.

Milan to Verona, Verona to Venice, now Venice to Florence, with side trips to San Gimignano and Siena, this is all sounding very predictable. Of course you had to see Florence, the Uffizi. My parents remembered the flood, seven years before, read about the young people who came to help, to save the treasures.

The first night in Florence, my mother woke up, she had a nightmare. The nightmare was this: She was back in Co-op City, waiting and waiting for the elevator and back in the midst of the gray towers, the vast empty Greenway, if only de Chirico could have painted it. But it was only a nightmare, there were still three more weeks of unreality to enjoy. She went to the curtain, and looked down at the gentle Arno. No, no, what am I saying, we didn't stay beside the Arno. *You kidding, we couldn't afford that.* I don't remember where we stayed in Florence. *There are a lot of things I don't remember, what was it, 1973?*

There were too many people, too many tourists, that we remembered, and that the Florentines were ornery, as if we needed them more than they needed us. *These Northerners, they think who the hell they are.* The Ponte Vecchio seemed too commercial, the jewelry looked cheap, *what's all the fuss?* The famous bistecca Fiorentina is just a grilled steak, *big deal.* But it was paradise, that's why everyone was here, why the Florentines were the way they were, and why, if you woke from a nightmare about an emphatically ugly corner of the Bronx, one where you lived, you took a sip of aqua minerale on your night table, blotted out the sweat with a tissue, and thanked Christ above, even if you had issues with Him, that you were here and not back there.

My father was almost obsessed with seeing long-lost family still in Italy, the ones who hadn't left fifty years before, who stuck out two world wars and were now enjoying an economic miracle, with some snags. He kept saying, "We have to see the cousins, we have to see the cousins." So we headed west, to the coast, to Folonica.

The first thing these cousins did was give us three bottles, three heavy bottles of Vecchio Romagna to lug the remainder of the trip down the boot and back to the Bronx to give to the New York relatives. Well, no, the first thing they did, this is Italy, was feed us. All this spaghetti, and they just watched us eat. Just watched us. And then all this wine at the table, bottle after bottle—we weren't used to it. Our siesta lasted until early evening. That part we could laugh about.

In Rome, there were more cousins. There were long lunches, siestas, wasting time, or maybe not, talking about whether Italy would go Communist, how the Red Brigade was gaining momentum. *Who was behind that bombing in Milan four years ago anyway?* Maybe we would never see them again, either us here, or them in the Bronx. This could be it, they said, we should brace ourselves for it. My father said, no, it wouldn't happen, Italy would never, ultimately, go Communist, that communism would never outlast the Catholic Church. I don't know what the response was. My mother rolled her eyes—*the Catholic Church*.

And if the Catholic Church were so important, why in the hell did we miss the Sistine Chapel? Because of the cousins—was it these same cousins or still other cousins? Okay, we saw St. Peter's, Bernini's colonnade, and the aunt made pasta, homemade pasta, marinara, with a simple bistecca, once over, and a green salad, but for that we missed Michelangelo's masterpiece. *For that we missed treasures?* Then it was Sunday. Everything in Italy was closed.

It's overwhelming. This is Naples we're talking about. Just the smell of the place, as soon as we got there. It smelled like salted cod, *when it's kept out drying*. We were supposed to be there for a day. One day, we could stick it out. And we got a good recommendation for dinner, from my father's cousin, Michele, in the Bronx, but a real Neapolitan with gourmet tastes. He said, "Go to Zia Theresa's, right on the water, order the clam sauce." Which is what we do. They have these teensy-weensy clams about this big, you don't get here. The food, what food, *this is the best food in Italy, this is why people love Italian food, not because of forcemeat and risotto.* I have the pizza. The pizza can't be put into words; it's best not to try. It must be something in the water, they said. It's only this good in Napoli.

As we eat, the kids, little kids, we're talking six, seven, eight years old, they'd come in row boats, and stand up, and push themselves along the wall, with people like us eating, and they mumble, in dialect, "*sordi, sordi,*" money, money. *Now it's coming back to me, there was a lot of begging in the street in Naples. It was very disturbing.*

Later that day, we were walking and there was this kid, sitting in the street, against a wall, in shorts, he was filthy. He couldn't have been more than five or six, my age, and it looked like he was sitting in a puddle of urine, and he said to my mother, in dialect, "*Signora, sordi, sordi.*" She looked at him and said, also in dialect, "*Che fa ca?*" what are you doing here? He looked back at her and said, also in dialect, "*Chi na sa tu?*" as in, what do you know?

Daddy gave him some money, some bills, but he was six years old going on fifty. The kids there weren't like kids, my mother said. They knew how to steal, bargain, finagle. We spent the one night and left.

We left to see more cousins, one outside Naples. Somewhere, I went to an outhouse. I remember because it frightened me. *How come the bathroom's not in the house?* This one cousin, an old woman, she was hard to find. We kept asking, where is this address? My father wanted to see her, whoever she was, we don't even remember now, but she served liquors, coffee, and cookies. For that, more masterpieces went unseen. But Cousin Mario's, that was nice, in Sarno, the hometown, where old ladies were snapping beans into pots in the front of their doors, *a real peasant town.*

They called it *a gaaz,* dialect for *la casa,* the house, even if it was really an apartment. It looked like nothing from the outside, but when we took the elevator to the second floor, wow. My father's aunt was waiting by the front door, a large, dramatic wooden door, with a bouquet of tiger lilies. She gave them not to my mother but for my mother to give to Mario's wife, Sara. Strange, but the lilies were beautiful. The furniture was the best stuff, the finest ceramic tile in the bathroom, everything in the apartment gleamed, it was immaculate.

The dining table was set with white linen, *you don't remember?*, and silver coasters at every setting, with emerald green glasses. Then the dinner, *she was a cook like I don't want to tell you.* She started the meal with a huge bowl of mussels, frutti di mare. Everything Sara made was out of this world. At the end of the meal, she brought out eel, baby eel, fried or deep fried—they're famous for eel down there. *Absolutely out of this world.*

The next day, Mario took us to the Amalfi Coast, a grueling, winding drive, for an ordinary lunch. *It was very touristy, even then.* Nothing like the night before, the home-cooked meal, in the hometown of my father's father.

The plane from Naples to Palermo was small, maybe with propellers. Nor was it TWA, Eastern, or Pan Am. It might have been Alitalia, or maybe even something else. *I was a little nervous.*

But what was there to be nervous about? We met that guy on the plane, the young guy, *he was a dreamboat*, blond hair, how can we forget his name? He started talking to my mother, *talking, talking, talking*, told her he worked in West Germany and was coming back home to Palermo to visit his family. My mother told him her grandparents were from Sicily, that this was her first time, that she couldn't believe it.

He said, "Where are you staying?" We told him the name of the hotel and he said how are you going to get there, do you have anyone to pick you up, the airport is far from the city. He said, no, no, no, that's no good, I'll have my father drive you, he'll be there waiting for me. The father wasn't waiting there, this is Italy, but the Palermo airport was small and sleepy and we talked more. He already knew my name and called me Michele Semolina, because I had freckles.

We said, "Are you sure this won't inconvenience your father." He said, "No, no, don't be silly." The father arrived in a big station wagon, he appeared stern, and the son said, "*Papa, questi Americani.*" The father motioned, enthusiastically, *yes, yes, get in the car.* And when he heard my mother speaking dialect, Sicilian dialect, what she still knew from her grandmother, even if it was Trapanese, he said, "You stay with us."

We said, "No, no, thank you, but we can't."

They said again, "No, no, stay with us." They rang the bell, the son did, this is on the outskirts of Palermo, there are mosquitoes everywhere, and said, "Mama, we have friends, we're bringing them up."

The mother had red hair and blue eyes. We say, "*Scusata Signora...*" and she said, "Come in, I was just making lunch." *She was Sicilian so she made the marinara with eggplant, just like we did.* She put out cured meats and cheeses, salamis we'd never seen before.

Then they start opening the rooms; they had this huge apartment. "There's plenty of room for you," they said, "never mind the hotel."

One room was under lock and key. "*Guarda signora,*" the redheaded matriarch said to my mother, "Look I'll show you." It was precious to her. *And there was the Christmas tree, the artificial Christmas tree, that was all decorated. This was July.* My parents thought this was hilarious, that they never undecorated the tree.

The younger brother took me on his Vespa for a ride around the neighborhood. The day was progressing, and we said we'd love to stay but we already paid for the hotel, we paid in advance in America, and we'd lose the money.

They said, "Well in a case like that, you shouldn't lose your money, but we'll drive you to the hotel, and we insist on taking you to Monreale, you know Monreale?"

"Yes, of course," we said, "the Norman cathedral, the cloister, we were planning to spend the afternoon there tomorrow."

"Tomorrow it is then, we'll pick you up, you tell us the time." And that's what they did, and invited us over for dinner again. *What they didn't do. They treated us like we were their own flesh and blood.* Better, even. Relatives don't do that. We sent them a gift when we got back home. *I have pictures of them in the album, in the Japanese album, go look.*

The rest of Palermo was like this: wide boulevards, horse and buggies, in disrepair but elegant, a lot under scaffolding, a lot was closed, not many people out, certainly not begging, *like those Neapolitans,* and by nine at night, everyone's inside.

We got lost, this is Italy, and that's part of it, like Venice at the beginning of the trip, and so on down the boot. It's part of the fun. And so we wandered around. It's Sunday, possibly, bright and sunny, and no one is on the street. The neighborhood gets more and more dilapidated as we continue on, not sure exactly where we're going. Then a man appears from out of his window, from the old school, really old school, with the handlebar mustache, wearing a cap. He just looks at us, and doesn't look away, holds his gaze. My father says, "Let's get the hell out of here." *These Sicilians.* My mother said, "What, what for?" She didn't feel afraid, she felt local, whether she was or not. But we left and found our way back to one of the boulevards.

Another day there was a feast, for what, I don't know. *No, not Santa Rosalia, nothing so big.* The signoras were making pizza, foccacia really, *it smelled out of this world,* and it was. They put a little *aleeg—alige,* anchovies—tomato, a little onion, just the way Jenny Rollo did it, the landlady back at 137 Jefferson, at the two-family house. We're back in Bushwick. You could smell that yeast rising, the windows would be open. She would come out in the hall and say, "Lilly, Lilly, I have something for you," and she would send up squares of pizza. *Oh, the taste.* My mother had no appetite as a kid, her father always made her nervous, but that she could eat. It was light, like air.

The drive to my mother's hometown, not her hometown, her grandfather's hometown, was west, along the coast, to Trapani. My father didn't drive, from East Harlem you didn't have to. My mother was in the process of learning. The Cohns were teaching her.

We hired a driver to take us to Trapani and Marsala. The Super 8 footage is from out the window of the backseat. It's flushed now, the color, or was the sea that pale a blue? There's no one on the road. The breeze is hot. The windows, all four of them, are open. Our hair blows around wildly.

My mother didn't bother trying to find family. She was one more generation removed from the old country. She could've asked her uncle who they still had there, but why? Family, yeah, it's great, but they complicate things at best, ruin things at worst. There was an uncle, or was it a cousin, who came to visit her grandfather in Brooklyn, used to cut his hair. He was a barber back in Sicily, this uncle or cousin. But she didn't even ask. Her mother's family, did they have anyone left here? My mother didn't know, and didn't ask. She wasn't on the best of terms with them since her wedding, *that whole thing*.

We had lunch by the sea. My mother ordered couscous, that was the dish to order in these parts. It was just like her grandfather's. They pronounced it *goosgoosu*.

In Trapani, there were churches everywhere, more than in Rome, it seemed, maybe one per block, sometimes two. The salt pans, the famous salt pans, we didn't see. Her grandparents never talked about them; they were real city people. Oh, and the lemon trees, did I mention the lemon trees? Along the roads, lemons everywhere, like in the pages of *Il Progresso*, but in color. *Can we pick one, is that allowed?*

In Marsala, we saw where they made the wine, Marsala wine, dense and sweet. *Did we bring bottles home? That and the porta.* My mother's grandmother talked about the porta Garibaldi. This is Italy, everything is named after Garibaldi, but this for good reason: Garibaldi invaded Sicily through Marsala.

And that was it. We only hired the driver for the afternoon; it was getting late. "I would have liked to get in deeper, stay longer," my mother said of her hometown. Not her hometown, but her grand-mother Fidele's hometown.

She couldn't, we couldn't. We had to get back. There was a final stop in Taormina—might as well end in style, the last scene in *L'Avventura*—but our vacation was over. Who gets three, four weeks' vacation anyway? Maybe we were where we belonged, here in Italy, despite those Northerners, the encroaching Communists, obligatory visits to cousins. Maybe this was the place we should have been all the while. Maybe we, those before us, should never have left, fifty, seventy years before.

"I don't want to go home," my mother said. *I was almost sick to my stomach, the thought of that place, Co-op.* Why was that even home? When would we get out?

Just look at it: In Italy, everything seemed to be in marble and stone, even the cousin's apartment in a small town in the hills out-side of Naples, where they ignored building codes. Co-op City was all concrete—concrete on top of concrete.

"Don't worry," my father said. "We'll come back." He was talking about Italy. "I still want to see Agrigento, the baroque Siracusa, Peru-gia, Assisi, and Turin, to see the shroud."

Daddy said: "Every three years we'll go to Europe." There's so much more to see.

SHEA STADIUM, 1974

My first baseball game was—I don't remember when my first baseball game was, to tell you the truth. I can remember my first football game and against whom; first basketball and hockey games, but not baseball. Maybe because it came before the others, so much sooner.

It was at Shea and it was either 1973 or 1974. Let's say '74, when I was six. It was the summer, a bright perfect day, maybe a little hazy. We went with the Cohns, our closet friends. Tom Seaver was pitching. I know this from the Super 8 film, my mother still had the camera, the one that filmed her wedding at the Plaza, the World's Fair in Flushing, the gypsies in Milano-Centrale, and the western coast of Sicily. Seaver had that delivery, such a beautiful motion that whoever held the camera for those few seconds focused only on Seaver warming up between innings. We were in the lower deck, third-base side, it looks like.

My father, who virtually considered himself a Yankee, would have wanted Yankee Stadium for my first game, as was his, but the stadium was being renovated for two years. To see the Yankees play in Shea was an incongruous, even offensive, sight to him. And the Mets were already becoming my team. I remember them losing in the World Series, Willie Mays pleading his case on his knees, at home plate, against this big, bad, hirsute club who wore white shoes. The Yankees were old, wore what looked like brooding white uniforms with black caps. The Mets were young, in royal blue and orange. Even their announcers were fun. Lindsay Nelson with those blazers.

So many kids in Co-op City, despite it being in the Bronx, were

Mets fans. Shea was still relatively new and, more important, it was safer and easier to get to. Maybe Robert Moses did get this right: Jump right on I-95, over the beautiful Whitestone Bridge, *what views*, and you were right there, at this circular structure with a gaping-wide opening, the Coliseum of Queens.

Not that my mother would find the courage to drive there, but the Cohns did, and would again and again with us over the years, even when, and maybe because, the Mets became a laughingstock.

Still, not to remember your first baseball game, at least who they played, seems unbelievable, even sinful. How can I remember that the Rangers played the Blues in 1975, that we sat in greens at around center ice; that we sat in orange seats, Sonics-Knicks, in 1978; that we were in the upper deck at Shea for the Jets-Dolphins in '79, *Monday Night Football*. But I can't say who the Mets played in '73, maybe '74? Let's say it was Houston.

My father remembered his first game: Yankees-Tigers, 1938. The Boys' Club took him and the neighborhood kids, before they learned how to gamble. He remembers Lefty Gomez was pitching. He loved Lefty Gomez. Maybe that's why he loved Lefty Gomez. He remembers sitting on the first-base side. He remembers looking right at Detroit's second baseman, Charlie Gehringer, and Gehringer looking back at him. *No really.* He thinks the Yankees won; it was Lefty Gomez after all. He remembers Joe D., everyone's hero, his too. He remembers Hammerin' Hank. Hank Greenberg, Lou Gehrig, Bill Dickey, Tommy Henrich. Half the Hall of Fame played that day.

He doesn't remember that Lefty got touched up for seven runs. He doesn't remember DiMaggio's brilliant catch in the fifth. He doesn't remember that DiMaggio had three hits, that Gehrig did, too. Or that the Yankees scored twelve runs. But Lefty got the win. About that, he was right.

I should remember all of that. Seaver must have won; he was Seaver. I remember the concession stands, all that royal blue, the caps, the shiny, fake plastic batting helmets, the smiling Mr. Met blow-up dolls, all the National League caps, piled on top of one another. I remember tall, elderly men, with ruddy faces and Mets hats, taking us to our seats, dusting them off, my father slipping him a two-dollar tip, the usher accepting in a seamless motion, then putting his forefinger and thumb on the brim of his cap: Enjoy the game, he said to us without saying it.

I remember being told to bring my baseball glove, that I'd have to be ready, that you never know when a foul ball would come your way. I remember being afraid of the ball. *Please don't hit it here.*

This was a problem in my own baseball career—I was afraid of the ball. Not afraid, petrified. I was happy to join the Co-op City Little League, probably the following year, when I was in second or third grade. I joined with Harry Cohn. We were the smallest kids, and the youngest, but since all we did was talk about baseball, our parents thought we should try out. The tryouts weren't challenging. All we had to do was know the basic rules of the game, do some running, and make contact with a big foamy rubber ball, not a baseball, or even a softball. So the League officials put us in the entry-level division, where almost everyone was a year older than we were. This was a mistake.

I was assigned to a team called the Sampans, sponsored by the Chinese Restaurant on Co-op City Boulevard, next to the movie theater. Our colors were royal blue and white. We had real baseball uniforms. My father took me to Herman's Sporting Goods, my favorite place in the city, and bought me a nice glove.

"Let me show you how to break it in," he said. "You schmear some olive oil on it, tie it up with a shoelace, and sleep with it."

He would take me out to play catch. I can't remember if he had a glove of his own. Even if he did, he looked ridiculous, insisting on playing in his dress slacks. He didn't own a pair of jeans or shorts or any kind of athletic wear, nor did he own sneakers, which he thought were for kids or professional athletes, but not for mature, employed adults. My mother was in full agreement, one of the few times. I never saw either of them in jeans, shorts, or sneakers. They didn't own any.

So when it was time to take me out to play, he'd wear slacks, usually an old pair, and worn-out wingtips. That was on a good day. Sometimes he would bring me down and play with me in his slippers, which embarrassed me no end, especially if I'd see other kids from the building.

"Hey Mike, I saw you playing catch with your grandfather from my window yesterday," I heard.

"That's not my grandfather," I'd mumble. "That's my father."

Even if he loved sports and played enthusiastically in his day, he never seemed to enjoy playing with me. It seemed more out of obligation. He seemed easily winded and pained if he had to bend to pick up a ball, and anxious to get back upstairs to the apartment, to his *New York Times*, his books, to accepting bets or placing them. Pretending he was Buddy Harrelson to my Felix Millan never seemed like his idea of a good time. He said: "Never refer to me as your old man, like some people do. Promise? Word of honor?"

He'd annoy me with stories of these old Yankees whom he wanted me to emulate, often with Italian last names: Crosetti, Rizzuto, Martin, Pepitone, and, over and over, DiMaggio. DiMaggio, DiMaggio, DiMaggio. I was almost relieved when my mother said: "Oh, would you give it a rest with that DiMaggio. What self-respecting Italian would have ever married her."

And worse, he'd evoke the boys from the old neighborhood: "Learn to follow through on your throws. Nick-a-Nick had a beautiful follow-through." "Break fast to the ball and camp under it, like Chubby." "Use your body and get in front of the ball, don't be afraid of the ball. Be like *abunam'* Bence." And most of all: "Use two hands, not like these guys today on TV. Use two hands."

I did learn to throw and catch, but with a rubber ball or tennis ball. When Little League started it was hardball and only hardball. These kids may have only been eight, but they threw serious heat. The ball was a blur and seeing how other kids, other kids older than me, started crying when they got hit by a pitch, I wanted no part of this. I stood three feet from home plate and went 0 for the season, making contact only once for a foul ball. I was lucky in only one sense: that the famous Co-op City umpire known as "Big Mike" never umped any of my games. Big Mike was a very fat black man with a loud, loud voice. If someone looked at the third strike, or if they'd swing and miss, it was not enough for Mike to say, "Strike three, you're out!" No, Mike had to have a signature call, something to remember him by, as if we'd ever forget him. He would say, or rather, bark, in the loudest possible voice, "STRIKE THREE. . . . GOOD NIGHT!" It was humiliation on a grand scale, as the Little League fields were in the wide-open Greenway, which was framed by several of these tall buildings. Sound would carry. So if you struck out, and Big Mike was calling balls and strikes, half of Co-op City knew about it. For that, at least, I was spared.

My only highlight was working out a walk—*good eye, Mikey, good eye*—and managing not to cry when, inevitably, I was hit by a fourth-grader who was having location problems.

Most of the games were scheduled on weekend afternoons when my father had his bookmaking to tend to. That was his excuse. More than once my mother yelled at him. "Aren't you going to watch Michael play!"

"I gotta answer the phones," he'd say. "What am I supposed to do?"

"It's okay, I'm not gonna do anything," I'd say.

"Ay, cut that out," my father said. "Don't talk like that. You're due. I think you'll get on base today. I have a hunch. Just don't be afraid of the ball." Every weekend he said that to me: Don't worry, you're due.

My mother was afraid for me. She'd only come to see me play once, and watched all the way down the left-field line, in foul territory, with what looked like a hand over her face. "What are you talking about," she said, impatiently. "I've seen how fast these kids throw that ball. And they're huge, some of them. He's a little bit of a thing. I'm telling you, one of these days a kid is going to get hit in the face with that thing and get killed. Mark what I'm telling you."

Now, maybe, I was off to my death.

"Would you cut it out," my father would yell back at her. "You're putting ideas in his head. You can't be afraid of the ball."

"Didn't it happen to that Italian ballplayer?" she said.

"Tony Conigliaro," he said.

"Yeah. Tony Conigliaro. He got beaned, didn't he?"

"Listen, Brother Michael," he said, now almost laughing, "just choke up on the bat and keep your eye on the ball. And step into the pitch. You'll be all right."

When I'd get home, he would be all excited and ask, "How'd ya make out?"

The answer was always the same. "Oh for two."

"Did you make contact?"

"Nope, struck out."

"Swinging?"

"Yeah"

"Well that's all right," he'd say. "You know Reggie Jackson strikes out a lot."

"You shouldn't have pushed him into this," my mother said. "He's too young and too small."

"Maybe you should bunt," he said, thinking out loud. "They teach you how to bunt yet?"

"Nope."

"I'll have to teach you next time," he said. "There's an art to it. Rizzuto was the best I've ever seen at it. You're a Rizzuto-type player."

I was so useless that my own team loaned me out one game when the other team was short a player. This was especially difficult because pitching for the Sampans that day was our flamethrowing right-hander Jimmy, who was by far the best, and hardest-throwing, pitcher in the Co-op City Farm Division. Before the game, I got Jimmy alone and said, "Hey Jimmy, can you take it easy on me today." "Yeah, okay, Mike, don't worry."

Maybe I wasn't good, but I was popular with my teammates, and

Jimmy was a nice kid. When it was time for me to get up, I was shaking in my stirruped socks. Jimmy was lights out that day. As usual, I stood way off the plate. Jimmy was a kid of his word, and was throwing not only outside but noticeably slower. The pop in the glove still scared me. One pitch went by, then another, then one more—you needed eight balls for a walk in the Farm Division for some reason, so this was an excruciatingly long at bat. Soon parents and coaches started to get on him: "C'mon, Jimmy, throw it." Same thing, low and outside. I'm up six balls, no strikes. But now he's being chastised, by his father, his manager, who's actually my manager, who knows how afraid I am of the ball: "Jimmy, burn it in." That's all I kept hearing. "Burn it in, Jimmy, burn it in." I looked at strike one. I still have the unheard-of count of 6–1. The next pitch comes streaking in, but it's in the dirt. Seven balls, one strike. I'm one ball away from getting on base against the legendary Jimmy, even though he's letting me. Then another white blur streaks by, this time closer to me. Strike 2! It's a full count: 7–2. Now, I thought, maybe, for a change, I'll get lucky. *I'm due.* Jimmy was going for the strikeout, I knew that; he caved in to the urgings of the psycho Little League parents, not his inner humanity.

So I was going to swing. I choked up, closed my eyes, and swung, as hard as I could. But this was real life, even at such a young age, and I missed, probably by a lot, I would think.

Way to hang in there, Mikey.

Despite me, the Sampans were a powerhouse. We finished the season undefeated and captured the Farm Division Championship. We were awarded a buffet lunch at a restaurant in the East Bronx, where each Sampans player was given a championship plaque. The plaque was presented to each of us by none other than current New York Met, Ed Kranepool. He was coming to the end of his career, and I only remembered him as a bad player, a pinch hitter, and automatic out. Still, he was a real live Met we were going to meet. He played in the World Series in 1973 and was part of the 1969 team I'd heard so much about. Some of my other Sampans teammates weren't as impressed on the way to the luncheon. "Kranepool stinks," one of them said. "Why can't Kingman be there?"

I don't remember much, except Kranepool giving me the plaque, and saying, in a very familiar voice, "Way to go, kid." He was from the Bronx and looked like he could've been a manager in the Co-op City Little League, not a big league ball player. I didn't care, I got to meet a Met. There's a picture somewhere.

And the game? The Met game, that first one, I mean. It was fantastic, it really was. I got a Mets yearbook, a Mets T-shirt, my sister got a Mr. Met doll. Harry and I wore our gloves all game, just in case, my father talked to Max about politics, the hot dogs never tasted that good, the Gulden's mustard never tangier, the kraut never as tart, the sun never stopped shining. The Mets won, all right, Seaver was pitching. He took care of the Astros, or the Padres or the Expos, no problem. My father won money on the game, let's say he did, and on the way back we sang the Mets song.

SAN JUAN, PUERTO RICO, 1975

Read to us, we said. Okay, she said, I'll read to you. Let's see what's here.

My mother's eyes combed the book shelf; it wasn't her shelf. What would be good for children? Ah, this will be good for you kids, and she began reading. *"Once when I was six years old I saw a magnificent picture in a book. . . . It was a picture of a boa constrictor in the act of swallowing an animal. Here is a copy of the drawing."* She opened the book for us to see the illustration.

My mother read to us before, plenty: *Aesop's Fables*, the first time I heard the word *moral*, *Curious George*, and the *Little Toot*, a Little Engine That Could but as a tugboat instead. We'd see tugboats all the time, from our kitchen window in Co-op City, on the Hutchinson River. See that small little boat, see how strong it is, that could be me, why not. But *The Little Prince* transported us. We may have been in an ostentatious high-rise in San Juan, Puerto Rico, with dim lighting, mirrors, *Playboy* magazines, which didn't exist in our house, shag carpet, a real bachelor pad, but now we were in the North African desert, stranded with Saint-Exupéry, his aircraft down.

My mother read this with great enthusiasm. She'd change inflection, depending on who was speaking, undulate pitch, and vary cadences, to keep my sister and me enthralled. *"Thus you can imagine my amazement, at sunrise, when I was awakened by an odd little voice. It said: 'If you please—draw me a sheep!' 'What!' 'Draw me a sheep!'"*

It made sense when kids always asked me, during a birthday party or a play date: Is your mother a kindergarten teacher? Maybe it's what she could have been, or should have been. *Would that have been better?* She could read a story, play a board game, sing a song, like no one else's mother.

"If they ask if you're a teacher, what should we say?"

"Tell the truth," she said, "that I work in the home, that I'm a housewife—no, homemaker. It's nothing to be ashamed of. Tell them it's hard work, that it's not easy. "

"And Daddy, what do I say when they ask me what Daddy does?"

"You say he works for the City, that he's an administrator for the City. That's the truth. But don't tell them about the phones. You don't tell that to anyone. Understand?"

This was our night, the three of us. My father was out with the guys, gambling at the La Concha, a hotel and casino just down the road, still in Condado.

He was never out with the guys, hardly ever; he was always home, with us, and he never went to casinos. He only did it here, in San Juan, at the La Concha. Maybe he'd been to Las Vegas on the way back from Camp Pendleton after the war. Or maybe once to Atlantic City. But casinos weren't my father's dream or weakness. Neither were late nights, women, drink, song. When he told Rino that he wanted to have a couple of kids, tuck them in, he was telling the truth. In Puerto Rico, he would go to the casino with his gambling associates—were they friends?—as a way to bond, with a different type, with associates yes, but men he liked. And he only played blackjack. In his mind, it was the only sensible game to put your money on.

My mother went on reading. She said, "The sheep, the desert, the downed plane, the baobabs, you'll read this again when you get older and it will be different then."

"What do you mean?" we asked.

"You'll know what I mean. It's for kids but it's also for grown-ups."

She didn't say this on the first night. She didn't finish reading us the book the first night. We wanted her to extend the pleasure, read it, act it, slowly. We told her, "The story can't end. Never finish." So she stopped at some point. And my father would soon be back and we should be off to sleep. I worried about nightmares, these boa constrictors and the funny-looking trees, they looked scary.

"Do we have those snakes in Co-op City, the ones that can swallow an elephant?"

"No," my mother said. "Not in Co-op City. They don't even allow dogs in Co-op City."

"What about in Puerto Rico? Do they have those snakes in Puerto Rico?"

"No," she said. "Everything is nice in Puerto Rico. Maybe you'll see some big bugs, but they won't hurt you. Now let's go to bed."

And we did. And we heard my father come home, late or whatever late is for a seven-year-old.

"How was it?" my mother asked.

My father, happy, said, "Would you believe I was up six hundred dollars. I'm pulling nineteens, twenties, blackjack, I caught a streak. Well, to make a long story short, I finish with a hundred dollars but what are you gonna do? We'll have a nice dinner in Old San Juan tomorrow. Who's better than us?"

My mother laughed this time. *Why didn't you quit while you were ahead?* If he only quit while he was ahead. If he had, would we still be in Co-op City? Would we be in San Juan, in this high-rise, right now?

He always envisioned a streak, not at the blackjack table pulling twenties for a few hands, but a substantial streak, the kind he had all those years ago, the one that ended when Wake Forest didn't cover and he put his fist through the gumball machine near Mount Carmel Church. His time would come again. Parlays were how he interpreted the phrase "Have your money make money for you." He would put something together. A package, he called it. What that package was, it was never clear. A down payment? A retirement fund? Savings for college. Any savings. Quit while he was ahead? *He can't, like I keep saying. He's an addicted gambler. He doesn't admit to it.*

The next day, that's what we did, we went to Old San Juan. That's what we always did in San Juan. We went to the public beach across the street—*you kids should learn how to swim*—or we went to Old San Juan, walked around, went to El Morro Castle, a museum for Pablo Casals (*that's the public school you kids will be going to in fifth grade, Pablo Casals, I.S. 181*), ate at El Patio de Sam, in the courtyard in the back. The waiters seemed to recognize us from last year. Or we'd go to La Concha and have an afternoon drink.

My father said: "They take us for wealthy Spaniards."

My mother: "Wealthy Spaniards? They take us for New York Jews."

My father: "No, they think we're Castillians."

We were lucky to be here. My mother told us that. "Kids, we're lucky to be here." The clean air, the warm sun, so what if the public beach was just a public beach and not the pristine kind written up in travel magazines produced in Manhattan. It was February, freezing in the Northeast, and we were here. Lucky.

This time last year, we were all here, and my parents by themselves, two years before that, their last vacation alone together. The year before, it was the same; it was perfect. We flew Eastern Airlines, a DC-10 out of LaGuardia, a plane full of Nuyoricans and us, to paradise. In the middle of our week there, we took a small plane for a day trip to Saint Thomas. Our next-door neighbor in Co-op City, Ricardo, was from Saint Thomas and he said, "Oh, you got to go." We did, and when we came back and told him what a beautiful place it was, he said, "Thank you," proudly. "And don't I wish I was there now instead of freezin' my behind up here." We all laughed.

We were in Puerto Rico because of football, the unpredictability of it, the drug it had become. My father was making money, bookmaking, then, brazenly, recklessly, gambling on top of that. He would earn three thousand dollars booking, gamble four thousand dollars. He'd tell my mother at the dinner table, with a small reproduction of the painting *Pilgrims Going to Church* by George Henry Boughton hanging on our wall, facing me directly, "More money is being gambled on football on the floor of the New York Stock Exchange than anyplace else." Could that be true? *Believe me when I tell you.*

If he was winning, someone else was losing. One was Stan Binsky, international business man, bachelor, jet-setter, based in Puerto Rico. My father met him in New York, on 271 Church. Someone in the diner downstairs made the introduction. He was in steel, Stan was, and he worked for his father, who once had holdings in Cuba, before the revolution. The friendship began slowly, with a small bet here and there, but mainly just talking, about my father's work in the department, about the welfare state vs. capitalism, the role of government vs. free markets. They spoke about religion, about politics, about race, about everything you shouldn't talk about in a business relationship. Stan introduced my father to more of his friends and work associates. It all, they all, just fell into my father's lap.

Stan's girlfriend was a stewardess for Braniff. I knew all the airlines and would look into the sky in Co-op City during punchball games, and identify the planes as they made their descent into LaGuardia. "Mike, what's that silver one, with the red and blue?" "That's A.A.," I said. "And that one, that crazy one with all the colors coming around Building 3?" "Braniff," I said, "that's definitely Braniff."

We never saw her, this glamorous stewardess. And we rarely saw him. He was tall, thin, bearded, world-weary. He seemed mysterious to me; I was just a kid, but he was a mystery to my mother. She'd say to my father: "How come he never talks about his son?" and "Stan must be Jewish, no?" "No, how many times do I have to tell you, he's Romanian."

"A Romanian Jew then," she said. "Binsky is not a Romanian name," she said.

"That's true," he said. "They end in the *u* usually. But it's his mother who's a Romanian Catholic. The father was Russian. I don't know if he was Jewish. He never said his father was Jewish."

There were never any photos around, not of his son or his parents, nothing of sentiment. In a way, just *The Little Prince*. Maybe he'd read it to his son.

He would vacate his apartment for us to stay for a week, rent-free, while he was overseas on business. This was generous; he was generous. It was also a way to pay his debt. He was losing piles of money to my father and didn't always have the cash to pay. His cleaning lady would leave the apartment immaculate. He'd leave ice-cream sandwiches in the freezer, a box of twelve. He knew us kids would like them.

His friend and colleague, professional and gambling, was Ron, half Puerto Rican, half Polish (*who's half Puerto Rican and half Polish?*). With his thick reddish gray beard, he looked like the country singer Kenny Rogers. He was more extroverted, more forthcoming. He also lived in San Juan, in Santurce, also in a high-rise, with shag carpets, dim lighting, and *Playboy* magazines. He also had a son somewhere; was it in Florida? My mother said to him: "Ronnie, why don't you settle down . . ." My father finished the sentence, ". . . find a nice Puerto Rican girl." "Eh," Ronnie said, "it's not so easy." He'd shake his head. If it were only that easy.

We'd see Stan and Ron the first night or two, my father might go to the casino with them, where he was always up five or six hundred dollars, then down, lucky if he broke even, then they were off—to Bonn or Frankfurt or I want to say Hamburg, maybe on Braniff.

My mother took *The Little Prince*. She stole it. The hell with it, she said, Stan won't notice. She didn't finish reading us the book that week; we still didn't want the experience to end, so she'd finish back home.

My father said to her, "What are you doing? Leave the book here." He liked to say, "I never stole a dime from anyone." She said we'd just be borrowing it, so she could finish reading to us. Think of it as a loan, she told him. This my father could accept; loans he understood. Okay, so long as we send it back to Stan. And, in his mind, you could never have enough books around.

My father was a compulsive book buyer, and reader, mainly of history, but also of art criticism and music. He didn't watch much television, the Yankees if they were on Channel 11, or a detective show, he loved Buddy Ebsen, *he's from the old school*, Jack Lord as Steve McGarrett, and Kojak.

Out of the blue, my father might shout, "Look, come look, it's Jake the Baker from my old neighborhood!" or "Ay, it's Blackie's cousin—he looks good, that son of a gun, go call your mother." Then he'd yell out, "Cora!"

My mother would be in the master bedroom. By then we had a small second TV where the last thing she wanted to watch were programs about urban crime. She was addicted to *Masterpiece Theatre*, the interminable *Upstairs, Downstairs*; *Poldark*; *I, Claudius*.

She might rush in and say, "What, what happened?" thinking there was an assassination or plane crash. He'd say, "Ah, you just missed it was Jake the Baker on Kojak, he was just there for a few seconds. He was the bad guy again. Ha!" She'd say, "That's what you called me in for? Everything is always about that neighborhood, and those *paisan*s, what did they ever do for you?" Then she'd go back to Alistair Cooke.

When his show was over, he was back to his books. They seemed to come in the mail or by UPS every day. Our large bookcase was bursting, there was no more room. Foreboding titles to a second grader: *Hadrian* by Stewart Perowne; *Memoirs of Hadrian*, by Marguerite Yourcenar; *The Outline of Music*, Edited by Sir Malcolm Sargent; *Ways of Thinking of Eastern Peoples: India, China, Tibet, Japan* by Hajime Nakamura; *Dante and His World* by Thomas Caldecot Chubb; *Garibaldi and His Enemies: The Clash of Arms and Personalities in the Making of Italy* by Christopher Hibbert; *Guide to the Art Treasures of France*; *Franco* by Brian Crozier; *The Great Conductors* by Harold C. Schonberg; *The Evolution of Man and Society* by C. D. Darlington; *Inside the Third Reich: Memoirs* by Albert Speer.

"A remarkable portrait in depravity," said *The New York Times*; *The Condottieri: Soldiers of Fortune* by Geoffrey Trease; *Karl Marx: His Life and Thought* by David McLellan; *Ivan the Terrible* by Robert Payne and Nikita Romanoff; *Joan of Arc* by Edward Lucie-Smith.

To make room for all these, Uncle Pep, carpenter and character, was brought in. He was short and thin and old, the brother of my father's mother. He came from Italy, Nocera Inferiore, in the 1950s. Either there, in the old country, or here, under the el at Castle Hill Avenue where he lived, there was a scandal, an affair (can I say a ménage à trois?), something. *But don't talk about that.*

He would make two bookcases in our living room—one ten feet long, floor to ceiling; the other slimmer, three feet, in the corner of our living room, and would hold more books but also vinyl recordings, jazz and classical, nothing popular, and copies of the academic journal *Daedalus*, those dreary, matte covers, one issue after the next, piling up. Then the uncle would make two smaller ones in my room.

Pep had come the year before, or maybe the year before that or the year before that. Maybe I hadn't started school. I remember him working all day at our house for days. He'd come in the morning, kiss my father on the cheek before he left for work, have a coffee with my mother, tell stories, then, finally, get to work. *He's a wheel and a half, my uncle.* My mother would make him a big, hot meal, usually pasta, with wine, and they'd talk and laugh over a two-hour lunch. He'd tell us more stories, of his childhood during the Great War, and of Africa, of his time there in the Italian army, in Ethiopia or Eritrea or Somalia. He was in the desert, he may have been stranded at one point. "The stars," he said to my mother in dialect, "they scared me, they were so big." He acted this out. He thought the world was coming to an end. Maybe it was the malaria. His two brothers, both officers, never made it home. One day, you must go to Africa, to the desert, he said. It's the most beautiful place on Earth, even more than Italy. He'd have another espresso, only from the maganette, the Italian coffee maker, a cigarette, then a siesta.

The copy of *The Little Prince* ended up on the bookcase Uncle Pep built, the big one in the living room, second shelf from the bottom, so my sister and I could reach it. It was never sent back to San Juan.

"They call me Professor," my father said. He'd say this the next morning, when we all had breakfast and we asked him about the casino. He never had delusions, but he was flattered by the attention these men, businessmen, well-traveled men, gave him. Maybe he woulda, coulda, shoulda, been a professor, or at least a high school history teacher.

"Don't let them patronize you," my mother said.

"What patronize? They take me for a learned guy."

"Why don't they pay you what they owe you then?"

"Well, we get to come to Puerto Rico, don't we?"

"Sure, I love Puerto Rico, but they hardly use their apartments here. They're flying around on business, they're with their girlfriends, they're everywhere and nowhere, these guys. They take advantage. If they paid you what they owed you, we could put that away and invest it in something." She didn't say "house" or even necessarily mean "house" this time. She wasted too much breath, thought, dream, on "house" before. Still, she hadn't given up on it. Maybe there would be a streak. If not this year, maybe next year or the year after or by the time my sister reached high school age. She said, "These guys gamble for sport, with their disposable income. They don't do it to pay the rent."

He didn't respond.

They did like him, these men. And they probably did think he was learned. Or maybe they were patronizing him. But they brought their business to him. They felt comfortable with him, and they knew he knew, what would you call it, the score, the street? He was low enough on the radar that they wouldn't get found out. It was a mom-and-pop bookmaking business, without the mom, but he was still big enough to absorb an ample wager. They didn't know Frankie Beesh or Muzz or Rudy, another East Harlem bookmaker who took bets from an NBA superstar for years, while he was playing, and kept it secret. They didn't know my father knew these men, but they knew they were in good hands. They were sharp and they were good businessmen. They knew he wasn't pay-or-die. They knew he was big, but knew he wasn't too big, that he wouldn't get rounded up at Super Bowl time, when the FBI made its busts every year. *Mommy, are they going to arrest Daddy for answering the phones like these other people on the eleven o'clock news?* They knew, these sharp businessmen, that he shouldn't even have been doing what he was doing.

PORTUGAL, SPAIN, MOROCCO, 1976

We went around the room, this was September, first day of third grade. The question was simple, one that had been asked again and again, September after September: What did you do over the summer? Did we have to answer the question or write something and recite it out loud? I don't remember. This is what I said and/or wrote: "Last summer, I went with my mother and father and sister to Portugal, Spain, and Morocco. We went for three weeks and had a very nice time. We flew on the Portuguese airline TAP and then Iberia. We went to the Alfama in Lisbon. It was very old. Morocco was also very old and very hot. In Spain, we went to the famous Prado Museum and saw famous paintings. We also went to a bullfight at the Plaza De Toros and my mother bought me a T-shirt and poster that I hung in my room."

The kids just stared. So did the teacher, silent for five, ten seconds. The other kids had gone to Lake George, Shorehaven, a pool club in the Bronx, or Co-op City Camp.

I wasn't trying to embarrass anyone. I knew I was lucky to be there, in Portugal, Spain, and Morocco—like in Puerto Rico or Italy or Shea Stadium. I loved these kids in school. I had my friends from my building; Harry, up on the twenty-fourth floor, was still my best friend. But at school you got to meet kids from all over Co-op City, still enormous and mysterious to a child. There were even little ones bused in from Boston Secor, a housing project across the highway. They had less than the Co-op kids; they were poor, or close to it, whether they were white or black or Hispanic. Their clothes weren't as nice, they went to Korvette's, a discount department store on Boston Road. My sister and I were lucky. (Did I mention we were lucky?) My father's brother-in-law, my uncle, worked at Saks Fifth Avenue, and we got 30 percent off. If my father was doing well, we'd buy our clothes there. And my aunt worked at B. Altman; we got 30 percent off there, too. The children's clothes at Altman's looked like grown-up clothes but smaller, so we preferred Saks. So did my father, he always had, back when he worked there. We shopped at Lord & Taylor and Bloomingdale's. My mother had charge cards from there, and they would go unpaid, month after month after month, surcharges and interest mounting, until my father broke a losing streak, usually when football season arrived, just in time for school.

These kids from Secor, that's what they called it, Secor, the way we called it not Co-op City but just Co-op, spoke street, even at five and six years old. Some of the Co-op kids also went to Korvette's or Alexander's on Fordham Road and talked street. You'd always hear "ain't" and especially "it ain't not." I kept hearing that turn of phrase, from seven-year-olds, in school and downstairs playing in front of the building. I liked the sound of this and used it back upstairs. I'd say it: "It ain't not, Mommy."

"Don't say that, ever, not in this house, or anywhere else," she'd scream at me. "Speak properly." Then she'd turn to my father and say, "See what he's learning in this place."

I started kindergarten at the public school, P.S. 178, in 1973, a few weeks after we came back from Italy. It was scary, as it is for everyone. No need to say more. But after that it was the most fun you could have. Except for the food so my mother would get me a new lunch box every year—Scooby Doo, Fat Albert, Spiderman—and pack a lunch every day. "You have to eat your lunch," she'd say. "You're a little bit of a thing."

That I was small I could see already. When we lined up in size order, I was at the shortest, maybe second or third shortest in the class.

Harry was my size. Maybe that's why we got along; we had that in common, that and our love of the Mets.

Somehow I escaped bullying. Maybe it was the era. The Peanuts Gang, *Captain Kangaroo*, *Zoom*, *Sesame Street*, the songs we'd hear on the radio and sing in the schoolyard: "Games people play, right, wrong, I just can't stop it"; or "You don't have to be a star, baby, to me in my show"; or "Rock the boat, don't rock the boat, baby, rock the boat, don't tip the boat over"; or "Summer breeze, makes me feel fine, blowing through the jasmine of my mind," the Isley Brothers version.

Maybe it was our teachers. Some were post-hippies, or still real hippies. Everyone's favorite teacher was Mr. Shaw, a tall, lanky young man, with hair well past his shoulders, long beard, bandana, old jeans, a smile this wide. He was the happiest man alive. I remember how he bounced when he walked. His classroom was a mess and the kids loved it. He lived somewhere in northern Westchester, I think it was, on a farm with all sorts of animals. He invited about fifty or a hundred of us one warm Saturday, for a cookout and a chance to play with the animals, to get out of the city.

When you got your final report card in June, with next year's teacher listed, you prayed it was Mr. Shaw. I never had him, but my sister did. My mother never met a hippie before. Karen and Russell were the closest. She didn't know what to expect. She always told my father: "See these hippies, in a few years they'll all be in suits and ties working in their father's corporations. Who are they kidding?"

"While those poor guys were spit at when they came home from Vietnam," my father said. "Now they're all whacked up."

So she invited Mr. Shaw over for lunch, during the end of my sister's year with him. He gladly accepted. My mother made her lasagna for him. Would he like it? she wondered. These hippie types, they weren't like us, they talked pluralism, equality, but did that include our people? Or were Italians too traditional, the bad guys to them, the troglodyte meatballs, the Frank Rizzos? My mother was a housewife, out of fashion then; she'd never been to an antiwar protest or a rock concert, indoor or outdoor.

Lasagna is still lasagna, especially hers, hippie, yippie, weathermen. He said, "Mmmm. Mrs. Agovino, just cut it right down the middle."

Our teachers were like this. Most were Jewish. Some were older and tenured and just there, going through the motions, for the pension. But most were young and enthusiastic, happy to be teaching in this brand-new school with a multiracial student body, part of the massive "educational park." That's what it was known as, the Northeast Bronx Educational Park. Harry S. Truman High School was in the middle, surrounded by two K-to-fourth-grade schools and two "intermediate" schools, fifth to eighth grades.

They taught us not to worry about penmanship; that it was the content that counted. It's what you say, not how you say it. It didn't matter if someone was black or white or Puerto Rican, Catholic, Jewish, or Baptist. *And Jehovah's Witness?* Or even Jehovah's Witness. We were all the same. They strummed guitars and sang songs. We sang "We Shall Overcome." We sang, "Oh Hanukkah, oh Hanukkah, come light the menorah. . . ." We sang a Christmas carol, I forget which one, and we sang, "Feliz Navidad."

Some just mouthed the lyrics, depending on their persuasion and the prejudices they were taught at home. Some black and Catholic kids lip-synched "Oh Hanukkah," some Jewish kids did the same for "Oh Christmas Tree," or whichever one it was. Was it genteel? You could almost say it was genteel.

It was genteel until an unexpected swirl of violence. It was first grade. I would walk home from school, holding hands with Debi, a classmate who also lived in my building and was a family friend. Her parents were friends with my parents, her sister with my sister. We were so close to home, within one hundred feet of the back of our building, where the bicycle and walking path met a plot of grass, some of the famous Co-op City landscaping that was supposed to make us different from Boston Secor across the highway or Parkchester in the central Bronx. Then, these men, raging young men, wild-eyed with long bats, stickball bats, approached with great speed. I don't remember if it was a group of whites chasing a group of blacks, blacks versus whites, or if race even mattered. I remember a long-haired white kid swing his bat at someone, so focused on inflicting pain he either didn't notice us, we were tiny, or he didn't care. He swung and missed and his follow-through caught Debi on the eye and me on the top of the ear. It hurt, but Debi received the worst of it.

The teenagers were gone, as fast as they came, running toward Baychester Avenue, toward P.S. 178, from whence we came, and the highway, perhaps to the other side, to the Bronx we were trying to run away from. I don't remember much else; I've tried to wipe this out of my memory. But I know this: I left Debi there. I was crying, we were both crying, and I ran to my building. I knew it was wrong as soon as it happened. My parents told me I couldn't do that, to leave a friend like that, they knew I was hurt and afraid, but I should have stayed with my friend. Debi had a black eye, but she would be all right eventually. My mother probably blamed my father. Maybe she said, "I told you this place would be bad for the kids." I remember my mother saying it was "a gang war."

Besides random mayhem, it was okay to be the smallest kid, or the second or third smallest. Or maybe I was just lucky. My best friend in kindergarten was Otis, a big, strong black boy with a small Afro and defiant streak. He'd go after kids, not little ones, but other big ones, as if to test himself, even at that age, and he seemed to enjoy talking back to teachers or openly ignoring them.

He was the opposite with me. He was my friend and guardian, through kindergarten, first grade, and second grade. If anyone thought about laying a finger on me, they'd have to deal with Otis. My mother gave me permission to invite Otis over after school, and his parents quickly reciprocated. My mother knew that Otis was developing a bad reputation in the school but she met his parents when they came to pick him up from our house and liked them. They were older, conservative, middle-class, better than a lot of what she saw in Co-op City's whites. For whatever reason, I had a calming effect on

Otis; he was a saint around me. I don't know why. We liked to touch each other's hair. I touched his hair and said, "It's so soft, I wish I had your hair." He touched mine and said the same. If only we could trade. What a promotional brochure that would've made for Co-op City.

Otis didn't have a dashiki, not that I remember, but one of the black kids did. And so did Stevie Wonder and since we all loved Stevie Wonder and tried to memorize "I Wish," I wanted a dashiki, too. I asked my father.

"You can't have one," he said.

"Why?"

"It's not your culture, it's for black people. It comes from Africa."

"So?"

"You'd be patronizing them."

"What does that mean?"

"In other words, that has a special significance in their culture, and you only like it because it looks nice. That's the wrong reason to wear it. They could take that as an insult."

At P.S. 178, they took us on school trips. Your parents had to sign a permission slip so you could go, just as they had to sign your homework assignments every night. What parent wouldn't sign? They took us to the Bronx Zoo, the Bronx Botanical Garden, and Wave Hill in the west Bronx for what seemed like every year. "It's hard to believe we're still in the Bronx," a teacher or volunteer parent would say at all of those places. They took us to the Museum of Natural History and next door to Hayden Planetarium. Once, they took us to the Empire State Building. They took us in big yellow school buses. We could see the depot, a mile away beyond Bartow Avenue, from our twenty-second-story terrace, an unsightly yellow sea. The city was broke, dropping dead, but there was still money for public schools. Or maybe just our public schools, the Northeast Bronx Educational Park. The last few bucks.

When the school year ended, I transitioned to the friends in my building. The kids from school would somehow vanish. They might have been from Building 1 or Building 5 or Building 13 or Building 24 or miles away in Section 5. That's where Building 35, the last building, was; it was identical to ours. But these kids were nowhere to be found. They went to sleep-away camp or Co-op Camp or a few whose parents had a little more to Westchester Day Camp or stayed near their buildings or in central-air-conditioned apartments.

My mother asked me if I wanted to go to camp, but discouraged it without saying a word. She wondered about the supervision at these camps—and camps were for joiners. On this, my mother and father agreed. "We're not joiners," they'd say at the dinner table. They said to my sister and me, when we were little: "Never follow the program; never follow the crowd."

She knew it was important that I learn how to swim—*you never know*. Look at what she did the summer before at the little motel just beyond the Waldbaum's supermarket, on the edge of Co-op City. She took us with a friend and her young daughters to the outdoor pool there, for sun, to cool down. *And don't you know, a little girl falls in and no one notices, there's no lifeguard. What was I supposed to do?* She never learned how to swim in Bushwick, or Island Park, but she dove in, saved the small blob of a child, somehow. She was the heroine of the afternoon. *What if I didn't see the kid?*

But instead of me learning how to swim, she had me play with the building kids. And besides, traveling was an education by itself, maybe the best education, better than camp. She said this over and over.

We were all young, six, seven, eight, nine years old, our gang. That's what we called it, the gang. There was a core of six of us, but often more kids came down. It depended on the season. Some we didn't like, but we let everyone play. The leader was a kid two or three years older than me. His name was Stevie, and he lived on the fourteenth floor. Or maybe it was the eighth floor. He was the first to arrive, he had the ball, and he had the personality. His mother was Jamaican and had a thick accent. His father was a quiet man; I never heard him say a word.

Stevie came down at one o'clock every summer afternoon and started buzzing our intercoms. My mother liked him because he was polite, well-spoken, and his mother appeared strict. And he didn't hold his finger down too long on the buzzer in the lobby. "He was raised well," my mother said. "Hi, it's Stevie. Can Little Mike come down?" That's what I was called, being one of the youngest, the smallest, and the second Mike in the building.

"When you play ball, you still choose up sides like we used to do?" my father asked.

"Yes, we still choose up sides." I hoped I ended up on Stevie's team. He was the best athlete but also the most encouraging. If you made a mistake, he'd say, "That's all right, good try, good try." Jack was the same, he was white. Maybe he lived on the eighth floor. There were hardly any Italians in our building, maybe five or six or seven of the building's 396 apartments, but one kid who invited himself to play was the opposite of Stevie. He was short, a Napoleon of a child, and yelled if you made a mistake. *Please don't put me on his team; put me on Stevie's team.*

The group stayed close to the building. We used the gray concrete monolith, its pillars and sharp angles, as our playing fields and courts.

Punchball was the most popular. For that, we played right behind our building, where there were six rectangular patches of grass, and in the outfield a wall, above which was a sand garden. It was a natural; a wall for real-life home runs, if only for left and center field, and the grass rectangle, made for something close to a diamond. The base paths were concrete, as was the left-field warning track and foul territory. And the grass wasn't really grass, not anymore, so we weren't violating the ubiquitous signs: KEEP OFF THE GRASS. That and: NO DOGS ALLOWED.

We used the left-field wall for another game: "off the wall." We used the same super-pinky sponge ball and had to throw it, on one bounce, off the wall. If it wasn't caught off the carom, it was a single, double, triple, or home run, depending on how far it went and which outfielder flubbed it. There was a variation on this, played against a pillar; there were pillars everywhere. At the base of each pillar that held up this massive building was a layer of concrete that jutted out at a ninety-degree angle. If you threw the sponge ball at this strip, the ball would take off with great velocity and provided the game with a deep, home run threat. Depending on our collective mood, we played this on a pillar in the back of the building, but also in the front of the building; maybe the sun was brighter or not as strong or maybe we wanted an audience, attention.

If we did, there were usually old people ready to chase us away. If the old people didn't chase us away, then it was a group of middle-aged Jewish women who sat under the building in lawn chairs. They would watch the world go by and provide a loud, running commentary on anything and everything. That or they gossiped about anyone and everyone coming in and out of the building. They were known, by some, as "the yentas." If the yentas didn't chase us away the Co-op City Security did. We were part of the NYPD's Forty-fifth Precinct, but we had our own security officers. They looked like cops, they had navy uniforms like cops and cars that looked like cop cars, but didn't carry guns. They'd say, "C'mon fellas, break it up. Go play ball on the Greenway. That's what it's there for."

The Greenway began about two hundred feet from our front door, but we never played there. We loved our concrete. We were still munchkins but after we played our games we would watch the older kids with envy play touch football in the street, in the loops of Defoe Place and De Kruif Place. There were loops all over Co-op but the end zone of these two fields was in the middle of a busy street, with a constant flow of buses: the BX15 to Gun Hill and Fordham roads; the BX17 to Allerton Avenue; the QBX1 to the Pelham Bay Park subway station then over the Whitestone to Main Street, Flushing. Plus, the red-white-and-blue private express buses to midtown Manhattan. But these kids, teenagers they were—their long stringy hair, their Afros, their bandanas; the boxes blasting Salsoul and Philly soul—they were fearless, running precise patterns, buttonhooks, posts, fly routes. *Everyone go deep, fuck the buses, someone come down with it.* Wow. What games. What athletes. We knew we weren't allowed to play, by our parents or by the teenagers themselves, young, cocky supermen. But one day, it would be us, prancing in the street.

You go play on the Greenway! And why should we listen to you, mister. You're not a cop. And when we got upstairs we watched from our windows, partial view, twenty-two stories up or thirteen or five or thirty-three stories up. My mother said: "One of these days, a kid is going to get hit by a bus, with their bravado."

We played running bases and slap ball, both under the building, either when it rained or if the sun was too strong. Slap ball was a punchball derivative, but with a pitcher. If the ball was hit at the pillar that stood in for second base, and at such an angle, it would deflect out from under the building and into the shabby grass and bushes—sorry, the landscaping—usually at least an extra base hit, sometimes a home run.

We played skully, a game with bottle caps filled with clay, flicked on the asphalt. We played a game called errors, the rules of which I don't remember anymore. We played manhunt, something like tag, with teams and diffuse, conceptual boundaries. We would hover and hide around the building, in and around sandboxes, and on what we called the little rock, which was just that, a rock formation in the middle of the town houses at Defoe Place. Next to Building 1, close to the thruway, was "the big rock," with still another sand garden, sliding pond, seesaws, and monkey bars. During summers, kids (cousins, nieces, nephews, grandchildren) from everywhere (Westchester, New Jersey, Massachusetts, Pennsylvania, Ohio) might visit a relative in Co-op City. They might stay for a weekend, a week, or a month. They loved those sand gardens and monkey bars and playing manhunt with us, and punchball. *Oh, we love Co-op City,* they all said that. And we asked, being serious: "Why don't you move here, you can play with us all the time. We play football in the snow." Then they'd go home.

We played touch football, not with the big kids in the street yet, but behind the left-field wall, on concrete. We played in hallways sometimes, the long hallways, if parents wanted us close. The old people hated this. The voices echoed, a long, fluorescent bulb could get smashed by a ball, even a Nerf ball. This I couldn't do. "No," my mother said. "Not in the hallway."

Never follow the crowd. My parents meant it. The year before, in 1975, 80 percent of Co-op City's residents withheld their rent in escrow to launch the largest rent strike in the country, in the world, of all time. The tenants hired a famous attorney, Louis Nizer, to represent them. They were going to stick it to the United Housing Foundation, boy. You weren't going to kick these union folk around anymore.

My parents didn't buy into it. They thought it out, they discussed it at the dinner table. Yes, the rent had gone up 60 percent in the last three years already. Yes, my father was still a product of Vito Marcantonio's district, still an admirer of the New Deal. Yes, he still worked for the Department of Welfare, still appreciated it, loved many of the people. But the 1970s were limping on, weren't they? He could see, up close at his day job, money squandered, he could see programs failing, the city bankrupt, good intentions gone awry, liberalism at its pious, suffocating, bullying worst. He was ambivalent. He began a subscription to *The National Review*, "Buckley's magazine," he called it, to keep his objectivity, to see how the other half thought, how the rest of America thought. They piled up relentlessly, beside *Daedalus*.

This is what my parents reasoned: Co-op City is going down, people who were full of hope were already moving out, as fast as they could, *just look out the window, the moving trucks are triple-parked.* There was talk of crime, rumors of crime. There were urine puddles in the elevators, how embarrassing. My mother saw our neighbor Beverly with rubber gloves and a mop, cleaning the floor of the elevator. "Bee," my mother said, "what are you doing?" "There was urine in the elevators again, and we have company coming over tonight." If she didn't clean it, who knows how long it would sit there. There were graffiti-covered walls in the stairwells, floor to ceiling, and smashed lightbulbs. After I'd play with Harry, either he in my house on the twenty-second floor, or me in his on the twenty-fourth, we would wait by the stairwell door, sometimes with a parent, to make sure the other got up, or down, those two scary flights safely.

"Better to let the rent go up," my mother said, "and keep the better people here."

"Yeah, but that kind of defeats the ideology of Co-op City," my father said.

"Ideology?" my mother said. "You think I care about ideology. I've got—no, we've got—two kids to raise here. I've given this place a chance at least, and I'm supposed to worry about preserving the ideology of Co-op City? C'mon."

"All right, all right," my father said. "I understand your point."

If Charlie Rosen heard this, could you imagine? He was called the "Lenin of Co-op City," by Jack Newfield in the *Village Voice*.

My parents didn't read the *Village Voice*, but since it covered the strike, my father brought it home.

They read what Newfield wrote: "What has all this done to the people of Co-op City? It has galvanized them. It has turned them into a community as nothing else could ever have done. It has excited in them a sense of original power they never knew they had before. . . . This sense of power they can easily trace to their extraordinary solidarity. This, in turn, has naturally produced an enormous camaraderie among them. Hundreds, thousands, of people in Co-op City now know each other who never knew each other before."

"Oh, please, what nonsense," my mother said. She always used this phrase: liberal propaganda. *That's liberal propaganda they're spouting.* "If it's so great why don't these liberal newspaper editors move here. They wouldn't move here in a million years. Who are they kidding?"

My father nodded, halfway agreeing. But Newfield he liked. He said: "He means well, Newfield. He's from the old school." Maybe he just knew that Newfield loved boxing, that they had the sweet science in common.

Rosen was a printer at the *New York Post* and the leader of the strike. He was fearless, charismatic, a bully standing up to a larger bully. He spoke at tenant gatherings in English, Yiddish, and Spanish. He was a local hero. Imagine what he would have thought had he known us. What would we have been to him? Bourgeois wannabes? Sellouts? Betrayers of the cause?

That was the blessing, the curse, but in this case the blessing, of Co-op City. It was so big you didn't have to feel the wrath of Charlie Rosen—"that Maoist," the Socialists at the UHF called him—if you didn't join his fight. He lived in who knows what building, 14, 24, a town house next to a giant sandbox for the kids, which were everywhere. You couldn't make one out from the next, even us, and we lived there.

If you wanted to defy the defiers, there was no retribution. And if we were part of that minority 20 percent, that meant there were a bunch of us—whatever twenty percent of sixty thousand is. We weren't alone.

The strike lasted fifteen months, well into 1976. New York's secretary of state, an articulate Italian American by the name of Mario Cuomo, was a negotiator. And we won, I mean they won, a few days before July 4, 1976—what symbolism. There were more fireworks than usual that year, everywhere in Co-op City someone was selling illegal fireworks. Third-graders were selling fireworks. The blockbusters and M-80s that were set off in the giant green Dumpsters boomed and echoed. The sound was terrifying. It frightened me as much as the powerful winds that rampaged over our flat plain. There was nothing more frightening than the wind on the twenty-second floor. When there was a storm, I'd hide in the bathroom, where there were no windows, no howls. *What if the windows blow in, then what will we do?* The wind, the Fourth, and soon Halloween, *Don't go out on Halloween.*

"What did they win?" my mother said when the rent strike ended. "They'll have their project now."

My father agreed. "It was a Pyrrhic victory," he said.

"What's that mean?" I asked.

"You ever hear of King Pyrrus?"

"How is he supposed to know King Pyrrus?" my mother said. "He's not even in the third grade."

"Right, well he was a king who thought he could defeat the Romans, and he did, but in the process his army was devastated. In other words, he won, but at a cost."

Anyway, we had a plane to catch. It was July 1976 and we were headed for Lisbon.

My father had said, "Every three years we'll go to Europe." There was still no house, Franco was dead now, Salazar, too, so by July we were, like I said to my third-grade class, on the Portuguese airline TAP.

We went for three weeks, and did the things I said we did. Should I have told them more? That we went to Sintra, that's where the photo's from, with me and my father, fading now, or was the sky that pale? Look at the ninth-century Moorish castle in the background. That was from the Nikon my mother had just gotten. A gift from my father. I remember how heavy that camera was; it was my job to carry it. "Don't let it out of your sight," my mother said.

The Portuguese, who knew they were so nice. We'd never known a Portuguese before. *You know where they settled, up New England, Massachusetts, Rhode Island.* Morocco was next. We took a plane over the strait. *Kids, we're going to Africa, can you believe it?* We stayed in Casablanca. Don't ask why, it's too embarrassing. We hired a driver. He had a beat-up car. The upholstery was burgundy leather, with tears in it, and masking tape covering the tears. There was no air-conditioning, this was North Africa in July, and that burgundy upholstery smoldered. Our legs were covered, *thank God for that.* Neither of my parents owned a pair of shorts. But even for my sister and me, my mother said, no shorts. This is a different culture; they cover up.

So we wore our little platform shoes, tie-dyed shirts my sister and I made in school, our bell-bottoms, they allowed bell-bottoms in Muslim countries, and we kept the car windows open, all four of them, our long hair splashed around, and were thankful for that hot, dry breeze. He drove us to Mohammedia and Rabat, *that's where we should've stayed.* There was a picture, from the Nikon, of my father and the driver leaning against that old car on the side of a road, both with their arms folded, foreboding, looking at the camera. That one I can't find. But why didn't he take us to the casbah? *We asked him and he said, "Eh, the casbah."*

In Spain, we went to the Costa del Sol, the Alhambra in Granada, and Madrid, the Prado, the bullfight. We took a day tour to Toledo, to the great cathedral. We never took tours; my mother hated the idea of them, of flocks of tourists, of beat-the-clock tourism. We always went solo, but we lost time being sick, and had to see Toledo. The bus trip was an ugly one, all of these generic high-rises. *God, it looks like Co-op City.*

I didn't tell my third-grade class about getting sick. Maybe they would have said, Good. Or if not them, their parents, if they told their parents. It started in Portugal. Maybe the water, maybe food poisoning. It hit my mother and sister first. Then me and my father got it, whatever it was, in Spain. My father's stomach cramps were debilitating; he spent most of the days in Costa Del Sol in the hotel. My mother took us to the beach. *They never ripped me off, not once.* She said this about the Spanish, the men who sold umbrellas on the beach, or sodas and snacks. Nor did they leer at this attractive thirty-four-year-old in a bathing suit. My father said it was because they were Latin, they were Catholic. *They're honorable.*

It wasn't the Italy trip. After all those meals at El Faro with Karen and Russell—*I wonder whatever happened to them? I wonder if they're still married?*—my parents thought they'd eat with abandon. My father's pain seemed unusual, scary. Maybe it was the beginning of an ulcer, dealing with all the stresses of a gambler's life. Things were good, money was coming in, going out, but coming in again. But it was still up to Steve Grogan and Bert Jones. Could they get a field goal out of this last drive?

So I left out any talk of stomach trouble when I told the class. No one wanted to hear about vomit, diarrhea, sometimes at the same time. I just mentioned the good parts. After I read it, after the pause, one of the kids, a friend, said out loud, in front of the class: "Is your father in the mafia?" The teacher paused. They waited for me to answer.

"No," I said. What else could I say, I couldn't think of a retort more clever or, better still, a snap. *Your momma's so fat.* . . . The teacher chimed in, finally, with something like, "Well, that sounds very nice, Michael," and moved on to the next kid. She may have said that I was very lucky.

I told my mother. "He said, what?" she said. "After I had that kid up here, treated him like my own, that's what he says? That's because he told that *ginzo* mother of his how we lived, that we went to Italy for a month, and they're jealous. He's getting that from the parents. That *cafoon* mother, and his Jewish father, both of them."

He was half-Jewish, half-Italian, much bigger than me, a rough-house kid, bordered on being a bully, but wasn't with me. This word *cafoon* was a variant of the word *cafone*, which meant a low-class person. The dialect version was *gavon'*. *Cafoon* was either Sicilian dialect or a Bushwick-Sicilian dialect word. Or maybe just an invention of my mother's father, Jimmy. He was the only one I ever heard pronounce *gavon'* this way, but he said it with great joy: "Look at these *caf-OONS*," he'd say, telling a story. "Ha, ha! What a *caf-OON!*" That and *ginzo*. "These *ginzos* from the other side, look at 'em! Ha!" My father, you could see him get angry, the blood rising to his forehead. *Why does your father have to put his own people down? Aren't there enough doing that already?*

My mother told my father what this little *caf-OON* said to me in school. "These are ignorant people, what are you gonna do?" my father said.

She said to me: "You tell that common trash that your father is up at six o'clock every day, and works for the Department of Welfare. And that he's home for dinner by five-thirty, where we have a home-cooked dinner around the table every night. Tell him that he knows Romare Bearden, that he spoke at his farewell luncheon. What a common piece of trash, that kid."

My father said, "Well, relax, who cares what people say? They don't define me."

Then she said to me: "Don't be like these people. Never be common."

And then: "Jesus, when are we going to get out of this place?"

THE CITY, 1977

He was never afraid. Maybe fathers never seem afraid. When we rode those rancid city buses through the Bronx, with crumpled McDonald's bags, roaches congregating and imperious, and worse the subways. There was nothing scarier than the subways, scarier than the Fourth of July and the wind gusts on the twenty-second floor. The stairwells in Co-op City came close—all the graffiti, the smashed fluorescent bulbs, the stretches, two, three floors at a time, of complete darkness, the ominous footsteps of someone walking down or up, it was always hard to tell. One of our little gang, one of those summers, pointed to something in the stairwell and said: "You know what that is?"

"No," we said.

"It's a prophylactic," he said.

"A what?"

"Man, let's keep going."

The subways were on a different level of menace. They were loud, brawling, confrontational. They traveled through what appeared to be hell, burnt-out shells of buildings, rubble, blight, despair, name the cliché, and kids, my age, playing in it and through it. It didn't seem right.

My father moved through these urban dioramas as if it were normal. It may have been a different landscape from thirty years ago, but he wasn't going to run from it. He said this to me: Never be intimidated. Never show you're afraid.

Eventually, it would heal itself, all this. And if he were confronted with danger, an old-timer, a *paisan* or a Puerto Rican from East

Harlem or a black man from the old school, would stand with him. And that's what would have happened.

He wasn't a big man, five foot six, but he had a sturdiness to him, thick arms and chest, legs too, and wide feet. His wingtips were all triple E. Not a tough guy—how do you look tough in bifocals—but sturdy. Then why was I so little? "Don't worry," he said. "I was like that at your age. Or maybe you'll be like my father. He was small-boned, a more delicate type." He said: "Some of the greatest prizefighters were lightweights, featherweights, bantamweights, a-hun-twenty, hun-thirty pounds." *Did I ever tell you about Willie Pep?*

We had these Saturday morning outings in the city, he and I, sometimes he and my sister, sometimes the three of us, more often he and I. I would have preferred to go on Saturday afternoon, to sleep in. But I had no choice; they had to be mornings. For one, he was a morning person; he loved the mornings, the earlier the better. He said: "Don't sleep too much, it'll make you dopey and lazy." I wanted to get angry, but I suspected he was right.

And he had to get back by eleven-thirty, noon the latest, to get to work, his second job, to answer the phones. The bookmaker. There were games; there were always games. If it was January, February, and March there were Saturday afternoon college basketball games, dozens of them. There were prep races for the Derby, and he always put a bet down himself on the Wood Memorial, the big New York race. *The Wood's the Wood.* There was pro basketball and hockey, even if only the Irish bet hockey. In April, May, June, July, there was baseball. Baseball made him American, baseball was the greatest game invented, but baseball only brought us financial misery.

By August, thank God for August, there was preseason football, and the junkies needed it. If they could've bet on an intrasquad scrimmage they would have. Then the college games, September, October, November. Baylor, Vandy, Brigham Young, Rice. "Daddy, where's Rice?" "It's down Houston. Excellent school, by the way." "Where's

Vandy? That's in Tennessee, another good school." "And Clemson?" "South Carolina. It's an agricultural university."

December, the playoffs and the bowl games started, the wagers, the risk, the rush, got bigger. So did the chance for opportunity. The cycle would begin again, with the Bluebonnet Bowl on New Year's Eve. I didn't mind his second job; it gave me a chance to stumble around and discover more about sports.

My father got a postcard from Stan. I don't know if it was from 1977, the stamp is gone, but it must be from the summer. The postcard's from Prague, of the Staroměstský Orloj, the old-town clock. Par avion; *letecky*; air mail. He wrote: "Dear Vince, Hope all okay and straightened out. September just around the corner. Are you ready? My best to the family."

My father's office was this: his half of the dresser and his half of the bed. Herodotus and Thucydides next to *The Sports Eye*, a touting newspaper, and stacks of football sheets with small boxes where he would scribble the line fluctuations during the week. The phone lay next to him on the night table; he had to be next to it because he was hard of hearing.

He'd say to his customers: "Excuse me, can you repeat that, I don't hear well."

My mother would say: "He's deaf as a goddamn doornail."

I'd ask, "Daddy, how come you don't hear well?"

He said: "That goes way back. I never told you that story? What happened was, I never wore a hat. I never wore rubber shoes. I was always downtown, I could never change, I would walk in the rain, and I had a severe sinus problem and got bad earaches. As a matter of fact, in the service, I went to the V.A. hospital, and they told me I had perforated eardrums. When they go and send me to San Diego, they send me to radar school. And I spent the whole week in the San Diego Naval Hospital, and my ear was oozing mucus. I was totally deaf that whole week, and I was frightened. The hearing came back, but it was never the same. They wanted to give me eight or nine percent disability, which would have been eight bucks a month. Looking back, maybe I should have taken it. . . . But I was ashamed, you know. They were very solicitous, the nurses, but they had to put penicillin in my backside, it was embarrassing. Remember, I was seventeen, eighteen years old. But both my ears were perforated, the nerves were shot. Never the same. Like your mother, she can hear water running. She should be in the CIA, if you ask me."

And my mother said, "Yeah, but he hears what he wants to hear."

The books piled, his legal pads piled, the *Sports Eyes*, the sheets of NFL schedules piled. I studied these sheets; the thick *History of the Peloponnesian War*, like the stacks of *Daedalus*, were too intimidating if not off-putting. All these piles. My mother yelled: "You need your own office, this is ridiculous. We should have a house with a den."

This is where he ran his business, in his room, over the phone, where he conferred with Albert, his trusted partner. Albert was Chubby's kid brother from the old neighborhood. This meant he could be trusted in ways that didn't exist anymore. *He was a prince, believe me when I tell you*. He earned a living putting down linoleum floors and remained in East Harlem, one of the few who did, on *a hun' sixteenth* and Second, where he got the line on Monday mornings.

He never got married. Neither did Chubby, who wound up at the Parks Department, a full-embracer of leftist causes. I never met Albert, not like Stan, Ron, or some of the others. I only knew his voice over the phone. He was a serious man. When Roy called, and he heard a small child's voice, he'd make a big production. "Hi Honey, how are you today? How's school? Good, good. Is your daddy home?" You could tell he was a father.

Albert, even to an eight- or nine-year-old, was all business, never rude, just professional. "Can I speak with your father please." But he was ethical—*honorable as the day is long. That's another thing that saved me, dealing with Albert. That and your mother.*

This office, this bedroom, twenty-two stories in the sky, is where my father charmed clients—*Sir Stanley, as I've said before, you're a gentleman and a scholar*—or yelled at clients, never threatened, but yelled when he had to—*if someone was tryin' to pull a fast one.* And some did try. They would say they bet something else after the fact. They were called "claimers." One claimer tried to use my father's hearing impairment against him. But my father had a gadget added to the receiver so he could increase the volume. And he'd repeat all of a client's bets back to them at the end of the call. He yelled at this man: "Don't you make a jerk outta me! Don't you ever!"

Office hours were Monday through Friday, six-thirty, after our dinner, until eight; Saturday, noon to four and six-thirty to eight; and Sunday noon to four, with paperwork at night after the NFL games. Sunday mornings were for *The New York Times* or a visit to his mother's and sisters' or, sometimes, if he was alone, church, especially for a holiday. He'd bring back a palm on Palm Sunday.

Friends weren't allowed over during office hours. The phone would ring and ring and questions would likely follow, even from kids, especially from kids. A few years before, we had a second phone line installed, just for my father's clients. So on big sports weekends, any sports weekend, the ringing was constant. If a little friend called, we'd tell them we'd have to call back, that I was busy doing homework. Which was true, but it was also Monday night, and Cincy was playing someone, Kenny Anderson vs. Kenny the Snake maybe, and Joe D.—no, two Joe D.'s—had to phone in their bets, and Stan and Ronnie and Lenny and Roy and Ned, and friends of theirs, and this one who knew that one—a dime here, two dimes there, Cincy minus the points, a hundred times. Then he'd repeat it back to them.

I knew our household was different, but it was all I knew. What was different was normal. *And what's normal anyway?*

We'd go to museums on Sundays, the Met, the Frick, the Guggenheim. The first time we went to the Modern was 1971 for a Romare Bearden show. We'd say that we were going to the city, or going downtown, even if it was Eighty-sixth Street. My father would get Albert to do the phone work, maybe once a month. My mother wouldn't take the subway—*you get killed now on the subway*—so we took the express bus. It may have been safer, cleaner, free of *you never know*, but the blighted landscape was just as pronounced—and from an even better vantage point, the Bruckner Expressway, the despair interminable, ongoing.

When we got off the Bruckner, in the southern tip of the Bronx, there was a stoplight, and on the corner, a building that once was. It was rubble now, hills of rubble, and when it was covered in snow, kids played on it with their sleds. When we turned onto the Third Avenue Bridge you could see, in the distance, the lettering YANKEE STADIUM in blue lights. I'd always make the effort to look, not that I liked the Yankees, but just because. The bus turned into Harlem, to Mount Morris Park. There was an undulating building that said SANS SOUCI, and around the corner another building, abandoned and partially collapsed, with the words BECOME CATHOLIC spray-painted on the side.

And then, like that, you were on the Museum Mile. We'd get off at the first stop, Eighty-fifth Street and Fifth Avenue.

Saturday mornings weren't as grand as the staircase of the Met or Frank Lloyd Wright's spiral. They were for my father to run errands, his meditation time, and he preferred if my sister or I came along.

He'd go for a haircut, he'd look for a book, he'd have us pick something out for ourselves. He'd meet a friend to pick up or drop off an envelope. *This is my little guy.* I knew what was going on, and I can't say I minded. It made me feel like one of the grown-ups, and these friends were always slipping me coins or crumpled dollar bills, just because I was Hugo's little kid. "Here, Mike," they'd say.

He'd look in the well-appointed window at Herzfeld, a men's haberdashery store, his favorite, on Fifty-second and Madison. "They got good stuff here," he'd say. "Real quality, tasteful. It's a family business, they must be German Jews. They're from the old school."

Then he'd pause. "Should I go in, you think?" he'd ask me. "I bounced a check on them a few months ago."

What could I say?

"Oh, what the hell," he said. "I always pay them." And they gave him a rousing hello. *Mr. Agovino, howareya?* He wasn't a great customer, merely a good or occasional one. They never mentioned the bounced check or checks.

"Let me ask you something," he said. "How much would it be to monogram that shirt in the window?" He liked his initials on his shirts and his book collection. For that he bought an engraver: FROM THE LIBRARY OF H. V. AGOVINO.

If he was picking up money, he'd spend it right back, unless he had to pay someone else. When he would argue with my mother, and she'd scream, "Why don't we save money so we can get the hell out of this place?" His retort was, "I'm good for the economy. People like me make the wheels turn." He'd say this again and again, sometimes thundering. "I make the wheels turn!"

When he had money, he spent it on us. He might take me to Herman's, the sporting goods chain. I could spend hours there. Or Paragon, the big sporting goods store near Union Square. I'd beg for anything with a Mets, Knicks, or Rangers logo. He'd say, "I don't want to spoil you," and then relent. A baseball cap, a mini-basketball in blue and orange, a hockey puck even if I didn't ice-skate or play hockey. "You can use it as a paperweight," he said.

He'd tell me: "You know, this is a business what I do. You know that, right? Your mother doesn't understand that. We couldn't do what we do on my city salary. No way we could. You have to tell your mother this."

I'd shrug my shoulders. Did I have to take a side? I didn't know myself. It was one thing to be with the adults, to get a Susan B. Anthony coin slipped into my palm by men with East Harlem accents, but I couldn't think as an adult, and even if I could, how do you choose between your mother or father? So I'd shrug again and say, "I dunno, Daddy." Or change the subject: "Daddy, who's Susan B. Anthony?" *Are you familiar with the term* suffrage?

He once asked my sister, since she was older: "Do you think I should claim bankruptcy?"

She was only eleven and said, "I don't know." Then she said, "No, don't. That doesn't sound good." She never said anything about this.

My father would go on food excursions, there's nothing he liked more, for wine, cheeses, bread, meats, cakes. If what was owed to him was a good chunk of change, and he didn't owe it to anyone that week, he'd go to DiPalo's in Little Italy for cheeses and cold cuts, pecorino romano, Locatelli Romano, fresh mozzarella, smoked mozzarella, scamorza, prosciutto, mortadella, salami, capicola, soppressata, the ones hanging from the ceiling, one hot and one sweet, gigantic tins of olive oil. These delicacies were spelled one way, pronounced another.

He'd go to various butcher shops for veal cutlets that had to be pounded thin. If they weren't, my mother would start a fight. *What am I supposed to do with cutlets this thick?!* There were at least two major screaming matches a year because of thick veal cutlets. And how could you eat thick veal cutlets?

For sweets, he'd go to Ferrara's in Little Italy or Veniero's if he had the money. The pastries were cannoli, obviously; sfogliatelle, the second-greatest invention from Napoli; and the two great secrets, pastacroce and pastachiotto. These, too, were spelled one way, pronounced another.

He knew someone at Ferrara's—"I don't know who he is, some *paisan,*" my mother called the man—who would throw in some cookies, the anisette sponge or pignoli or tricolors. At Veniero's, a well-known East Harlem gangster, Louie I, who my father knew from the old days, was working there now, as cover.

He'd say to me: "See, this was what my old neighborhood was like, markets like this, everyone knew one another. It's a shame you didn't experience it." He'd say this over and over. And over and over, I'd hear my mother's voice: *Well, you were the one who wanted to move to Co-op City.*

When we needed a change from Italian, and my mother didn't make a pie or cake, he'd go to the Upper East Side, Yorkville, and go to the Kleine Konditterei and Kramer's and Mrs. Greenburg's. *They're miserable bastards those Germans, but they make good cake.*

If he didn't have money for DiPalo's, Ferrara's, or Balducci's, he'd go to Arthur Avenue in the central Bronx. If he didn't have money for that, we would get a few things from the new Italian deli that opened up across the street from us, adjacent to the pizzeria. The pizzeria did so well, the owner expanded. My parents didn't like the owner. They called him *o strunz*. He was young, show-offy, drove a fancy car, had a thick mustache, wore gold jewelry. He wasn't a *ginzo*. If he were, my mother, like her father, would have referred to him as "that *ginzo*" or "that *ginzo* across the street." But he was American born. And she was first to admit that the ones from the other side knew their food, that they only used the best ingredients, that no Italian food in America could please them nor could any American-born cook, even if they were 100 percent Italian. *The ones from the other side are impossible; they'll send the food back, that's how obsessed they are with the food.* If the Co-op City deli were owned by an Italian-Italian the quality would be better. But *o strunz* across the street was lucky: He catered to non-Italians who didn't know the difference. *And now he's got a gold mine.*

But even average *gaba-gol* was better than no *gaba-gol*. My father just needed the *gaba-gol*, the rest he would do himself. A thin layer of meat, a few slices of tomato, black pepper, a drizzle of olive oil, semolina bread, a kaiser roll might do. *I learned from the Chief. He used to go and make us sandwiches in the club.*

But my father wouldn't go to the deli across the street. He didn't like *o strunz* because he wasn't from the old school. *Like one of these guys, they come into a little money, and then it goes to their head.* Instead, he sent me or my sister. I fought with her. *No, you go!*

Both of us were too embarrassed to ask for *gaba-gol*, it was a ridiculous word, an ugly word, it sounded like a vulgarity. What if other people heard us, maybe someone we knew from the building or school? They might make fun of us. Even if we didn't know them. Black girls once laughed at me when I said it, when I tried to say it. *Ewww, what's that? That sounds funky.*

"Who eats *gaba-gol*?" I or my sister would say. "No one eats *gaba-gol*."

"What are you talking about, it's a delicacy. It's delicious," my father said.

"Yeah, but you shouldn't eat too much of it," my mother said. "That stuff will kill you. It's all fat and salt. You should cut back on it."

My sister avoided going; she was getting older, reaching puberty, and young guys were always hanging out in front of the deli, sometimes playing football in the street, but usually just sitting on iron bars, smoking cigarettes, playing music, spitting, being crude. My mother didn't think a young girl should have to walk through this, risk comments, leers.

It became my job. *Why do I have to be Italian? Why do I have to have a last name no one can pronounce? Why do I have to go to the store and ask for things like* soob-ra-saad?

My sister: "Michael, Michael, you can say *pra-shutto*. That's easier to say."

That's ridiculous, what are we, from Kansas? It's brrro-shoot.

So I'd think out a strategy: Is it better to ask for the *gaba-gol* and proscuitto at the end of the order or to just get it over with and ask for it at the beginning? I'd ask for the normal-sounding foods first: the quarter of a pound of American cheese, of roast beef, even Genoa salami, there was nothing inflected or ethnic about "Genoa salami."

"Anything else, small fry?"

"Yeah, and a quarter of a pound of"—I'd lower my voice—"of pra-shutto."

"Of what?"

Pause, then whisper, like my sister said "pra-shutto," the American way.

"Quarter pound of *brrro-shoot*, you mean?"

"Yeah."

"You got it." One clerk was nice. He'd bounce quarters on the counter so they'd ricochet straight back up. Then he'd hand them to you. He had red hair and a mustache.

"Is that it?"

"No." I'd take a deep breath. "A quarter pound of *capa*. . . ."

"What? Speak up, little man."

"*Capa* . . . , I mean, *gaba*. . . ."

"*Gaba-gol?*" He'd say this loud, without apology.

"Yeah."

"You got it."

After the Saturday-morning excursions, my father would count what he had left. He was always counting money in public. This was his worst habit. That and waiting for the subway on the edge of the platform, with his head sticking out. Sometimes he'd count money while waiting on the edge of the subway platform.

I told my mother. She yelled: "Hugo, don't stand on the edge of the subway platform. It scares the kids!" And: "What are you doing counting money in the subway. You'll get knifed."

"What the hell are you so afraid of?" he said, annoyed.

If, at the end of the outing, he didn't have anything for bus and subway fare on Monday morning, he'd say to me, and I'm nine years old, "Do me a favor, lend me your allowance. I'll pay you back by Tuesday, with an extra half-a-dollar."

"Daddy, no!" I'd say. "I want to buy a comic book."

"Don't worry," he said, "we'll get you the comic book. When have I ever let you down?"

"Well, all right." How can you say no to your father.

"Atta boy, Brother Michael. You're a good kid. And do me a favor, don't tell your mother."

———————

This time my father did seem afraid, for the only time. It wasn't the subway or the Bronx or any street characters that scared him, but this pain in his stomach. Since the trip to Spain last year, the pain would come back. He thought it was from a bad slice of pizza; he was always looking for a slice of pizza as good as in his old neighborhood. He could never find it. He told the story: "I was in Midtown and I was desperate to use a john. So I run into Saks Fifth. I get there just in the nick of time. And guess who's in the stall next to me, doing a number two? The old-timer, Burgess Meredith!"

It was funny for a moment, that Daddy did number two next to the guy from *Rocky*. We'd seen *Rocky* last year in Co-op City, in a packed theater, people talking, yelling, at the screen, as if they were at a real fight. They all wanted Rocky to win, so I decided to root for Apollo Creed; someone had to, and I was sick of hearing about all these Italian athletes.

But then it wasn't funny. My mother said, "Why does this keep happening to you?"

"Well I went and had a quick slice of pizza," he said, "that's what probably did it."

"What are you eating that junk for," she said. "They use that cheap olive oil, I keep telling you. You're not going to get the pizza that you were used to. They make it for people who don't know the difference."

After the Burgess Meredith sighting, it continued. My father called them "attacks." *I had another attack today.* When he went to the doctor, he was sent immediately to New York Hospital. It was his gallbladder and pancreas. Surgery was needed. There were already complications.

My mother told my sister and me that we would be taken to spend a week or two with my grandparents, her parents, in Smithtown, Long Island. She'd be at the hospital every day and it was Easter break anyway. Besides, we loved Smithtown, right? It was like going to the country for us. A real house, a backyard, a driveway, a barbecue, a dog, the massive, vaguely threatening Saint Bernard, Bernie. It's where we spent Christmases the last few years, after another peace was made, and Thanksgivings and Fourth of Julys. So Grandpa was a little crazy but never around me. He was my favorite relative—he had that smell of tobacco and he sounded like Baretta, the TV character. And Grandma was always fun.

"Okay," we said. "But is Daddy gonna die?"

"No," my mother said, but that's all she said. We heard her on the phone. She said this word again: "complications."

My mother drove us out there. She hated driving but since my father didn't drive, she was the reluctant family chauffeur. She learned late in life, when she was in Co-op City. The Cohns upstairs taught her and she found an instructor, a lugubrious middle-aged Jewish man named Lewis. He had a name for his driving school, it was something that didn't fit, like "Grand Prix Driving School." She liked him because he didn't panic, like she did, while driving the tempestuous streets of the Bronx, with the double- and triple-parking. He would simply shrug. He told her: "Look far into the distance, not right in front of the car."

Our car was a used, very used, Buick LeSabre from the early or mid-1960s. It was gray with a black roof. My father called it "the Gray Comet." He got it through a friend for a few hundred dollars. Soon the passenger-side door wouldn't open. The passenger would have to get in the driver's side and scoot over. The upholstery was black, there was no air-conditioning, and not all of the windows rolled down all the way. It was one of the uglier cars in Co-op City.

My mother only knew how to get to her mother's in Smithtown, Lord & Taylor in Scarsdale, where she longed to live, and my father's parents nearby in Pelham Bay, and these were the only places she would drive to. It was traumatic for her.

Smithtown was the longest drive, an hour, maybe more, *depending on that damn LIE.* She hated Smithtown, for several reasons. There was the drive, the fact that her father lived there, and it wasn't the kind of suburb she imagined for herself. It wasn't Westchester. *It's lunk-heads from my old neighborhood.* There were the Bensons next door,

a genteel, older couple, *real Americans,* but there were teenagers with
sports cars who played loud hard rock and smoked. *And God knows
what else.*

When my mother left us there, she told her mother to keep us in
the house or in the yard, to make sure we didn't go near those kids.
She told her to make sure I ate enough, what foods she should make
for me, and to watch the Saint Bernard, that the dog was bigger than
both me and my sister. She told her mother to make sure we read
our books, did the school assignments our teachers gave us knowing
we'd be out possibly two weeks, and not to let us watch too much TV,
but that a Met game was okay. "And make sure that loon doesn't do
anything crazy." She was talking about her father. My grandmother
laughed.

My grandfather, Jimmy, didn't do anything crazy. He'd go off to
work in the morning, in his sky blue Chevy Impala. After he sold the
store in Bushwick and moved to Smithtown he got a job in construction, even in his fifties. He wore a hard hat and smelled of cigarettes.
For lunch he would take two cans of Schaeffer and two packs of Bel-
airs. When he get home he'd invite me into his den and watch the
Met game with him. It was mostly light gray static, the reception
was that bad, especially on Channel 9, the antenna hardly a help. He
never went crazy when I was around. He'd talk to me about baseball
but he didn't know much about it, I could tell. He would say things,
a player's position, a statistic, that was wrong, and I knew they were
wrong, but knew better than to correct him. When my father spoke
of baseball, even if it annoyed me, these old-timers, I sensed he knew
what he was talking about. All these names, Yankees or not: Warren
Spahn, oh, did he love Spahn, used to go to the Polo Grounds when
the Braves came in to play the Giants, when they were still the New
York Giants; Johnny Sain; Lefty Gomez; Bob Feller; Larry Dobie;
Musial; Clemente; Killebrew; Koufax; Drysdale; Gibson. I didn't
know who these players were, but my father made them sound like
historical figures.

My grandfather, on the other hand, said things like: "These dut-soon ball players, they run like the wind, watch 'em," and "This Lee Mazzilli looks like a real *ginzo*."

I just nodded and agreed and laughed. Then he'd tell my grandmother: "Hey, Lilly, he's a smart little kid, this one here."

Daddy didn't die. My mother called her mother to say the surgery went well, the gallstones were removed, that he'd have to stay in the hospital a little longer, that he was weak, but he was okay. She got on the phone with us and said he had a wonderful doctor, a serious, dignified WASP who took time to explain everything to her.

"What's a WASP?" I asked.

"Oh," she said, "that's right, how would you know. It stands for white Anglo-Saxon Protestant. We don't have any in Co-op City. Anyway, your father will be okay, and he was asking about you and your sister. How's your grandfather treating you?"

"He's funny. He has a funny way of talking."

"Funny?"

"Yeah, he calls Lee Mazzilli a *ginzo*. What's a *ginzo*? And a *dut-soon*, what's a *dut-soon*?"

"Oh great, that's great. No, you don't want to say those things. I'll explain why when you come home. Don't say that in front of your father, he'll have a fit. Meantime, listen to Grandma."

She told my grandmother that she lost her appetite, that she'd get to the hospital at eleven in the morning and stay until six. She would take the express bus back to Co-op City and head straight to the lobby. There was a serial killer shooting brunettes, some even close to Co-op City. You couldn't get more brunette than my mother.

The night the lights went out, when the great blackout of 1977 rolled in, my father was home, as he was every night, reading a biography of Joan of Arc. He said: "*Oh Madon'*."

The first thing my parents did was talk about the last blackout, twelve years before, when they lived on Bruckner, how my mother was on the subway, pregnant with my sister, in the last car, on her way to meet my father on the platform of the Brooklyn Bridge station, how she had to walk the catwalk with everyone else through the tunnel, how nice and cooperative people were, even if she wasn't showing yet. They talked about how things were different then.

She remembered how she called her mother—they still had the store in Bushwick—and said to her, "When Hugo calls tell him I'm on Canal Street, that I'll wait here." She remembered how people reached out. She remembered a flashlight in her eye, and thought, "Oh, no," but it was my father.

Now they had to get to the north Bronx. She called her mother again. "Can Dad pick us up?"

"Yes, he'll leave now."

She remembers waiting one hour, then another hour, and her father never showed. She called her mother again. "Where the hell is he?"

"He's back here," her mother said. "The bridge was closed."

"I can see the bridge from here," my mother said. "I see cars—the bridge isn't closed." She asked a cop, "Is the bridge closed?"

"No, the bridge is open," the cop said. "Can't you see the cars?" *Leave it to my good-for-nothing father.*

She remembered that they shared a taxi, that they had to walk up the seven flights, that they got home after midnight, that they were starving, that time flies, that that was then. What will happen now?

After the 1977 blackout, after the entropy, the loss of all coherence, there was overtime. My father's day job called. The Department of Welfare had to assist, to provide compassion, to sign checks. They had to improvise to make things right; everyone, anyone, could be asked to do anything. My father was sent to the Bronx County Courthouse to calm the masses, to sign checks. If you were affected by the looting, and could prove you lived in the area, you might get a few hundred dollars to help tide you over; if you owned a business, you could get a few thousand, to get up and running again, if you even wanted to.

My father told this story: "One guy, he comes in and says he was a business owner, that he needed full compensation. I said, 'Okay, what is the name of your business, I'll look it up here on the roster.' He says, 'Well it doesn't really have a name.' I said, 'What do you mean?' He said, 'It was a number bank.' I bust out laughing."

They had a party for these department workers like my father, the social service folk, for their work that summer. It was at Gracie Mansion, the only time he'd been there. He was given a certificate, something about the outstanding work he did serving the citizenry of New York City during the Blackout of 1977. *Something like that. It's up there somewhere. Or no, maybe it's in storage.* The mayor, Abe Beame, might have been there. His signature is on the certificate. My father never got promotions or big raises, we never celebrated his achievements, not for his day job. But he got a certificate from the City of New York.

Mayor Beame was in Co-op City when the blackout hit—at a synagogue, giving a speech. It was an election year. The Democratic primary was in a couple of months and Beame had to outmaneuver Ed Koch, Mario Cuomo, Bella Abzug, Percy Sutton, and Herman Badillo, just to get his own party's nomination.

Over dinner that summer, I said, "Mommy, who are you going to vote for?"

"I don't vote," she said.

"Why not?"

"None of them represent us. I only voted once, and that was against John Lindsay and he still won."

"Who's John Lindsay?"

"Oh, you don't remember, you were too young, but he ran for mayor. He was very good-looking, from the Silk Stocking District. But he hated people like us. He said Italians were base people. I couldn't stomach him."

My father said, "He was what they call a limousine liberal."

"But the teachers in school always say it's important to vote," my sister said.

"Yeah, well, this election they can't vote. It's for the mayor and they all, conveniently, live in Westchester, and they don't have to deal with the city's problems. They spend seven hours a day in Co-op City, they get in their cars, and they go home. So tell them to mind their own business."

My father laughed. A laugh of agreement.

We didn't go anywhere that summer. My father had good health coverage from the city, but it was still three weeks in the hospital, New York–Cornell, and the bills were coming in, vacation days down to almost none. Plus, it had been a bad year, wins-and-loses wise; football season couldn't get here soon enough. We would sweat it out in the city, like everyone else.

That spring, I began to accompany my mother to the supermarket for her big weekly shopping every Thursday night. We'd go to the Co-op Supermarket across the street or to the bigger Waldbaum's, né Key Food, about a fifteen-minute walk on the edge of Co-op City. I would serve as her protector against this nutcase shooting brunettes with a .44 caliber. Several of his victims had been Italian.

When they finally caught him, the Son of Sam, word was he used to live in Co-op City when he was a teenager. He'd hang out in those early days by Buildings 1, 2, and 3. That's what our old babysitter told my mother by the elevators, that she knew him. *Would you believe that?*

And a few nights later, when the lights came on and everything was back to normal, my mother sat in front of the TV, forlorn, and watched Bushwick burn. She said: "Look at that. It's my old neighborhood." The fire started, they said, in an abandoned knitting factory.

NANTUCKET, 1978

I wasn't allowed to see *Saturday Night Fever*. There were dirty parts, my mother heard, and when it opened at the end of 1977, I was still only nine. My father didn't want to see it. *That stuff isn't music. You call that music?* Duke Ellington, that's music. Benny Goodman, Basie, Sinatra, Nat Cole was music to him. Bebop, okay, it wasn't his thing necessarily, but it was music, played with great skill and speed, by virtuosos. The later Coltrane lost him, so did Miles Davis, Cecil Taylor, Lennie Tristano. They eschewed melody as they evolved, but it was music, cerebral music, worth listening to. He said to my mother: "How can you listen to this crap on the radio?"

"Jazz, the big bands, swing, it's passé," she said. "Who listens to it anymore?"

My father turned to me and said, "If anyone ever tells you Benny Goodman was just a pop musician," he said, "be sure to correct them. He was a serious musician."

"Huh?" I said.

My father knew of John Travolta from the TV series *Welcome Back, Kotter*, and he did our people no dignity in his portrayal of Vinny Barbarino. *That's the last thing we need—ooh gray-deen*, my father called him in dialect, an idiot.

So even if he loved movies, and cherished an afternoon out with his family, *Saturday Night Fever* wouldn't be on his list. He may have come out and said it: It's beneath me. He made the exception for *Rocky*, because that was boxing. *Why are there no good movies anymore? Not even from Europe.*

This left my mother, fifteen years younger than my father, and sister; they couldn't wait to see it. It was all anyone was talking about, even going into the new year. Even black people admitted Travolta could dance. *Oh, that John Travolta, that white boy can move.*

"Yes, we were portrayed as morons in the movie, but we have types like that," my mother said when she came back with my sister.

"So, doesn't every group?" my father said. "Why are we always the laughingstock? We have doctors and lawyers. Look at Mario Cuomo."

"Oh, he's a walking liberal cliché. That's why he lost. All that's failed he still espouses," my mother said.

"Maybe you don't care for his politics, but he's well-spoken. And just the other day there was an Italian American byline in *The New York Times.*"

"One. Thank you."

"No, there's more now."

"The media, the elite, know they can dump on us, because we sit back and shut up. We don't complain, we don't write letters."

"You're right," he said, "but maybe we should. And I write letters to papers if I don't agree with something."

"But they don't publish them," she said.

"No."

"That's what I'm saying," she said. "They tune us out."

"And it doesn't help that we stab one another in the back," he said. "The Jews help one another and we hold one another down."

"Why shouldn't the Jews help one another? No one helped them. I would do what they do," she said.

"The Catholic Church tried to help the Jews."

"The Catholic Church?" she said, laughing and yelling at the same time. "Pope Pius XII was an anti-Semite, who are we kidding? Let's be honest here."

"You don't know what you're talking about, many clergy risked their lives to save the Jews. You don't read what I read."

My sister and I, we're looking at each other: *Here we go again.*

"I don't need to read!" my mother yelled back. "You read so much you get stupid. No one protected the Jews, no institution, and not the Catholic Church! Okay! The Catholic Church didn't do a damn thing for anyone except the Catholic Church. I don't need to read. I lived it. Those German nuns? They hated nice little Sicilian girls in Bushwick, and we were Catholic—can you imagine what they thought of the Jews."

"You're wrong! Average clergy sheltered people. The French Resistance is being uncovered as a myth, but the intellectual classes in this country are all Francophiles. They hate us. The Italians had a resistance movement. Remember that Rossellini movie we saw, when they gunned down the priest and Anna Magnani, that was a true story."

"Maybe Italians did," she said. "There's a difference between Italians and the Church. Didn't he have a Jewish mistress, that Mussolini?"

"That's right, he did. And many Jews were Fascists in the 1920s and the early, even the mid-1930s, especially in the North."

"I never heard that, and let's not make excuses for Mussolini."

"No excuses, but at least the Italians themselves strung him up."

"After how many years? The damage was done. And we were talking about Pius the XII. Don't make excuses for the Church. They're full of shit—pardon my expression. Who helped my uncle Sal, Jews did. He was undersized, five feet tall, and they had compassion, the Hellers in Brooklyn. They took him for one of their own."

"Well, your uncle was a prince of a guy," he said. "He was impossible not to like."

"Look, the Jews stressed education and they left us in the dust in this country. With us, it was always family." And then, putting on a working-class accent, she said it again: *The family. My family.* You say you could've gone to Colgate. Why didn't you?"

My father paused, then didn't answer. "We're starting to come up. There's a guy on Channel 4 who's very good, Tony Guida. But he annoys me, he tries to Americanize his name—*Guide-a*. He should pronounce it the right way: *Gwee-da*."

"You know why he doesn't? Look at what they do to this Italian girl on Channel 7, Rose Ann Scamardella. She worked so hard to be a news anchor and now they make fun of her on *Saturday Night Live*. Roseanne Roseannadanna."

"That's awful," my father said.

"I think you're agreeing," my sister said, "so why are you yelling at each other."

Then my mother said, "Oh, but is that skit funny: *This is Roseanne Roseannadanna*!" She said it in Gilda Radner's voice. My sister and I laughed.

"Now you're contradicting yourself," he said. "It's a beautiful name, Scamardella, and someone has to go and make fun of it. You like to laugh at your own people—"

"Oh, here we go—"

"Like your self-hating father."

"Yeah, he's twisted," she said, "but at least I admit it. And he's not the only one who's self-hating."

My father said, in a lower voice now, "I know. Look at Vito."

We knew Vito's story by now. Vito was my father's friend from East Harlem, one of the few he still kept in touch with. Not one of the tough guys, not one of the street guys, the opposite, if anything. He could draw. He painted the scenes of Venice on the walls of my father's social club, fifteen years before. He could also write. When he heard from my mother that we loved *The Little Prince*, he said he'd been working on a script, maybe a pilot for children, and would my sister and I like to read it and give our opinion. We did. And we liked it. I don't remember the details, but it was good, with bright dialogue, never boring, maybe too smart for kids, my sister said. "It's not babyish," she said.

He loved the big bands and would make tapes for my father. In the '60s, he'd go to the movies with my parents. He was one of the only ones from East Harlem whom my mother could spend time with. He wasn't like the rest of them. *He's so nice, Vito, he doesn't have any of the street nonsense in him.* Every year he sent the smartest Christmas card, the most original, one from a specialty card store or a Manhattan museum, you could pick it out among the dozens that sat on the shelves that Uncle Pep built.

Why hadn't he done better in life? He lived on the Upper East Side. He got out of East Harlem and lived on Seventy-something Street, between First and Second. He was proud to live there, and lost all traces of his accent from forty blocks north. But it was a studio, a rental, *a crackerbox*, with his vinyl records, his books, and drawing pads. Still single, pushing fifty, a few years younger than my father, barely paying the rent with a real estate job while he did his writing. He came to visit us once, for Christmas, brought a German cake from one of the bakeries in Yorkville, but never came again. He called, he always called, but never came back.

He changed his name once, *did I ever tell you that story?* When he first went into real estate, he changed the E at the end of his last name to a Y, so it would sound more Irish, less Italian, and the Vito to Vincent. He showed my father his business card. *I said to him, "What, are you out of your mind?"*

When Vito called, he spoke to us, asked us how school was going, what subjects we liked best, what we watched on TV, what books they had us reading in school. This wasn't like my father's other friends, who when they found out I took a liking to the Minnesota Vikings would ask me if they had any injuries that week, *and do you happen to know if they play well on artificial turf?* Those friends were the friends who would always have Susan B. Anthony coins or crumpled two-dollar bills at the ready for me; Vito gave us puzzles, books, drawings, something to make you, the eight- or nine- or ten-year-old, think.

After every conversation, my sister or mother or father or I would say, "Vito, when are you going to come visit?" He'd say yes, that he would, that he was just a little busy but that he'd come up, definitely, that he was looking forward to seeing us all again.

My mother said: "He'll never come."

My father: "Yes, he will."

Mother: "If he wanted to come, it's forty-five minutes on the bus from Eighty-sixth Street. He doesn't even have to take the subway. He could come tomorrow if he wanted to."

Father: "Well, you know, he, he . . ."

Mother: "He doesn't want to come to the Bronx. It's like going backward to him."

Father: "No, it's not that, it's . . . I don't know what it is."

Mother: "That's it, I'm telling you." Accents he didn't want to hear, smells he didn't want to smell, petulance he didn't want to deal with. Stale, crumbling madelines. Guys, wasted potential, standing on corners, spitting for no reason, not because they chew, no one chews in the Bronx, but because they did it since they were kids, and still do, while sitting on car hoods, while tossing a football. All that he left behind and no longer had to hide from in his rent-stabilized walk-up on Seventy-something Street.

And then my mother said: "But I guess I can understand. Who wants to go backward?"

So when my father said, "Look at Vito," what did he mean? That his self-hate held him back or that it pushed him forward? That at least he gave the writing and illustrating a shot or that his ethnic insecurity doomed him?

Vito never sold his pilot or published the children's book he wrote or did anything with his drawings. He remained single, in the studio apartment, the rental, on the Upper East Side, Yorkville. Over the years, he asked my father about his youngest sister. She was pretty, a graphic artist, and she, too, was single.

"How's your sister doing?" Vito asked.

"She's good, she's good," my father said.

"Oh, good. Well, tell her I said hello."

"Yeah, yeah, I will."

But she wasn't interested.

He had lacked something, maybe ambition or not knowing the right people, maybe confidence. Maybe he was unlucky.

My mother said: "Vito's a wonderful person, but Vito's a loser."

"Why do you have to use that term. Human beings aren't losers, how many times do I have to say that?"

"You're not living in reality." Then, to us, quietly, she said: "As usual."

It might have been a movie, just a movie, nothing more, but it was taken, by the masses, as documentary. That April my sister had a party, it may have been a slumber party, for her twelfth birthday, and *Saturday Night Fever*, while it wasn't the theme of the party, its sound track played over and over. We danced around our living room like little kids, impersonating Travolta and his gang, but these girls weren't little kids anymore, they were in the sixth grade, sixth grade in the Bronx, at I.S. 181, the junior high school, and my mother saw where this was going: Too many of these girls were already talking about boys. Maybe they shouldn't have even seen this movie, maybe they were too young. But they all had, and in public school in the Bronx, you picked up on all kinds of things.

After the party, my mother didn't want my sister to have anything to do with most of these girls anymore. *They're all boy crazy.* Soon they'd all be chasing boys around, these trashy boys, with poor upbringings, and where was that going to leave them?

Maybe my father was right, maybe *Saturday Night Fever* was junk, maybe if you see something enough you start believing it, that you'd work in a paint store your whole life, nothing more, maybe it was bad for us.

My father said, "Why don't they make a movie about Italian Americans who were sent to internment camps in this country during the Second World War?"

"What?" My mother said. "That was the Japanese."

"Mainly the Japanese, but a lot of Italians, too. It's a little-known fact."

"I never heard that growing up," my mother said.

"That's because your father thinks he came over on the *Mayflower*."

The more we tried to upend the "John Travolta-type," as my mother now called it, the more popular it became. If you didn't have that haircut, the D.A., if you didn't speak that way, with that sound, that inflection, adamantly inarticulate, you weren't really Italian. "Ain't goin' nowhere" was a destination point to be proud of.

"You don't sound Italian." People said this to me from then on.

What's an Italian supposed to sound like?

My friends talked about the movie. Stevie, the leader of our ball-playing group, said: "The Bee Gees sing like faggots." Another black kid said, "Yeah, and they stole from black people. What do you think Gamble and Huff have been doing this whole time?"

I asked my mother at the dinner table: "Mommy, what's a faggot?"

"What? Where did you hear that word?"

"Downstairs today. Stevie said the Bee Gees sing like faggots."

"I'm surprised he said that. I wouldn't have expected that from him. That's a bad word, don't use it." Then she glared at my father: "See what he's learning."

"Well, what do you want from me? I can't control what comes out of every kid's mouth." Then he said to me: "See, Michael, a lot of these rock singers, they sing in what's called a falsetto, meaning they sing in a higher pitch. It's an Italian word, many words in music are Italian, like piano, the word is *pianoforte*. If the falsetto is done right, it's wonderful, but these rock singers, they're just screachin' and hollerin' to hide the fact that they don't have any talent. You can't even understand the words they're singing. That's why I don't listen to this rock music. It's an abomination."

"It's not rock," my sister said. "It's disco."

"What's the difference?" he said. "It's all the same. It's a debasement of our culture. I blame the Beatles and that Elvis Presley before them. He wasn't even original, he stole the rhythm and blues from the blacks and he went and got rich on it."

"What are you talking about?" my mother said. "The Beatles wrote great songs. They had something to say; they changed the world."

"What did they change?" he said. Now the voices were getting louder. My sister and I, directly opposite at the dinner table, looked at each other.

"You're out of touch," she said.

"I'm out of touch? Mozart is great. Beethoven is great. Satie is great. The Beatles won't endure."

With that, he looked at the clock, dinner was over, and he had to work the phones for the night's baseball games, take the bets, make his own. He said: "Brother Michael, wait until I get to the bedroom and put the phone back on the hook."

My sister, or I, said, "Ma, why do you have to yell at each other."

She said, "Oh, cut it out! Don't be so delicate. This is what people should talk about. That's what the dinner table is for, discussion, debate. What do you want to do, eat frozen TV dinners and watch *Hollywood Squares* at dinner like other people? Not here." Then she said this to us: "Never take the easy way out."

"And besides," she said, "he's full of it. When we were courting, he said he liked the song 'Yesterday.' "

My parents talked about a late spring vacation that year. He was tapped out. This was a year-and-a-half string of bad luck. A bunch of people owed my father money, but they didn't have it. And when he got it, he'd first have to turn around and pay the half dozen people he owed. There were still his doctor bills from the surgery last April. The bills would come, sit on his half of the dresser, and two months later the same bills would come in the mail again.

"But let me see," he said. "Maybe I can cobble something together, pay by personal check, and worry about it later." He wanted to get away himself; last year was tough for him, and even if he loved the city, he could use a week away.

"We could do something close," my mother said. "It doesn't have to be fancy, just let's get out of this dump. It's not good for the kids."

My mother wanted something completely opposite to the Bronx and Co-op City. She wanted something quaint, she kept saying. We went to Nantucket. We took Co-op Cab to LaGuardia, to the Marine Air Terminal, on the airport's outskirts, so out of the way, the driver missed the exit for it. When we walked in, my mother said: "Kids, this is what is called Art Deco. Take a good look." The plane was small and propellered, the scary kind, the kind we flew from San Juan to Saint Thomas.

We rented two rooms in a guesthouse for five or six days. It may have had a kitchen so we could save money on food. Some of the restaurants were expensive. My father would adjust his bifocals and look at the menus outside and shake his head and say: "Madon', they charge telephone numbers." Then he'd say: "Like *abunam'* Bence used to say, 'All you need is a thousand a week.' "

"Daddy, tell us a story about Bence."

"No, please, no Bence stories," my mother said. "We're in Nantucket, I don't want to hear about East Harlem. Let's enjoy it while we're here, enjoy being out of Co-op. Take a deep breath. Feel how clean that air is?"

Instead, we had sandwiches in the guesthouse. "Mommy, tell us a story. Did your parents take you anywhere when you were little?"

"Those two? They didn't take me around the corner. Once we went to Florida—it was awful, I never told you that one?

"My father got the car in '55, I think, and everything was Florida, Florida, Florida. First we went to Niagara Falls. That was all right, but when we went to Florida, it was summer. They closed the luncheonette in Bushwick for two weeks and we rented a house on the beach, somewhere near Daytona. He was too cheap to stay in a hotel. 'That's not for us,' he said.

"The house was cute, it had jalousies, you knew you were in Florida. But the drive down was hellish. There was no air-conditioning. This was in July or August—oh, my God. He wanted to show that he could get down there faster than anyone, so we didn't make any motel reservation along the way. We went through Virginia, it seemed pretty, then North Carolina, which was all trees, and we're going and going, no vacancy signs, no vacancy, no vacancy. I don't want to tell you: the heat! We were dehydrating. And the bugs. The windshield was splattered with bugs.

"Finally, we found a juice stand—a paper cup for fifty cents. 'Can we have another?' we asked. He said, 'Yeah, okay.' 'And another?' My mother said, 'The kids are still thirsty.' 'No, no more,' he said. 'Who are they kidding, fifty cents for that little paper cup?' We were like, with our tongues hanging out.

"We ended up finding a room the following morning in Georgia, at about six in the morning. The Dreamland Motel, it was called. It was brand-new, the linen, the pillows. It was booming. What I remember most was that drive. And all the fast food along the roads. We had chicken in the basket. It felt like Americana."

"What," I asked, "is Americana?"

There's a photo of my father on the beach in Nantucket. He's not in a bathing suit but, again, in a sports coat, slacks, collared shirt, and wingtips. He's standing next to an unoccupied helicopter, abandoned for some reason, there on the sand.

We did spend time on the beach, without formal clothes and wingtips. We brought bathing suits but didn't spend much time in the water. My mother said, "This is the Atlantic, it's treacherous. Just go in to your ankles. There's no lifeguard here and I can't save you."

"Don't put fear into them," my father said. "I'll save them."

"How are you going to save them?" she asked.

"I swim. Here, watch."

"No, come back. Okay, kids, watch this. This is the U.S. Coast Guard at work."

We watched from a safe distance, like we did on the public beach in San Juan and Orchard Beach in the Bronx. He splashed around, clumsily, barely moving in a coherent direction. We laughed. He did this for two or three minutes and came back to us. "See," he said. "Don't say I can't swim. I was in the Coast Guard." He looked at me and my sister. "You know that, right? My oldest brother was a war hero in the Pacific theater. When I die, they'll wrap the coffin in the American flag. These people in Nantucket aren't the only patriots, that they're flying the flag everywhere. They'd have you believe they all came over on the *Mayflower*."

My mother rolled her eyes. Under her breath, she said to us, "Uh, well, they kind of did."

It was up to me or my sister to change the subject. I said, "When am I going to learn how to swim?"

If my father couldn't swim or drive or look just so in boat shoes, he could place a bet. We were there for the Belmont Stakes, late spring, we must have missed a few days of school. We watched the race in a large elegant TV room, either at the inn where we were staying or some-place else. As people gathered for the race, my father excused himself. He put a call back home to New York, to one of his associates. Albert, probably. But you'd never know; he was discreet.

When it came to horses, my father lacked the gumption he had when it came to football. In the fall and winter, he would think noth-ing of putting down his own bet on the ten-point road underdog. With the horses, he bet the chalk. "Always go with the quality horse," he said. He didn't get much action on horses, especially since the state cut in eight years earlier and created Off-Track Betting, but liked betting the big races, like the big fights. First the state cut in on the horse play-ers and now there was talk it would do the same with the numbers. *How's a guy supposed to earn a buck?*

What he bet was the same result of the Preakness, three weeks before: an exacta, amount, as usual, unknown to us, with Affirmed on top and Alydar second.

Everyone in the stately room was glued to that one TV. How could you not be? Is this the greatest race ever? It was just as it was three weeks before, Affirmed, Alydar; no Alydar, Affirmed; Affirmed, Alydar; no, it's too close to call. *Affirmed*. Trip, or part of it, paid for. *Tonight, we'll order a nice Bordeaux.*

ENGLAND, THE NETHERLANDS, 1979

Was the fight in York, outside a Protestant church that my father refused to go into? Was it in Dover, within eyeshot of the white cliffs? Or was it in Bath, over a postcard? Was there even a fight?

Everyone remembers it differently. I remember it taking place in York, outside the Protestant church. My mother thinks it was in Dover. My father doesn't remember a fight. *Whattaya talking about, fight? We had a wonderful time.* My sister says no, that it was in Bath, that it was over a postcard in which my mother wrote to someone that England was "awesomely beautiful." My father looked at it and said, "No it's not." *Here we go.*

He'd been on edge since he arrived in London. Was it that he was in Protestant country for the first time? *Death to the Papists!* He reminded us, almost upon landing, how brutal the English were to the Irish, how they robbed the Irish of their language, the worst thing you could do to a people. And look what they did to India? Was it this brand-new prime minister of theirs, Margaret Thatcher, whom my father was suspicious of immediately? *She's gonna be for the fat cats.* Or was it the money, the fact that we shouldn't have even been here, with or without the poor exchange rate? That this time it was a case of beg and borrow. That maybe he should finally have paid off New York Hospital. But he had said it in 1973: *Every three years. . . .*

My mother, on the other hand, couldn't have loved it more. She had watched *Masterpiece Theatre* all this time and now she was here. Money would be tight, but bless the English, they were bad with food. Which was good; we would save on meals at least. We stocked up on scones in the breakfast room of Durrants Hotel, where we stayed. It was our favorite hotel of anyplace we stayed so far. What characters these English were. An ancient man with white hair, someone out of *Upstairs, Downstairs*, served the morning scones, and asked, every day, "Strawberry jam?" Another just served the tea or coffee and asked, "Coffee? White?" My mother loved this. Not "milk" but "white." *These British, they're hilarious. It's like* Fawlty Towers. *All we need is John Cleese.*

At six P.M., my sister and I would walk to a McDonald's we found on or near Baker Street. It was about a ten-minute walk, but my parents felt it was safe and my sister was thirteen and feeling independent. For my sister and me, this was a treat. We could only eat fast food on rare occasions, on a road trip with relatives, at a birthday party, a quick bite while on a trip into the city. For my parents, this would save them money. They went out after we finished, maybe to a pub or for Indian or for Chinese one night, and a fancy English meal another night. They had Beef Wellington. "You didn't miss anything," they said.

We were lucky; our mother cooked and cooked well. Most of the kids we knew in Co-op, their mothers either worked or cooked one or two things or cooked poorly. "These women today, they think cooking is beneath them," my mother would say. "But I'm no women's libber."

"Mom," my sister and I asked, "how come you don't work?"

"Why, who asked?"

"Kids at school," we said.

"What kids at school? That's coming from their parents. And that's none of their business, what I do and what I don't do? Who else?"

"Ah, no one."

"People are nosy—boy, oh boy. And they like to stir up trouble." She paused. "Even when I did work, your father took my paycheck. The same thing would happen now. I wouldn't see any of it. See these Jewish women, their husbands give *them* the paycheck. I never even saw his pay stub, much less a paycheck. Every time I started a little savings account, he came to me, hollering, 'I need the money!' " She looked at me. "He didn't even have the money to get you out of New York Hospital when you were born. He had to run somewhere and borrow it. He thought it was funny at the time."

My sister and I didn't say anything. *Wasn't it funny?*

She said: "If anyone asks, tell them I work in the home, and it's hard work. They should try it some time before they criticize it."

Every night was a ritual. My father would get home by five-thirty, after an eight-to-four day, and by five forty-five we would all have to be around the table. No excuses. If I was late from playing ball, I wouldn't get punished, my parents didn't believe in official punishments, nor would I have food withheld; I always needed the calories. Instead, I would get reprimanded. First my mother and then my father. My father would say, "Your mother works very hard to prepare a meal like this. Don't you appreciate that? Don't you know it's better for you to eat a home-cooked meal? You know how many people out there would love a home-cooked meal? You don't want to eat junk the way other people do. Do you?" And that was that. I was allowed to state my case, that the touch football game went into overtime, that it was so compelling, people from the town houses behind our building were watching us as they came back from work, that I couldn't just walk away. No, this table was where I belonged, not on the asphalt running slant patterns. Now was the time to eat and converse.

The only night he missed dinner with us was at the annual reunion dinner with his former colleagues at the Non-Residence Center within the department. It was in Harlem, *near the old Polo Grounds*. He liked his job, but he didn't bring it home with him. There was little room for advancement, anyway. Instead, my parents would discuss the news of the day. They argued about topics and people. Jimmy Carter, for instance. My father: "He's a compassionate man; he's a great man." My mother: "He's genteel, but he's weak."

Or Woody Allen. My father: "He's one-dimensional; he only knows a certain sliver of New York. And he's self-absorbed." My mother: "What artist isn't self-absorbed? Fellini wasn't self-absorbed? Picasso wasn't self-absorbed? He writes of his milieu, but he makes it universal!"

Or Billy Martin. My mother: "He's a psycho case, that one. He shouldn't keep coming back to the Yankees. He should tell them to keep their job." My father: "He's a wheel-and-a-half, but he knows his baseball. And he never backs down. He's never intimidated."

Even when they agreed, it sounded like they were fighting. Like when the subject of psychotherapy came up. Father: "It's a substitute religion for the elite. It's a racket." Mother: "It's a cop-out. People want answers. Sometimes there are no answers in life."

Him: "Exactly!"

Or Norman Lear. Father: "His programming is liberal propaganda." Mother: "That's why I don't watch that stuff anymore. I watch *Masterpiece Theatre*."

Or movies. Mother: "*Days of Heaven*, oh what a movie. You kids have to see it when you get older." Father: "It's a great picture, a masterpiece." Mother again: "It's like a painting."

These were loud, brawling discussions at dinner. My sister and I were free to interject if we had a question or something to add. *Who's David Susskind? Who's this Dick Cavett guy?* But we were eleven and thirteen; we didn't stay up to watch Susskind late on Sunday night.

Did I mention there was wine at the table?

These meals were often feasts, especially on Sunday. You couldn't drink soda or water or juice with this food. And no, you couldn't drink milk. Even we children were discouraged from drinking milk with dinner. You had wine. Not expensive wine, unless it was a Catholic holiday, Thanksgiving, or my father had a windfall. Then he'd go "down the Astor Wine Shop" or if he was visiting Vito in Yorkville "go up McCabes" on Third Avenue, combine that with a strudel or linzer tortes from Mrs. Greenburg's bakery. He'd buy French and Italian reds and whites for these occasions. Otherwise, it was table wine, or if my mother made something like meatloaf or pork tenderloin or, for Saint Patrick's Day, corned beef and cabbage, then beer, Ballantine Ale if it was domestic, Beck's if we could afford imported that week.

The wine they shared with me, probably before I was ten. You can have a little, it's good for you, they'd say, but just a little. They might mix it with water or ice or both but it was what we'd drink. With veal cutlet Milanese once a week, roast lemon chicken, baby lamb chops, sausage and peppers, fried Sicilian meatballs, no sauce, with a hint of lemon (her paternal grandfather's recipe), steak pizzaiola, London broil. There were always two or three vegetables. On Friday's we didn't eat meat. My father wanted to keep that tradition, Vatican II or not. So Fridays were peppers and eggs or potatoes and eggs or spaghetti marinara or a tuna and tomato salad in the summer. A couple of times a year, to give my mother a night off, we'd order a pizza, "from that jerk across the street. He has the Midas touch that one, and he can't even open his mouth to speak. Unbelievable."

Sundays were the thick rigatoni with ragu sauce, meatballs, sausage, braciola, or chicken cacciatore ("gotch-a-dor"), a roast pork, or, if I was lucky, like Super Bowl Sunday, a roast beef. Christmas Day lasagna and a roast, Thanksgiving was turkey—no pasta, nothing Italian. My mother insisted on that. If we spent Thanksgiving at her parents' house in Smithtown, her father would say, "Can you believe, some of these Italians eat macaroni on Thanksgiving. They're in America now." My father let it go or didn't hear him or pretended not to hear. Easter was leg of lamb, Christmas Eve the seven fishes, of which I ate almost none. *You don't know what you're missing.* When my mother expressed concern that my tastes weren't varied enough, that I had to eat more than beef, that I had to eat more of everything, my father said, "Don't worry, in ten years time he'll be down Umberto's eating the clam sauce. That's where they killed Joey Gallo. I ever tell you about Joey Gallo?"

My father didn't cook. He did salads and sandwiches. "He makes good sandwiches," my mother said. "He learned from the old man in the Club, the Chief." And he was in charge of the fruit after dinner.

He peeled the pears or apples, sliced the watermelon or cantaloupe, divvied up the orange slices. His coup was peaches in the wine. Come fall, he'd travel all over the Bronx and Manhattan for a certain type of peach, the Neapolitan dialect word was *per-cog*. This was passed down from the old country; it was our thing. It wasn't in any magazine or cooking show. This wasn't trendy.

This bothered my parents, when they'd see something about our culture, especially food or drink, that was written by a non-Italian. *They act as if they invented it.* That we'd been eating/drinking/doing whatever it may have been for years, for centuries, and now we didn't even get any of the credit, as if we had nothing to do with it. But not hard peaches in chilled red wine; who cares if you're not supposed to chill red wine. No one, that we saw, ever wrote about this.

There was only a small window in September to find these peaches and he'd ask his sisters, brothers, his cousin from Naples, his old uncle, friends, acquaintances. He'd go to Chinatown—*ya never know*. He'd give strangers who worked at fruit stands his number, just to find these peaches or to chase down a rumor. Some years would go by without *per-cog*. You'd just have to live with that. When he found them, if they were the right texture—they couldn't be too soft—he'd gently skin them, cut them into chunks, and soak them in dry red table wine, for two or three days, in the refrigerator. Then serve as dessert.

All that wine. And then my sister began to notice, I hadn't caught on yet: The more wine, the louder the conversation, debate, argument got. She'd tell them this, and they'd say: "What, do you want us to drink milk with dinner, or Pepsi, like the other people." "Yes," my sister said. "Why can't we do things like other people?"

We argued, especially this year, about religion, the church. My sister turned thirteen and had to begin to prepare for confirmation. It never happened. There was a retreat for the thirteen-year-old Catholics of Co-op City who attended religious instruction after school once a week at Saint Michael's Parish. Calling this a parish, or a church, was a reach. It was downstairs in the community center across the street from us. There was nothing holy about it. It was a gussied-up, multi-purpose room that could have been used for anything. My father had Mount Carmel Church, my mother had Saint Leonard's, my sister and I had this, utilitarian Catholicism.

During this retreat my sister may have been withdrawn. But it was a retreat, she reasoned, not a social event. If it was a social event, she wouldn't have been there; most of her friends attended religious instruction at Young Israel.

When the nun in charge asked for a confession, something, anything, my sister didn't know what to say; she didn't have anything to say. She was a model student. She had done volunteer work at the Hebrew Nursing Home on Co-op City Boulevard and received an award from the B'nai B'rith. About the only rebellious thing she did was listen to Blondie and Supertramp records. *White music?* So she told the nun this: "I don't go to church on Sunday." When the nun asked her if she was sorry about that, my sister told the truth, as she was taught to do at home. "No," she said, "I'm not sorry." Now we had a problem.

My sister may not have taken this nun seriously since my mother didn't take the nun seriously—or Saint Michael's. This nun didn't wear the habit, and she was a chain smoker. My mother said: "She calls herself a nun? What nun smokes?"

The nun called my mother and told her that my sister, with that attitude, wouldn't get confirmed. My mother said, "You know what, I don't want to be associated with your so-called church, and I don't want my kids to be, either. Thank you very much." And after she hung up the phone, she mumbled in dialect: *Va fa Napola*, go to Naples, go to Hell in other words.

My father was furious. He yelled, "Never mind, I want my kids confirmed in the Catholic Church! They had their Holy Communion, they'll have their confirmation."

My mother didn't back down. She was a Catholic, but a weary one. She believed in the teachings, the rituals, the art of it all, she believed in its essential core. *It's poetic.* She loved Good Friday, and our own ritual. We'd fast, we'd meet my father in the city at noon, at Saint Patrick's, then we'd go to two more churches. We didn't stay for full masses; my father couldn't hear the priest and got jittery, but it always had to be three churches. We would end the fast at three in the afternoon at Paul & Jimmy's on Irving Place or Il Cortile in Little Italy. We'd go to DiPalo's, wait on line forever, on the sidewalk, and buy the meats and cheeses for the next day, Holy Saturday. She loved this, and Easter, preparing the leg of lamb, the seven fishes on Christmas Eve, all that work.

But the Church was something else. *They run it like a corporation.* She stopped going to Sunday mass after she graduated Saint Leonard's in the eighth grade. And she didn't like what she saw in some church goers. Like that certain someone in our building. *Don't get me started on her.* "She'd come out of church, cursing everyone, envious, jealous. And then she says, 'Well I go to church every Sunday, I go to confession.' You've got to be kidding?"

So when my father yelled, she yelled back. "Listen here, you didn't go through what I went through with the Church. Eight years of Catholic school, don't tell me. That nun downstairs, she's not a nun. She's in street clothes with a cigarette hanging out of her mouth. She's going to confirm these other kids, a lot of them are common trash, they're boy crazy already, and she's not going to confirm our daughter, who's a good kid? Please."

This fight my mother won, but not without lingering animosity. So if we were standing outside an Episcopal church in Yorkshire, and one parent wanted to go in and the other didn't, and one said, "Oh, would you get over it," then, yeah, all hell could break loose on this quiet street in the original York, Old York, screaming accusations of her self-hate, her Anglo-philia, of *that father of yours*, and her retorts of his insecurity and ethnocentricity. *I'm ethnocentric, and Anglo-Saxons aren't?!*

The silences after these fights, especially after the money fights, about why we had none, lasted for days, sometimes weeks, sometimes months. This one, in England, as ferocious and personal as it was, didn't last. There was still more to see: Stratford-upon-Avon, for one, which would be good for us, my mother said, especially since two Shakespeare plays were taught to I.S. 181's advanced seventh and eighth graders.

The rest of the trip, at breakfast, wherever we were, we imitated the waiters at the breakfast room of Durrants Hotel in London. "Madam, strawberry jam?" "Coffee? White?" Even in Holland—where the food was possibly worse, as was the weather. It rained only one day when we were in England. And we took a stroll in it. "It reminds me of Gramercy Park," my father said. "Down near Paul & Jimmy's."

In Holland, it only rained. We landed at Schiphol in the rain, and it never stopped. We were ripped off, immediately, by the cabdriver upon arrival. He seemed so nice, too. He spoke perfect English, *they speak such perfect English*, and pointed out all the historical points of interest—and so many on just the ride to this hotel. He acted like our best friend. At the hotel, we asked how much it should have cost. *That sonnuva . . . What are they, Presbyterians these people?*

When we walked the streets, even canal-side, tall, skinny, long-haired entrepreneurs, offered my parents drugs, they offered me and my sister drugs. They spoke perfect English. They said it was the best stuff. "This is worse than New York," my mother said. "What a horror show."

"We should've gone to Ireland," my father said. "They're a Catholic country, they respect the family. There's none of this, offering drugs to little kids. How dare they."

"You wanted to come here," my mother said. "You wanted to see the Rijksmuseum, *The Night Watch*."

"The Flemish were giants of Western civilization."

"And look what it's come to," she said. "Europe is washed up. They have nothing left to offer. They've become too tolerant, too hedonistic."

"We can still have a good time," he said. "We just can't let the kids walk by themselves like in London." Besides, *The Night Watch* was worth it, wasn't it? And soon we'd be in Delft and The Hague, more masterpieces at Mauritshuis.

"If your teachers ask you what you did over the summer, be sure you tell them you came here," my mother said to my sister and me. "The teachers at the junior high school are more astute. Don't just say you spent the summer in Co-op, playing ball in the street because you want to fit in." *We are lucky to be here.*

For all of Amsterdam's decadence, for all the bad food—*who eats French fries with mayonnaise?*—the rain, the August chill, the crooked cabbies, *damned Presbyterians*, my mother said this at Schiphol, as we readied to depart on KLM, a white 747 with blue trimming, the Royal Dutch Airline: "I'm glad we came to Holland." My father: "So am I. What great paintings. They're in a decadent phase right now, but these things are cyclical."

In Amsterdam, the hippies hung on; in New York, they were fading. My English teacher in I.S. 181, a strict, middle-aged black woman who would teach us Shakespeare, told us it was time to learn how to speak correctly now, to start thinking about our futures, not to imitate that music we listened to. "See all those hippies, their rich daddies stopped paying their way and now they cut their hair, wear shirts and ties, and work on Wall Street."

When I told my parents what she said at the dinner table, my mother, impressed, said, "Really? She said that?" My mother repeated it, louder, to my father, as she often had to do. "Hugo, you hear this, what his English teacher said."

My father laughed. "She's perceptive," he said.

I.S. 181 was junior high school, a Bronx public school. Childhood was over. P.S. 178 was public but we were cute little peanuts, with Afros and long hair. Now we had a hallway connecting us to the towering, dreaded Truman High School, where we had gym class. We heard rumors of fights between invading kids from I.S. 180, adjacent on Truman's other side. In P.S. 178, there was the chant: "A fight, a fight, a nigger and a white, the nigger turned red and the white dropped dead." A black kid usually initiated the ditty, but it meant little, the fights were harmless, and at least we were going to school together, living together. Where else could you say that? Still, my parents said, no matter how innocent it seems, or how funny, don't ever say it. If black kids wanted to use that word, that was their business.

I was in one of these fights. I was the white. Luckily, no one was there to sing it. It was third grade, after Otis, my protector, was sent off to military school. A black girl in my class bragged about her little brother, Greg, and how he was the strongest, toughest kid, how he'd whoop anybody, any of you white-boy honkies. A few of us stood there, silent, even the kid who asked if my father was in the mafia, the half Italian, half Jew, who had the look of a budding athlete. They all said nothing. I heard my father's voice: *Never be intimidated.*

I once asked him what I should do if someone called me a honky. "First of all," he said, "you never call them a name back, never use any slur, not even this word Polack that people throw around casually. It's highly insulting. So never use those words. Remember, we were called guineas and dagos."

"Are Polish people really stupid?" I asked.

"No," he said. "That's ridiculous. They're not stupid at all. See this new pope? He's Polish and I think he'll be a very fine pope. Now, if they call you a honky, you tell them we're not honkies. The word *honky*, and you shouldn't use it either, it's a disparaging term, but it's meant for Central and Eastern European Slavic people. In this country they settled in places like the Midwest, Chicago, Western Pennsylvania, like this movie *The Deer Hunter* you've heard your mother talk about, excellent movie, by the way, for when you get older. They're tough people. They produced a lot of football players. But we're not honkies. If someone calls you that, just ignore it. Tell them your grandparents are from Naples."

My mother, to my sister and me, under her breath, just enough that my father couldn't hear, said, "Oh God, don't say that. Say you're Sicilian. Always say you're Sicilian."

My sister said: "Mom, I don't think the kids in Co-op City know the difference between Naples and Sicily."

But in school, when this kid called us honkies, it didn't seem the time to debate, to say that my grandparents were from Naples, *no, I mean Sicily*. So I, the smallest kid, said, "I'm not afraid of your brother."

The others looked at me. I shocked them—and belittled them.

"Okay," she said, "then you want to fight him?"

"Yeah, I'll fight him," I said. "I'm not scared." Why did I say that?

"Be in the schoolyard, a half hour after dismissal when no one's around," she said.

"I'm there every day anyway, playing scully." Now I couldn't back down. What would they think of me?

The fight, simply, was this: Greg's friend Mark, who was in my grade, grabbed me from behind, by my shoulders, and said, "You want him, Greg?"

I looked at Greg. He was younger by a year but much bigger than I, like everyone else. He had a weathered look for a second-grader. He answered, "Yeah." Mark pushed me hard into the asphalt, on our chalk-drawn scully board, where a few minutes before we played with our bottle caps filled with clay. My pants ripped at the knees and my palms were scraped and bloodied and burning. I stayed down, trying hard not to cry, and covered my head, awaiting the barrage, what I imagined would be fists and Pro-Keds.

Instead, I heard Greg say to his friend, "C'mon, let's get out of here." And they walked away. My friends dusted me off, asked if I was okay. When I went home, I told my mother I tripped and fell while running full speed. She said: "Be careful in that schoolyard."

That was as bad as the fighting got. That and the time I got beat up by Jordan, a Jewish kid, a bit of a nerd but bigger than I. This time there was a large group after school that followed us up to a grassy little hill outside Building 4, the designated fighting destination for P.S. 178. The fight was this: Jordan easily threw me to the ground, got me into a headlock, and gave me a couple of slaps that messed up my long hair. That was it. But at I.S. 181, I knew better than to get into any fights, these were real fights. *Yo, there's gonna be a throw-down.*

The student body was different. More of the kids I went to P.S. 178 with had moved. Our family friends from the twenty-fourth floor, the Cohns, first sent their son, Harry, to a Jewish day school and then moved to Westchester, to Scarsdale, near my mother's favorite store, Lord & Taylor. Harry and I once had big plans. He envisioned us starting a magazine exclusively on New York sports teams. This from a seven- or eight-year-old. My mother liked me having a friend like this. *See, the Jews are always thinking, even at that age.* She didn't blame them for leaving; how could she? They invited us up to their new house, three or four times, but soon it was only an end-of-the-year holiday card. My mother thought Sara would send Max over with some potato pancakes. He was still teaching at Truman High School, so close. Every Christmas they would come down to look at our tree. They loved the tree, the fragrance, and they would always leave my mother, every year, with potato pancakes for Hanukkah. My mother inhaled them. And then, no more. My mother felt bad. *The high school was right there. I thought she'd send him over with some. You got the feeling they didn't want to be associated with Co-op City.*

In junior high, at I.S. 181, there were more kids from Section 5, accepted as the worst part of Co-op, and still more from Boston Secor. They both spoke of marauding bands from "the Valley," a mysterious territory, on the other side of I-95. The Secor kids talked about dog fighting; we didn't know whether to believe them or not. There were no dogs allowed in Co-op, and signs everywhere reminding us, but there were auto-body shops and junkyards just on the outskirts, near where my mother parked her car on Rombouts Street, and sometimes there they were, stray and menacing. *Never go near those dogs!*

They talked about DJs and B-Boys and turntables and they brought vinyl records to school, funk records, 12-inch singles that you didn't hear on the radio, not even on WBLS, "Frisco Disco," and "Smokin' Cheeba Cheeba." *What's Cheeba?*

If the numbers said 50–50, black-to-white or 55–45 black-white, 60–40, 65–35, 75–25, depending on what classroom you looked at, the dominant culture was clear. *Somebody say Sugar Hill!* If you listened to rock 'n' roll, you were listening to the wrong thing. *Yo, that shit is devil music, man.* If your sneakers weren't a certain brand, Puma or Adidas, or tied a certain way, with thick laces, with an extra sock underneath so it would puff out, if you didn't polish your Adidas Superstar with white shoe polish, if you didn't have a toothbrush to stroke your suede Puma Clydes, you were wack.

I did all of the above. It helped that I didn't swim; in the eyes of my black peers, I was one of them. Reality was upside down; it was cool not to swim. In fifth grade, we had swimming classes for a two- or three-week span in place of gym.

We missed gym. We missed our gym teacher. Besides athletics, it was his job to teach us about things like sex education and drugs. Even he couldn't bring himself to go too much into sex. That we could learn from our homies. But about drugs he said, "Yo, fellas, I'm tellin' ya, stay away from drugs." And every year he told the story of how some kid, in I.S. 181 or I.S. 180 or Truman, high on angel dust jumped out of a fourth-story window. We didn't believe it; he swore it was true.

For swimming, they took us to Truman High School's immense pool and where there was a short, mean, chubby instructor. I was afraid, but I wasn't alone. My father suggested that I try it. I told him I didn't want to, that I didn't like the instructor, that less than half the class was planning to participate. My mother said: "You better not, it's too dangerous. And you're a little bit of a thing, if you drown, who's going to see you. No, you stay with the black boys and watch from the side. I'll write you a note."

We handed in our notes, signed by our parents, took off our sneakers, rolled up our pants, and sat on the side. We didn't acknowledge our fear or embarrassment. Instead, we made fun of the kids trying to learn. The black boys sang the Joe Tex song, "Ain't Gonna Bump

No More," *with no big fat woman* when the girls came out in their bathing suits. We said, look at this one, look at that one, we laughed, doubled over, instead of trying to learn. *Check that out, that nigga be drownin'. Ha!* We enjoyed these forty-five minutes of inverted reality. We made it cool.

After England/Holland I entered sixth grade, my sister eighth. Next year, for her, was high school. She was an excellent student, better than I, but on the standardized test she just missed out on Bronx High School of Science. My father had his fingers crossed for Stuyvesant, where he went, but that was even harder to get into than Science. She made Brooklyn Tech, but that would be two hours each way on bus and subway. This wasn't advisable for a fourteen-year-old in 1979 or '80. We didn't know of any kid in Co-op City who made that journey, one that was out of *The Warriors*.

At dinner, my mother asked my father: "So what are we going to do about high school?"

My sister and I looked at each other. *Oh boy.*

"I don't know," my father said.

"Oh, you don't know. Well, what are we supposed to do? We can't send her to Truman, it's even bad by New York City public school standards. The Forty-fifth Precinct is here almost every day on account of that school, not even Co-op Security, but the police cars. I see it, I hear it, every day, from our bedroom window. You're not home to see it. I am."

"I said I don't know. We'll figure it out," he said, yelling. "We'll figure it out!"

My mother didn't back down, she never did. I never saw her cry. "Well, if you listened to me and we had gotten the hell out of this place when we had the chance, but no, you had to do things your way."

"So you have complaints with life, is that it?" he said.

"No," she said, "I don't have complaints, but what about our future?"

"We still have time," he said. "Don't panic."

"Don't panic?" she said. "You gamble away whatever you win."

"That's the only way to win a lump sum," he said. "I can still put a package together. That's the only way we'll get out of here. We can't do it on my salary—how many times do I have to say that!"

"Your way is only going to make things worse," she said.

"Would you give it a rest," he said, yelling louder. "I don't sleep at night. Why do you think I don't sleep?" Then, in a softer voice, to me, "Brother Michael, put the phone back on the hook. I have to get back to work."

"He sleeps just fine," my mother said to us. "He's out like a light, snoring. I'm the one who doesn't sleep at night. We've got nothing. No life insurance, no retirement account, no savings, no real estate. Just a car that barely runs."

"Maybe we'll be left an inheritance," my sister said.

My mother let out a sarcastic left. "Forget it, kiddo," she said. "No one's going to leave us a dime. And I could never stand these people who grovel and kiss rear-end to be left in someone's will. It's disgusting, frankly." She paused. "I only wish we would be able to leave you kids something. Parents are supposed to leave something to their children, but at the rate we're going, that's not going to happen."

Then she continued. "Remember, never tell him where I keep my savings. If there's an emergency, and God forbid I'm not here, I keep whatever I can, a few tens and twenties, in the James Beard cookbook. That's only if Michael gets sick and needs a prescription filled or if we don't have money for food. Does he ever ask you kids where it is?"

"No," my sister said. My mother looked at me. "Nope," I said. It was true; he never did ask. For my allowance yes, but not for her secret stash, not that it was much. If he did, would we have told her?

"But we went to England and Holland and lots of other nice places," I said.

"That's nice, yes, and we always have a wonderful time, but we're not saving long-term. Every time I try to start a savings account at the Amalgamated Bank across the street, he drains it. If I tell him, let's buy stocks or bonds, he yells at me, 'What do you think that is, it's gambling!' Why can't we save, like everyone else? 'No, that's bourgeois!' "

"Daddy says he wants to go to Yugoslavia next, or maybe back to Italy," my sister said. "No one else in Co-op City does that."

"But they save for a house. You see the moving vans when you come home from school. Everyone's moving. I'd rather move to a better area with good public high schools, than go to Yugoslavia, as beautiful as it is. Save for our future. The fact is, your father is an addicted gambler, and he doesn't admit it. The bookmaker is always supposed to win, but he gambles on top of it. He's been doing it since high school." Then she paused, and said, "I'm going to end up out in the street. Homeless."

What could we say? We said, "Mommy, we won't let you become homeless."

But already I was terrified.

PART III

THE 1980s

Manhattan makes it, the Bronx takes it.

—*Local aphorism*

NEW ORLEANS, 1980

The night Ronald Reagan was elected president, my father cried and not out of joy. It was the only time I saw him cry. No, the second. He cried the year before, when his father died. Everyone cried that day; no one tried to hide it.

On Election Day, 1980, he tried not to show it. He wiped tears from his eyes when the returns came in and quietly excused himself. He played his Ellington and Basie tapes, as he did in times of despair, if Goose Gossage blew a save, and hundreds, thousands, of potential dollars for us, or if the football team he needed, whatever team it was, didn't cover in the last West Coast NFL game Sunday, seven-ish, perfectly ruining the fine meal we just ate and wiping out the rest of the day's winnings. He turned to Duke and the Count, then early to bed, for the Department of Welfare the next morning.

My sister cried, too, the first Tuesday after the first Monday in November. It was in the wind, especially among schoolteachers, that if Reagan won, we were headed for certain war, nuclear, Co-op City included. My father knew better. He cried for another reason: something would end, not the world—he wasn't having that, *the liberal propaganda, they should quit while they're ahead sometimes*—but a system, maybe what made America great. That would be dismantled.

My mother said this to me now, I was the only one left in the living room as the final returns came in: "Maybe it's for the best. This country has gone to hell in a handbasket. We couldn't even get those poor hostages out. Look at how we bungled that."

———————

"I like this kid Ravi, he's like a Sicilian kid, a real zip. He's wise." My mother said this about my new best friend, co-best-friend, really. And he wasn't Sicilian, he was from India.

I don't remember how this happened exactly, the aftermath of a very complicated, bitter breakup of a circle of close buddies, most from the same building, our building. All these cute little kids, friends from when we were this high, some older or younger by a couple of years, playing punchball, slap ball, fly ball, chuck ball, off-the-wall, running bases, British Bulldog, manhunt, always outside, in the summer. Then in the ice-cold winters, touch football, snowball fights, all at, under, or near our home, Building 6. Kids with baseball caps, tube socks up to the knees with colored hoops around the top, navy blue Converse All-Stars, canvas, all the perspiration in those, the stink, after all those summer hours on scalding asphalt.

Then something happened. Someone said something to someone else or did something or misunderstood something, and the gang, more Peanuts than Warriors, was no more. It didn't involve me, but there was a clear schism, and I had to take a side. I want to remember what it was, but I can't. I did what I thought was right, and I took the side of the minority, Ravi and Calvin. I remember feeling, knowing, that I did the right thing. I sided with the two I thought were right, with the two who were wronged, and left aside the core of the group, about five or six of them, including Stevie.

It was so bitter a split, we all stopped speaking to one another, very awkward when we would be waiting for elevators in the lobby, which was more and more now; they regularly broke down. Waiting and waiting for elevators, sighing, exhaling, rolling the eyes.

The worst thing you could do to someone in Co-op City, the most disrespectful act, was not hold the elevator door for someone. They'd have to wait who knows how long, perhaps run into an overly chatty or inquisitive neighbor: who, what, where, when, and why. *Some people.*

There were ways to retaliate: You could say "thanks a lot!" sarcastically just as the door closed with the elevator riders who didn't hold the door for you still within earshot. Or, there was the street thing to do: kick the door after it closed. If you did it hard enough and just so—with your back to the elevator, you had to pound the flat bottom of your sneaker into the door—you could cause the elevator to get stuck, which was an even worse inconvenience, and scarier, than missing an elevator. *Thanks a lot!* This was done usually by young people, and usually by angry ones, of which there were more now.

The less time spent in the lobby, the better. So when our group dismantled, it was awkward running into them by the elevator banks, the mailboxes, the intercoms. When I'd ring Ravi's buzzer and wait for him to come down or vice versa—*yo, you comin' down*—it was best then to stare blankly out of the big glass windows so as not to see any of our former friends coming or going. Soon enough, we stopped caring and they stopped caring. We just ignored one another—and that was how things were.

Most of the group had about reached high school age and were changing. The former leader, Stevie, who was black, was growing his hair long and joined a rock band, a white rock band oddly. He began to wear white rocker clothes, jeans, black leather jacket, a bandana. The others, of course, followed his lead and dressed the same, listened to the music he did, hung out with the new guys he hung with. Stevie was still a leader but wasn't imploring anyone to bend down and put their hands on their knees, in the ready position, to assume the ball was coming to them. He wasn't saying, "It's okay, good try, get 'em next time." He changed. He was listening to heavy metal.

"That shit's devil music," said Calvin, who was black. Calvin and Ravi, combined, would be my new Stevie.

Calvin's parents were divorced and his father lived someplace in northern Westchester, maybe Mount Kisco. Ravi was two years older than I, but Calvin was another year older than that.

I remember the day I first met him. It was a few years before, after school, when we all gathered to play ball. There were two new boys that day, one was Indian, the other black, and someone introduced them to our group. This person, I forget who, knew them from I.S. 181 and announced that these two would be playing ball with us regularly. I remember Calvin's jacket, it was a blue Mighty Mack—it must have been cold out. I remember because I had a gray Mighty Mack as my winter jacket. Calvin looked quiet, even a little nervous. The Indian kid, Vijay, was more talkative, outgoing. He lived in Building 4 or 5. We hadn't known anyone from that building before. There weren't many Indians in Co-op City, but with Ravi and this new kid Vijay there were two in our circle.

Calvin lived in one of the town houses off the loop known as Defoe Place, about a three-minute walk from the back of Building 6. We knew this cluster of town houses since it was facing a peculiar rock formation that jutted out of the Co-op City concrete. We called it "little rock" and played on it as small children. It was an integral part of the manhunt game, a place to hide. I had played there, too, with Harry as an even younger child. Harry's father, the science teacher, if he didn't take us to the blue-and-yellow Sukkot tent beside the parking garage, would have us collect stones from little rock and teach us about their properties and characteristics. We may have pretended to be Kirk and Spock, turned it into a make-believe planet searching for McCoy and other members of the landing party, who suddenly vanished. I brought my model tricorder and communicator and spoke into it, as if Harry could hear. These were the models my father bought for me a few years before at the grand opening of a store called the Star Trek Trading Post in Midtown. We stood on line, outside in the freezing cold for two hours. He was sick, we both were sick, for two weeks after that. *Don't remind me of that night with the Star Wars.* All for a few tribbles and blueprints of the Starship *Enterprise*.

This planet of ours was "little rock" and not simply the "rock" only because there was a bigger rock formation around Buildings 1 and 2, closer to the New England Thruway. This was "big rock."

Children played on it, too. It had a sliding pond that scooped down into a sand garden.

Calvin's door faced little rock, but his room window faced Building 6. My room window faced west, to Defoe Place, Calvin's exact bedroom window, and beyond that Building 1, I-95, the number 5 subway. Beyond that, only lights.

My mother liked Calvin as much as Ravi; she allowed me to invite both boys up to the house. They both looked out for me, and as more and more of the Co-op City originals began to flee and the place became more—not sinister, not darker—just more and more like the rest of the Bronx, without the fires, she was happy two decent boys like this, with good parents, were there for me. Calvin's mother worked at a school in another part of the Bronx. She knew Mr. G., Irv Gikofsky, the friendly weatherman on WCBS Channel 2, who was once a teacher there. She was always nice to me and called me "baby" or "honey" when I called or came over. I probably seemed young and small to her. I was young and small. But Calvin didn't like her new boyfriend, a man I never met. Soon he would have to contend with another boyfriend, that of his older sister's. He often grew quiet whenever the subject of family came up. Early that summer, his father had let him down, even if he didn't say so. I felt guilt-ridden about it, maybe I could've done something.

It was June, and there was a big fight coming up. My father still called them prizefights. Sugar Ray Leonard was going to fight Roberto Duran. Sugar Ray was youthful, innocent-looking, had a small Afro, the kind Calvin and my friends at school had, and the kind I still wanted. He had a cute little son he did TV commercials with, won an Olympic Gold Medal in 1976, was American, and a hero to me. To my father, he was a pretty boy, talked too much, was a show-off, the second coming of Ali. But worst of all, he used the great Ray Robinson's name in a kind of vain. There was only one Sugar Ray in my father's mind. *Who does this kid think he is? Big deal, the Olympics.*

To me, Duran was evil, a kind of beast, foreign. He didn't even speak English, or refused to. "He speaks English," my mother would say while watching the interviews leading up to the fight, "but he's sly like a fox, this Duran."

My father said, "So what if he doesn't speak English; he speaks Spanish. It's a beautiful language."

Duran's nickname was "Manos de Piedras," which meant, and my father loved this, "hands of stone." In fact, he loved everything about Duran. The way he was never intimidated, the way he took a punch, stood toe-to-toe, the way he wasn't a ready-made endorsement deal. Duran was simply this: he was old school.

"I hope he knocks Leonard through the ropes," my father said in the weeks before the fight. It was all anyone was talking about in Co-op City in those last few weeks of school, in the Italian deli, by the elevators.

"What sucks is that it ain't gonna be on no TV," one kid said as sixth grade came to an end.

"Yeah it is, it's on Channel 7," said another. Sugar Ray's fights had all been on ABC, Channel 7 in New York.

"It ain't not," the first kid said.

"He's right," I said. "It's on closed circuit, and I'm going. My father's taking me."

"Word?"

"Yeah."

My father came through. There was no way he was going to miss this. He loved the lower weight classes, more than the heavyweights. He hadn't watched Ali-Frazier I on closed circuit ten years before. He was afraid Joe Frazier would lose and he liked Frazier. Smokin' Joe was from the old school and to my father's eyes just as proud a black man as Ali. Frazier didn't belittle his opponents, didn't call them ugly. For that, my father was never a fan of Ali's, probably the only white person, and liberal, in the New York City Department of Welfare who didn't love Ali. No one would come up to the Rock and Joe Louis for my father. *If you're the greatest, you don't have to go around saying it all the time.* But he still loved boxing, the middleweights, welterweights, lightweights, even feather- and bantamweights. There was great technical skill there, delicate footwork, tactics, thinking, guts. He was convinced Duran wasn't going to lose to Leonard. My mother wanted Sugar Ray to win but she called him a "powder puff." "He looks like a powder puff, not a prizefighter," she said. "They'll make him an announcer when he retires, he'll go right into the media. He's good-looking and listen to him, he's super articulate."

We had three tickets. I don't know if the third was intended for my mother and she changed her mind at the last minute or if it had always been for my sister. She, like me and my mother, wanted Sugar Ray.

When Calvin heard that I was going to the fight, he asked his father to buy tickets. Calvin loved Sugar Ray, much more than I did. His favorite athletes were Sugar Ray Leonard, Ervin Johnson, and Tony Dorsett. He told Ravi and me that he was going to the fight. Ravi was unimpressed with both of us. He didn't love spectator sports as much as we did and was always thinking about money, how to save it, how to make it, what to spend it on, what not to. Fifteen bucks to watch a fight on a movie screen was not worth it, he said. What if it ends in the first round or if it's a boring fight or it ends in a draw. Would you get your money's worth then? Video games were worth it. Atari cartridges yes, you could play them over and over, and we did; closed-circuit boxing tickets no.

Then, a day or two before the fight, Calvin told us he wouldn't be going. Why, it wasn't clear. The tickets were lost or stolen or sold or never bought in the first place. I felt bad for Calvin, but there was nothing I could do. My sister made up her mind now that she was going to see this—she would spend the night out with the guys. I was twelve, she was fourteen.

Our tickets for the closed-circuit telecast were for the Felt Forum, adjacent to Madison Square Garden, which also broadcast the fight. They were both sold out, as were just about all the locations across the city.

"You sure it's safe, Hugo," my mother asked before the fight.

"Whatta you talkin' about, of course it's safe."

"But is it a place for kids?"

I thought it would be like watching TV at home. I was wrong. We got to the Felt Forum early. There were live boxing matches going on when we got there. The seats looked dirty. Some had graffiti in black marker, and others, like mine had the outer upholstery cut up, as if with a knife or razor blade. Stuffing was spilling out of my seat. There were no concession stands, no hot dog vendors, no older men with ruddy noses to take us to our seats. There were no kids, absolutely none, and no other girls besides my sister. It was not like a baseball game, sunny, with families, souvenirs, and Cracker Jack. As the crowd began to fill the place, it got scarier. It was men with gold jewelry, rings, bracelets, many necklaces. These were tough guys, all of them, white, black, Hispanic. I began to think my mother was right. Maybe this wasn't a place for kids.

A big white man was next to us. He was young and much bigger than my father. He smiled at us. My father seemed to know a person's nationality not only by their last name, but by just looking at them. This man, he later told us, was Irish.

"How did you know?" I asked him.

"All you had to do was look at him," he said. "He had the map of Ireland on his face. He was right out of County Kerry."

In the second round, after holding and grabbing and not much happening, Duran hit Leonard square. Leonard had never been hit like that, ever; I'd seen all his fights on ABC. His knees buckled, my father and everyone else in the Felt Forum leapt to their feet, either to implore Duran on or urge Leonard to stay up. The roar, as loud as any I'd ever heard, and the ensuing, collective leap, caused the pull-out seating to shake. I thought it would cave in. I grabbed on to my sister out of fear. I wanted to be in my living room in Co-op City. My father didn't seem to notice, so intent was he to see Duran put Leonard through the ropes. Which didn't happen. It went the full fif-teen rounds. When Leonard went to shake Duran's hand, Manos de

Piedras slapped him away and yelled at him. His fans in the Felt Forum were in the same kind of mood, and when Duran was announced the winner on points, half the crowd seemed furious that Leonard had been robbed, the other half, not so much happy, but vengeful in victory. Everyone was seething, and only now did my father notice. He said to the big Irishman next to us: "There's gonna be a race riot over here."

"Just wait," the big Irishman said. "Let everyone leave the building first."

"And would you believe it," my father told my mother later, "the big Irishman, he waits there with us, just so nothing happens. He even says to me, 'You gonna be okay from here?' Helluva sweet guy."

"Well, sure, he's probably wondering what you're doing bringing two little kids to boxing."

"Cut it out," he said, "nothing happened. If anything, the blacks and Hispanics would have gotten into it. No one was going to bother a man and his two kids."

Even if we waited for the Felt Forum to clear out before we left, Eighth Avenue and Thirty-third Street appeared to be chaos. People were spilling out of the Garden, running every which way, screaming in English and Spanish, cursing in English and Spanish. Everyone seemed mad at something, traffic couldn't move, horns honked, sirens blared, and there were mounted police. My father got us out of the scrum somehow, maybe heading east on Thirty-second Street, and zigzagging finally to Thirty-fifth and Madison, to the safety and calm of the Co-op City express bus. Or did the buses stop running by that hour? Yeah, I think we took a yellow taxi.

"And besides," my father said to my mother, "it was some fight. And we had a good time. Ask the kids." Did he mention, he won a ton of money?

When Calvin wanted to hear all about it the next day, I didn't tell him that I was afraid and wanted to come home, that I'd never go to the Felt Forum or to a boxing match ever again. I didn't tell him it was a great fight or what he missed. I just said, "Yeah, it was okay." I didn't want him to feel bad that he hadn't gone. "No one was knocked down. And they're talking about a rematch already."

"Told you," Ravi said. "A waste of money."

The summer of 1980, we didn't go to Europe like the previous summer. My sister was starting high school and it would be a private high school, a small little converted house called New Rochelle Academy. It wasn't a name-brand Westchester private school. It was where either wealthy misfits from north of the border went when they weren't accepted to the swank private schools or kids from the north Bronx, mainly black and Hispanic, whose parents wanted better for their children—or feared for them in the local public high schools. My sister was in this second group.

If it wasn't the priciest of private schools, with one of the best reputations, or any reputation at all, it would still be an unprecedented expense for my father. Instead of Europe, we'd make two return trips, first to Nantucket. I don't remember much from Nantucket. There were no Triple Crown horse races in communal TV rooms, in quaint inns, no screaming outside Protestant churches. This is what I remember: We saw Hugh Downs, from ABC News. "Don't stare," my mother said quietly, "but there's that Hugh Downs, from ABC." He was with his son, or grandson, a boy of about my age, smartly dressed, and with a white sailor's cap.

"See how nice he looks," my mother said. "And look at you, with those sneakers and those big shoe laces, like you're in the Bronx." She paused and said, "That kid's success is assured. There's no way he can fail."

And then she said this: "Money begets money."

Later that summer, it was back to New Orleans. For whatever reason, my mother wanted Ravi to check our mail. Maybe it was superstition. We had gone to New Orleans, the city of Armstrong as my father always promised himself, three years earlier, in '77, also in the summer. During that trip, the car, our ancient car, the Buick LeSabre, was stolen.

The Forty-fifth Precinct found it dumped in some far-off corner of the east Bronx. Kids just joyriding, they said. It was ours again. But my mother couldn't help thinking: Someone knew we were away. It's why she never had the post office hold our mail when we were gone a week, two, three at a time. The mailman appeared nice but my mother thought he was a little too friendly with some of the building tenants and what if he, or they, knew someone who knew someone. There were break-ins in Co-op City. Why let the world know you were gone, gone to some nice place they might not be able to afford.

My mother trusted Ravi completely, not only from her dealings with him, but from knowing who his parents were. Ravi's mother was a quiet woman, always dressed in a bright sari, *those are beauties the ones she wears*, never spoke loudly in the lobby, kept to herself. Again, my mother thought this was very Sicilian, a good thing. They weren't close, my mother and Ravi's mother, not at all, but they knew of each other through us, and would nod politely if they were waiting for the elevators. Ravi and his family lived on the fifth floor and used the two elevators that went from 2 to 18; my family used the other two elevators that went from 18 to 33, the express. So the two mothers had no time to chat in an elevator. A nod in the lobby would do; the same for our fathers. Ravi's father was a stern, conservative-looking man, who I remember in either blazers or loose-fitting, short-sleeve, white button-down shirts. Neither of his parents spoke much English, and to their children, Ravi and his two sisters, spoke what at the time I thought was Hindi but was probably something more local to their region.

In their apartment, even Ravi's room, were small posters, about three feet long by two feet wide, of Hindu deities. I remember one of Shiva in his room. In the apartment, there was a heavy smell of curry, which sounds like the most obvious stereotype. But when I would come back from Ravi's house, my mother would catch the scent in my clothes. She'd known where I'd been. She'd say: "You were at Ravi's."

"I dread going back to Co-op City," my mother said on the last morning at Café du Monde, after a week of jazz joints, a Superdome tour for me, and wondering how French, really, was the French Quarter. And when we did get back, we found that our car again was gone. Ravi had our mail, tidy, in a paper shopping bag. She told Ravi about the car, and he said, "What do you expect from this place? They're stealing cars every day here. Co-op City is like the highest or second-highest hotbed of stolen cars in the city. They even steal them from the garages. It's becoming a big ghetto. We all have to get out of here."

"Ravi is right," my mother said to me. "See, he's got more common sense than your father."

This time, the car was never found. "No more Gray Comet," my father said. "Who knows, maybe it'll turn up somewhere."

Later in the year, three weeks after Election Day, Leonard fought Duran in the rematch, in New Orleans, the Superdome, where we just toured. My father didn't get tickets for the closed-circuit telecast. He was depressed about Reagan, *dead broke*, and now, two days before the fight, crestfallen. There had been a major earthquake in southern Italy, in his father's region, Campania, and to the south in Basilicata, the poorest region in Italy. *That's all they need.* The epicenter was in Eboli. My father said that this was the name of a famous book, *Christ Stopped at Eboli*, by Carlo Levi. "Not Primo Levi, you've heard of him, haven't you?, but Carlo Levi. They're not related. You must read Primo Levi when you get older. He was from Turin."

My father might have been dead broke at the end of 1980, but he sent money to the earthquake victims. Who knows where he got it? My mother said, "Where's he getting this money from all of a sudden. One day he's desperate, the next he's sending money to Italy."

The second Leonard-Duran fight didn't seem to matter now. My friend Calvin got to go. His father bought tickets and took him to the Garden. I never saw him so happy. And then we heard the news, that Duran quit in the middle of the fight, in the middle of a round. *No mas, no mas.*

He did what?!

"They should refund the money," Ravi told us the next day. "What a waste. I told you."

THE DOMINICAN REPUBLIC, 1981

My father had a habit. No, not gambling. He gambled, more and more, on top of his bookmaking business, to inch his way out of debt, to pay for my sister's high school tuition, to land a big score. But he still insisted it wasn't a habit or an addiction or an illness or a problem. It would sound repetitive, but every one of those Saturday mornings he said this, something like, "Your mother needs to understand, this is a business." And as I got older, I wasn't sure what to say or think. I said what my mother said: "But Stan, Roy, all these Tom, Dicks, and Harrys, they're not gambling their rent money. They all have houses. This is sport to them." I was echoing my mother, but it made sense.

"Don't worry, I know what I'm doing," he'd say. "And let me ask you something, who does what we do?" Maybe they were both right, I thought.

Gambling was not, then, his habit. No, his habit was, every few years, when he was hard up for cash, which was often, he would hock my mother's engagement and wedding rings. He'd tell her he was tapped out, desperate. He'd yell sometimes, promise he'd get them back. She'd yell back. But she loved her husband, and if he was desperate, what are you going to do? Let him get the money from bad people, people who might possibly do harm to him? My mother wasn't a lover of jewelry anyway. It was too ostentatious. If she was going to be ostentatious, she would have preferred a fur coat.

During some of their epic dinnertime arguments, when my father yelled about all that we had and all that we did, my mother countered:

"So look at the Millers down the hall." They were the middle-aged Jewish couple, with the two Cadillacs, the house in Florida, and the season tickets to the Giants. Mrs. Miller had a fur coat, at least one, maybe more. "Other people have—they just have different priorities."

"Well, they can keep their Cadillacs," my father said. "That doesn't impress me. And how many years has he been saying when we see him by the elevators that he's going to take Michael to a Giants game? He hasn't and never will. He talks a good talk. So don't tell me about what they have."

The fur wasn't coming anytime soon for my mother, and jewelry, even that closest to her, wasn't of value. So when he said he needed money, she gave him the rings.

In February 1981, we went to Puerto Rico. This was the fifth time in eight years. The clients in the steel business, based in San Juan, the ones who traveled first-class to West Germany in brightly colored Braniff airplanes, who romanced flight attendants, and read *Playboy* magazine, were still gambling and still losing, and we were still invited to their Condado or Santurce high-rises, while they were in Frankfurt or Bonn or Hamburg.

In the middle of our weeklong stay, we went to the Dominican Republic. The February before it had been St. Martin/St. Maarten, half French, half Dutch. There wasn't much there, but we had a perfectly pleasant time in a very touristy hotel near the small airport. We spent most of our time poolside at this hotel, the kind that seemed to offer package deals to Americans. My friend Calvin and his single mother and sister would stay at this very hotel later that year.

This was on the French side of the island. No, make that the Dutch side, whichever side the airport is on. It was charming, we thought at the time, that the island was part Dutch and part French, not considering the social and economic scars of a colonial past. "The French were bad, but not as bad as the English," my father said.

Otherwise, we forgot our troubles by the pool, not the ocean for some reason, even though none of us, still, could quite swim. We splashed around and watched the planes land where the turquoise sea met the tarmac, cold black with bright white hash marks.

There was a great meal we had, on the French side, and my parents talked about the wine for years. It was the first time I heard the word Montrachet. "Kids," my mother said, "take a sip of this, learn what a great wine tastes like."

Santo Domingo was different. You could notice the poverty. People would stare and kids might crowd around you, not to threaten, but to ask.

We didn't have much to give these kids. We were there, yeah, but barely there, shouldn't, technically, have been there. We were there, not on credit, but the good-ish will of fortunate losers.

We couldn't buy much; we rarely did on these trips. We didn't have disposable spending money. If only we did. My mother, almost everywhere we went, Italy, Spain, Old San Juan, said, "Oh, what leather you get. And for half the price." But here, my mother bought something for herself, nothing grand, just a simple gold, or gold-colored, ring that fit just right on her ring finer. It shouldn't have mattered, it was so plain a memento; it could have easily been forgotten or tossed or put into the drawer with old, never-worn jewelry. What it became was this: her new, acting wedding band. Her rings were hocked, and would stay that way for fifteen years. This would now be a symbol of marriage, of bond, of death till you part, promises before God. This my parents believed in, despite the hollering, the doubts.

It was ten or twelve dollars, paid for in American currency, not much for us, a lot for them. It was the first time we felt guilty about being somewhere, as if we had too much. We asked one another: Were our tourist dollars helping them or were we taking advantage? We were going to stay at Casa de Campo, the resort conceived by Oscar de la Renta, the Dominican fashion designer of world renown. We couldn't afford it; now we were glad. How would that have made us feel?

San Juan, we were told by Ron, our half–Puerto Rican, half-Polish friend, was getting bad, unemployment, drugs, crime, but Santo Domingo was another kind of poverty. He picked us up at the airport a few days before, to whisk us off to his apartment. After pleasantries and us asking him about settling down, if he found that nice Puerto Rican girl yet—*eh, these women today, you don't want to know*—he warned us to be careful around San Juan, that there had been more crime lately.

"But not yours and Stan's neighborhood," my father said.

"Oh, yeah, even here," Ron said.

"Oh, my God. Since when?" my mother said.

"Eh, no one wants to do anything about it," Ron said. Then after a pause, he said, "But I'm protected," and patted the lower part of his trousers, where calf met shin met boot.

"What, are you going berserk, Ronnie, carrying somethin' like that around?" my father said.

"Just for self-defense," Ron said.

"Oh, my God," my mother said again. "Be careful, Ronnie."

"What about Santo Domingo?" we asked him.

"Worse," he said. "Just stay close to the tourist sites." When he went, he stayed at the Casa de Campo resort. He didn't leave. "You should see it," he said, "it's spectacular. But in the city, don't be surprised if kids ask you to bring them back to the States with you."

About that he was right. My parents met a young man on the beach, a teenager, not educated but intelligent, they said. He spoke English well and told them how hard life was there. "At first we thought he was up to no good," my mother said, reciting the story to my sister and me in the hotel. "But he was just a sweet kid. He wanted to come to America, he knew about New York. He asked if we knew anyone in government. Daddy gave him some money." My mother said we were lucky to be here, and lucky to be where we were from.

"Life here isn't what we as tourists see," she said to us. "I don't know how they get by day to day."

My father told us how the Dominicans fought for their freedom from Spain, that at least they had that knowledge.

"But what good does history do them now."

"Don't underestimate it," he said. Then he walked over to the piano player and asked him to play "Perfidia." It was my mother's favorite song.

It was on the plane to Santo Domingo that I told a lie, a recurring one, all because I never felt lucky to be where I was from.

As we boarded the half-empty Eastern Airlines plane, I wore a purple-and-gold-mesh baseball cap that said Minnesota Vikings and had a matching duffel bag. This was the age after I had been disgusted with girls but before the age of attraction. Thus, I was terrified of the opposite sex. So what to do when a young, chatty stewardess said to me, excited, "Are you from Minnesota?"

I had wanted to be from Minnesota ever since I chose the Vikings as my team, the day they lost Super Bowl X to the Oakland Raiders. No, they didn't lose, they were mauled. Still, it was complete devotion on my part. What would I tell her, this smiling, permed woman with curves bursting out of her polyester uniform, that I was from Co-op City, a place even my parents couldn't utter when other travelers we met asked us? Admit I was from a place my mother cursed in the beginning, middle, and end of each vacation. ("Oh, God, in four more days we're going to be back at that place.")

I nodded yes, that I was from Minnesota.

"Oh, I love Minnesota," she said.

Petrified, I put my head down, walked quickly to my aisle, grabbed the window seat, and closed my eyes and pretended I was asleep in case she'd further quiz me about the great state, the greatest in America.

My father, as usual, heard none of this, but my sister did, and told my parents when we landed in Santo Domingo. "Michael told the stewardess that he was from Minnesota."

They both laughed.

"Whaaaat?" my mother said. "Minnesota?"

"Ay, Brother Michael, what, are you losin' your marbles?" my father said.

Why couldn't I be from Minnesota? For one, they didn't say things like "losin' your marbles." This was the Midwest, where I imagined they spoke properly. The news and sports casters I listened to were all from the Midwest. Johnny Carson was from the Midwest. They didn't eat *gabagol*. They were real Americans.

From now on, I was from Minnesota. When people would ask me, and I was asked this constantly, in school, or in the street playing ball, "Why do you like the Vikings?" I would now lie, like I did to the stewardess, and say I was from Minnesota. No one bought it. "Man, you ain't from no Minnesota, you from Co-op like the rest of us," I was told by Jackie in the sixth grade.

"Nah, I'm from Minnesota, I was born there. My father is from there."

"Prove it then."

By now, I was prepared for this. The year before, I raised hell with my mother, demanding a subscription to the team's weekly newspaper, *Bob Lurtsema's Viking Report*. She discussed it with my father and though they were concerned about my developing obsession with sports, they felt any reading was good reading. So they got me the subscription.

The first issue arrived mid-season in 1979. My mother put it on the kitchen table so it would be the first thing I saw when I got home from school. Ahmad Rashad, one of my favorite players, was on the cover catching a pass. His purple jersey with the bright gold trim jumped off the page. That was the only color photo in the issue; inside it was all dour black and white, a lot of agate type, articles of last week's game, a preview of the next, photos of the players and coach Bud Grant, who never smiled. Of course, there were ads, all of local businesses in the Twin Cities. Soon I would remember street names from these ads and if someone asked, like Jackie had, I'd say I was from such and such a street, Lake Street, near "Waldo's Pizza Joynt" or "Bill Boyer Ford," in Minneapolis.

"Word?" Jackie said.

"Yeah."

He asked a friend of mine, Panamanian Rene, who knew I was lying but would happily lie for me.

"Yo, Alexis, Mike is from Minnesota?"

"Yeah, you didn't know that? That's why he's down with the Vi-kings."

If I couldn't be from Minnesota, could we at least go there?

"Ma, can we go to Minnesota this summer?" I asked.

"What are you crazy? No one goes to Minnesota."

"How come?"

"There's nothing there. That's where *Little House on the Prairie* takes place," she said. "That's Mankato, Minnesota."

"Mankato is where the Vikings have training camp," I said.

"When are you going to stop it with this Minnesota, it's not healthy anymore. And they're a bunch of losers. Your father keeps losing money on them."

"They made the Super Bowl a few years ago."

"Yeah, and they lost, didn't they? And they're not going back."

A Minnesota vacation may have been out of the question, but my love for this team remained unwavering. I began to love anything related to the state: The North Stars, the Twins, the Golden Gophers, Walter Mondale.

I would get there someday and see the lush grass field of Metropolitan Stadium. One day I would move to Bloomington and leave Co-op City behind.

My friends, and kids in I.S. 181, thought my loyalty to the Vikings was strange, but they respected it. It was different. There were mostly Jets and Giants fans, several Cowboys and Raiders fans, a few Dolphins fans, and a Patriots fan. I was the only Vikings fan, which made me special. People in school knew me as the Vikings fan.

On Monday mornings, on the short walk to 181, I'd often hear Mark, the class clown, yell my name out. If they won the day before, he'd say, "Mike MinnesOTA," with the piqued inflection on the last two syllables. If they lost, I'd hear him say, "Mike, Mike, Minnes-ohhhta," flat, as if to say, "What happened?" If Tommy Kramer had a good game, he'd say, "Mike, Kraaaaamer!" as in, "What a game."

Ted Brown, a running back from North Carolina, Ahmad Rashad, and Matt Blair were my favorite players, but Tommy being the quarterback made him the obsession of the obsession. He went to college at a place called Rice.

Who needed Fran Tarkenton? He was nothing but a host on *That's Incredible*, the stupid show on ABC before *Monday Night Football*. Kramer was young and cool, with long hair sticking out of the edges of his helmet. And he always wore eye black, in the rain, at night, in domes. If only I could smear on some eye black for my touch football games in Dreiser Loop.

It was almost impossible to see Vikings games on TV. It was always the Giants at one P.M. and the Jets at four, or vice versa. Instead, I was left with glimpses. Just as the CBS pregame show started at twelve-thirty, the host, Brent Musburger, would go to each NFC game they were televising and announce, "You are looking live at a sold-out Metropolitan Stadium in Bloomington, Minnesota, where today Tommy Kramer and the Minnesota Vikings take on the red-hot Detroit Lions and Billy Sims." In those five seconds the camera would pan over the field, and I'd see the players, in royal purple, running drills and stretching. It was always bright and sunny in Bloomington in the fall. But that glimpse, and halftime highlights, was all I'd see. Sometimes there were more substantial clips on this new cable channel that was available to us, Home Box Office. The movies were awful, but they had a show called *Inside the NFL*, with Len Dawson and Nick Buoniconti, both of whom, I was convinced, were anti-Viking.

To actually see the Vikings play, I'd have to wait for the rare Monday night game or until they played one of the New York teams. When one of these days did align, I'd mark it on my calendar months ahead. These games usually ended one way: In loss, tears, tantrums. And my father losing money. He never did ask me for tips, or inside dope on injuries, not that I had any, but he did see my devotion to Minnesota as some kind of sign, a team to continue to bet on until he hit it big with them, in a big game, whenever that would be.

I pleaded with my father to get tickets to the Vikings-Jets Monday night game at Shea in 1979. It was one of the few times he didn't come through. He was able to get Jets-Dolphins tickets the next season, but not for THE game. The kids at school wished me luck that afternoon. "Good luck tonight, Mike." The Shea fans chanted "Ho-ward sucks" in the background, and the Jets won 14–7. I cried myself to bed. "It's a good thing we didn't go to this fiasco," my father grumbled.

My mother was literally yelling. "Damn this Minnesota. What's wrong with them? Get a new team. I'm telling you, they're losers! And they're costing us money now."

The next season, 1981, they made it on to *Monday Night Football*: against Oakland, Denver, Atlanta. They lost all three times. This was embarrassing. *Yo Mike: Minnes-ohhhta.*

But they gave me miracles. There was the Miracle at Metropolitan Stadium. In the second to the last game of the regular season Minnesota was 8–6 and needed a win to clinch a play-off berth. They hosted the Cleveland Browns that day, an NBC game. The Browns were good in the early '80s, "the Cardiac Kids" they were called for their feats late in games. NBC would flash the out-of-town scores; Minnesota trailed all afternoon. My father let me call sports phone, 976–1313, obsessively, hoping for a more up-to-the-minute and favorable score. It was not forthcoming. It was still 23–21 Cleveland.

Then, finally, the unexpected. NBC went to an update, the kind where you held your breath. It was to Metropolitan Stadium. Don Criqui was in the studio and said something like, You won't believe this last play of the Vikings-Browns game. . . . It showed the following. With five seconds, no time-outs, Minnesota at the Browns' forty-five, needing a touchdown to win, Tommy dropped back, lofted the ball toward the end zone on the right, into a scrum of purple and white jerseys. The ball was tipped, by Terry LeCount or Sammy White, and before it hit the frozen turf, Ahmad Rashad was there to pluck it out of the air and fall backward for the touchdown, with no time on the clock.

I was screaming without reason, jumping up and down through the long living room. My father, seeing what I just saw in his bedroom/ office. "I DO NOT BELIEVE IT. I DO NOT BELIEVE IT!" I lept into his arms.

My mother was well into preparing our big Sunday dinner, which would start at halftime of the second game, about five-thirty, and came out of the kitchen. "What happened, those losers actually won? I don't believe it." To my father, she said, "Was it good for you?"

"Yes," he said, calmly all of a sudden. "It was good for me."

And I knew, immediately, that it wasn't. That he lost.

We may have watched football every chance we got, the two Sunday games and the Monday night game, but we no longer played it out-side in the loop at Defoe Place. There were only three of us now, me, Calvin, and Ravi. Now we played basketball more than anything else—that year, the one before, and the one or two after. Outdoors, on asphalt, in the I.S. 181 courts, no nets, no chains, just the iron cylinder. They never had nets.

I remember two brothers from Building 4 who Calvin became friends with, black brothers, fifteen or sixteen, amazing players, among the best at these courts. They looked tough, but were gentler than their appearance. A couple of times, one would climb on the other brother's shoulders to put a net up; they loved the sound of the twine. They were both good shooters. Within days, the net was torn down.

One brother was named Dexter, Dex we called him. He had some baby fat on him, but could do anything with the ball. He favored no-look passes and the crossover dribble. He'd go between his legs exces-sively and whip passes behind his back, all the while doing a running commentary in the middle of the game. "There's Dex, behind his back, finds the open man. What a pass!"

His brother Lamar had a leaner, fiercer look, like a young George Foreman, without the facial hair. He could put up a layup and with both palms slap the bottom of the backboard. He would block shots into the next court. Soon he would be able to dunk, it was just a matter of time. They seemed like giants to me.

They would let me play with them even if, on the rare occasion, Calvin or Ravi weren't around, even if they were much better. I was beginning to develop a good jump shot. I was short and couldn't penetrate through the taller kids and had to work hard on my outside game. They set picks for me. "Shoot up, Mike." "Do your thing, little man." "Yeah, Mikey." They didn't have to.

My father would ask me, "How's your set shot?"

"My what?"

"Your set shot, do you have a good one?"

"Daddy, no one does the set shot anymore. You don't see anyone doing it on TV, do you?"

"Yeah, this young fella Barry Bird does and in school, didn't they teach you in gym class? It's an effective shot. My friend Gussy had some set shot. Bob Cousy. You ever heard of Bob Cousy?"

"No. And it's *Larry* Bird and he does jump."

"I can't believe they don't teach the set shot no more. What about the underhand free throw, do they teach you that?"

"Daddy, that looks doofy, no one does that."

"But it's the easiest way to shoot a free throw."

"*Daddy.*"

Calvin was as good as Dexter and Lamar. He was one of the best on the courts, and by now, that was saying something. He was all arms and legs, a natural athlete, not flashy, but could shoot well, had a good low-post game, the more traffic the better, and above all, he could rebound.

This allowed us, and by extension, me, entryway into these courts, at any time, any hour. Long after the kids from 181 finished their after-school pickup games, we were there till dark, playing at the one corner court that caught some of the orange strobe light that hung over the school.

Ravi wasn't a great player but he was strong and tall and never backed down. Like Calvin, he was respected by the tough guys at the courts without being a bad kid. This was a delicate maneuver. He was thought, because of his brown skin, to be Puerto Rican. This didn't hurt. If you were brown-skinned in Co-op City, you were Puerto Rican, maybe Dominican. He didn't have an accent and spoke street when he wanted to. He liked the phrases: "Yo B., I'm down" and "I hear that."

His sport was handball, another game we began to play. With the old friends, when we were little, the handball and paddleball court, with its big imposing concrete wall, was off-limits. It was mainly used by Puerto Ricans, older teenagers and guys in their twenties, who excelled at these two games, which were even more inner city than basketball. Now we were regulars there. It was the first time I smelled marijuana, just a hundred feet from the back of my building. But since we were recognized, acted mature, didn't appear the types to squeal if we saw something we shouldn't see, and were decent-enough players, we were left alone. Even with that, badasses, the street Puerto Ricans, the ones who smoked pot and had leather brown cords hanging from their back pockets from their 007 knives, didn't bother with us. They were older, tougher, a different crowd. One regular wore a gun holster, the kind that looped through the shoulders, as a fashion accoutrement to store valuables, cigarettes, who knows what else. Before he'd play, he took it off, and gently put it at the base of the chain-link fence.

There was always music playing in these courts, the basketball courts and the handball courts. Dex and Lamar always had their box. That's what it was called, just a box, *yo, don't be touchin' my box.* All that music. It was different now. It wasn't "Kung Fu Fighting" anymore or the Jackson Five. It was Slave, Fat Back, LTD, Lakeside ("Fantastic Voyage") and this new stuff, The Sugarhill Gang and Kurtis Blow. ". . . And I want you to know, that these are the breaks, break it up, break it up . . . break down!" People couldn't get enough of it.

It was often just the radio, and only two stations, 92 KTU and 107.5 WBLS: Carlos DeJesus, Roscoe, and Paco, playing mixes by John "Jellybean" Benitez. And the Chief Rocker, Frankie Crocker.

Of course, we wanted to fit in, Calvin, Ravi, me; we didn't want to appear soft. So we bought knives for protection. We bought them on Main Street, New Rochelle, in Westchester County.

New Ro, that's how it was known, was just one of our destination spots. We would take the BX15 and go to Gun Hill Road for bowling, White Castle, and to buy a 12-inch single or 45s across the street at a small record shop, where no one ever seemed to buy records.

We took the BX17 to Allerton Avenue and White Plains Road to see a movie, along the lines of James Bond, and shop for sneakers. Ravi once got tired of waiting on line for the bus back to Co-op and said, "Fuck this, follow me," and entered through the back exit doors. I knew this was illegal, but he could do no wrong in my eyes. If we jay-walked across White Plains Road and I told him we were going to get hit by a car, he'd say, "Let them hit us, I'll sue." My mother said, "He's something else that kid. What a riot."

We took the QBX1 to Main Street Flushing to go to Crazy Eddie's to buy blank tapes that Ravi made mixes on, and we'd gawk at the boom boxes and turntables and talk about which ones we were going to buy. Ravi said there were only two brands: Technics for turntables and JVC for boxes, preferably platinum. Calvin talked about getting two turntables so he could learn record scratching. Ravi thought this was a good idea, deejaying and emceeing could make for a good part-time job. Rap and breaking was the new thing. He began splaying unfolded cardboard boxes on his bedroom floor so he could practice.

And we took the BX15 again, past Gun Hill Road, and onto Fordham Road, the central Bronx in geography, but in the early 1980s the northern border of the South Bronx. My mother in no way wanted me going there. Neither did my father. "I know that area," my father said, and there wasn't an area of the city, at least Manhattan, the Bronx, and Brooklyn, that he didn't know, "you'll stand out there." But all I had to do was tell them that I was going with Calvin and Ravi, and they reluctantly agreed. They trusted them completely. *They're good boys.*

This trip was exhilarating because it was dangerous and because we could come back with sneakers that you couldn't get anywhere else. We hid our money in our socks, *in case we get jumped.* One of the stores was called Onyx, and I did stand out. I was the only white person there and would have never walked in without Calvin, who was black and now approaching six feet, and Ravi. Onyx produced a brand of its own jeans that kids at school wore, but only black and Puerto Rican kids. I was obsessed with Adidas, the shell top or the Abdul-Jabbars and Puma Clydes, in colors that only Onyx seemed to carry, light-brown with a burnt-orange Puma stripe. We hooked these sneakers up, meaning we adorned them with thick laces, often two sets of thick laces or sometimes in a checkerboard pattern with an extra sock underneath so the design would protrude out. Our own bas-reliefs. We polished these sneakers if they were leather; if they were suede, we brushed them with a matching color toothbrush that we kept in our back pockets. Some black kids had the toothbrush showing from their back pocket next to the handle for their hair pick. Some had a pick with a black power fist at the end of the handle. I was jealous; I wanted one of these black power picks.

At school, in seventh grade at I.S. 181, kids noticed my sneakers.

"Yo, where'd you get them deaf sneakers," I'd be asked.

"Onyx," I said.

"Word? You went to Onyx?"

"Yeah, I went with my boys Calvin and Ravi."

"Word?"

"Word up," I said.

The trip to Main Street, New Rochelle, may have been in a safer neighborhood, but we were there to buy weapons. In addition to toothbrushes and black power fists in some of these back pockets of Lee and Onyx jeans, with the crease, were small leather chords, tied in a small loop, which were at the ends of knives called 007s. No one brought them to school, at least they didn't show that they did, but you'd see them at the I.S. 181 basketball courts, the handball courts, on guys hanging out by the deli, on the city buses.

We didn't have to use them, Ravi and Calvin agreed, but it would just send a message: that we were down. So we took the long, ugly walk to Boston Road, past the junkyards, gas stations, and auto-parts shops, near the Westchester border. There we took a bus that originated on Fordham Road and ended, probably two hours later, in White Plains. We got off on Main Street in New Rochelle. We went to a Chinese novelty store. Ravi had his own VCR and liked kung-fu movies. He knew of this store and that it had Chinese stars, nunchucks, and knives. The owners appeared to be a husband and wife, and they sold them to us, three 007s, no questions asked.

Ravi was becoming interested in weaponry and obsessed with self-defense. He was the one who told me that my neighbor carried a cane sword. My neighbor Ricardo, from Saint Thomas, my favorite neighbor, who worked as a porter at JFK, always walked around with a cane or walking stick, we were never sure what it was. Had he sustained an injury at the job? *Don't ask questions.* We knew he had been held up once in one of the garages in Co-op City, the one closest to us.

When I once waved to Ricardo from a distance, at or near our building, he gave a big smile, as he always did, and waved back with the stick. In the distance, he said, "Hey, what's up, Mikey? Say hi to you parents."

Ravi said to me, "You know your neighbor is carrying a cane sword."

"A what?" I said.

"It looks like a cane, but there's a sword inside there."

"Word?" I said.

"Word. Can't blame him. Co-op's getting bad."

"Word up, man," said Calvin.

Ravi was in high school, Truman, hearing more and seeing more, and was already looking to get out.

"It's horrible," he told my mother when he would come up. "You were smart not to send your daughter there. And make sure Mike doesn't go there." Calvin said the same thing. He spent one year at Truman, transferred to Mount Saint Michael, a Catholic school in the Bronx, but was thinking of going back to public school, Kennedy, in the west Bronx. He wanted to play football and basketball and had a better chance there. That, or his family couldn't afford the Catholic school tuition. Calvin told my mother the same thing, "Don't send Mike to Truman."

Ravi started carrying his 007 in his back pocket, never in his house, never in mine, never in Calvin's, no place where parents could see the leather chord. But he did carry it. He was down. Calvin did too. He had a job at Waldbaum's, the big supermarket on the edge of Co-op City. He worked late, and had to walk home. He needed protection. You kept hearing stories about muggings.

So when Ravi asked me about my 007, where I kept it, how it felt, I just said, "It's fine, I keep it under my baseball card stacks, under my bed. And it's only for protection, right?"

"Right," he said. "That's right."

What I didn't tell him was this: When we got home from New Rochelle that day, I closed the door of my room, turned up the music on my JVC platinum box, "the quintet," it was called, the same one Earth, Wind, & Fire endorsed in magazine ads, and started fiddling with it, snapping out the blade and closing it, snapping, closing, so it would feel natural in my hand. It only felt awkward and lethal and then when I closed it I cut myself—blood all over. I panicked. I couldn't tell my mother. I finally gathered myself, turned up the music louder, BLS played D Train's "You're the One for Me," I got my fingers to stop bleeding, cleaned up the blood, wrapped the knife in two old issues of *Viking Report*, got some other trash together to justify a walk down the hall to the garbage chute, and pushed it down the incinerator, relieved.

MARTINIQUE (OR BOSTON), 1982

July 11, 1982, was the day of the World Cup final between Italy and West Germany. Mine was not a soccer household of recently arrived immigrants or suburbanites. This new thing, soccer, came as a surprise a few weeks earlier, when a team in red-orange uniforms (Belgium) played another in white-and-blue vertical stripes (Argentina). They walked onto the field single file, both national anthems played, the two captains exchanged what looked like national crests, and then the eleven players posed for a photograph, six standing up and the other five below, crouched down like baseball catchers, with their arms around one another. How odd. This was different and foreign, and I immediately was drawn to it. When a Belgian scored the only goal, he ran and slid on his knees. This didn't happen after a home run.

Over the next days and weeks, my sister and I would wake up early and instead of watching repeats of *The Love Boat* as we normally would during the summer, we watched these magical games on the snowy static of Channel 41, in Spanish. My parents liked this idea because they thought it would expose us to a foreign language that was becoming more important.

When we had to choose a foreign language at I.S. 181, my father insisted on Italian. He had studied Spanish history and through the study of his own family lineage insisted that his last name originated from eastern Spain, but he wanted his children to be exposed to the language of his parents. My mother argued, loudly, for Spanish, for practicality. It was obviously more important internationally, even locally, she said, and could give us a leg up in the college-entrance race and the job market beyond that. That or French. My mother always wanted to study French and tried to teach herself. It had always been her dream, another dream, to go to France. The choice, to her, was clear, Spanish or French.

"Who speaks Italian, except these neighborhood types in the city," she said, referring to the first- and second-generation Italians in the Bronx and Brooklyn. "It will get you nowhere—like him. Listen to me. Noboby LISTENS!," she screamed I don't know how many times. "Everything is SPANISH. LEARN SPANISH. LEARN SPANISH."

"Italian is a beautiful language, whattaya talkin' about," he'd yell back.

"Yeah, like that disgusting dialect you speak," she'd say under her breath so just my sister and I would hear.

"Scholars learn it just to read *The Divine Comedy*," he said.

But it would be Italian for my sister and then, two years later, for me. My sister, now in high school by '82, would study Italian still more, without really learning it. I was embarrassed by it in seventh and eighth grades, especially as the school became more and more black. Italian was the last thing I wanted to be, its language the last thing I wanted to learn. I wanted to learn black slang, and was already as fluent as any white boy in Co-op City—the lyrics of Mellie Mel and Afrika Bambaataa easily came to my lips.

I was surprised any black or Puerto Rican kids—more than half the class—were even taking Italian. I soon realized why they were there. During the first week, Thomas, a broad-shouldered seventh grader with a steely demeanor, mature beyond his twelve years, said, to no one in particular, "Oooh, look at that ass." He was talking about the teacher, who had her back turned, writing the conjugation of the verb *stare* on the board. Someone else said, in agreement, "Word." They clasped hands. She did have an ample, shapely rear end, enough to make you take Italian and never learn it. As seventh grade went on, you'd hear some of the boys say just that: I only took Italian to look at the teacher's butt.

So these soccer broadcasts in Spanish, even if my mother didn't like the idea of my sister and me watching too much TV, placated her. She would be redeemed; we would all see, especially my father, that Spanish was the language to learn, that she was right, he wrong.

My father liked the idea of soccer for me, since it had already been said, over and over, that you didn't have to be big to play.

"Look at Pele," he'd say, even if he never watched him play and he had long since retired. "He was small but he was the DiMaggio of soccer."

By 1982, it was clear I wasn't going to get much bigger—I wasn't even going to get up to welterweight, my father's favorite division in boxing. He taught me how to throw the perfect left jab, *snap it, you gotta snap it*, upper cuts, combinations, and the hardest of all, the left hook. But I wouldn't be allowed in the ring. Soccer made more sense. It had been decided that I would not be going to Truman High School. It wasn't much of a decision. I didn't make Bronx Science, certainly not Stuyvesant, so my father would have to suck it up and send his second child to New Rochelle Academy, this "waste of money," as my mother called it.

But New Rochelle Academy did have a soccer team, anyone could make it and everyone would play, and I would be entering in September. My father thought it would be good for me to play on some kind of organized team, as opposed to just playing street pickup ball. So they let me watch game after game, and they bought me a soccer ball, a brand called Spartan, with the white-and-black hexagon-pentagon pattern.

All sorts of funny things happened that month in the World Cup. Algeria beat West Germany, who then went on to collude with Austria to prevent the North Africans from moving on to the next round. An imperious Kuwaiti sheikh ordered his team to leave the field when he thought the referee made a bad call. The referee capitulated. "Solidarity" banners were removed from the stands in the Poland-USSR game.

English fans swirled drunkenly and ominously in the stands. Were they fighting? Whom with? They sang loud; so did the French. The Brazilians scored beautiful goals, they all had one name, and Eder did flips when they scored. This was already the greatest sport I'd seen and it was only the first round.

Then something else happened. Italy won a game. I had hardly been conscious they were in the tournament. Who cared about Italy except *ginzos from the other side*. For me, it was all about these Brazilians in the yellow shirts and with the one names—Zico, Serginho, Falcão, they even had a stern-looking man named, impossibly, Sócrates, who apparently was a practicing doctor, chain-smoked, and played on a club team called Corinthians. I was used to team names like the Mets, Knicks, and Vikings, but Corinthians?

Italy, after three draws, beat Argentina, the defending champions, and would play this unstoppable Brazil team, this happy team, except for Socrates, who seemed to bear the weight of the world on his shoulders. Italy, I knew already, could not beat Brazil. Nor would I get to see it. We would be in Boston.

This summer there would be no vacation. *Every three years we'll go to Europe.* Not in 1982. In February, we made it down to my father's friends in San Juan and did three days in Martinique, Fort-de-France. We didn't Jet Ski or scuba dive, we never did, or swim, we still couldn't. We stayed in the city, a bustling place of commerce and hope, the first all-black city we visited. Mount Pelee, the volcano, hovered. It didn't really hover; it was in the north of the island, but it hovered in the postcards I brought back. I was now collecting them.

It was the hottest place we'd ever been, hotter than Morocco, hotter than New Orleans, hotter than Charleston, South Carolina, where we went the year before. I remember one afternoon, lunchtime, we were hungry, starving. I don't know why it took us so long to find a place. I remember being dizzy, from the heat and hunger. Maybe it was three o'clock when we walked in to one of the elegant restaurants. My parents were well dressed, not like many of the tourists in shorts and sneakers, but we were sweaty and guzzling down water. Everyone else was well kept, looking cool and starched. A stately man sat alone, next to us, in a suit, his manners impeccable, his newspaper folded just so. "Oh, God, what we must look like to them," my mother said. "*Shongad and morta de fam'*." Disheveled and starved to death.

It was upstairs, this restaurant. Were there ceiling fans? We asked about a menu. There was no menu, just what was cooked that day. It was in crocks and it was a stewed chicken. We weren't sure if we'd like it. My mother tried it first. It looked as if it had a tomato base. "You wouldn't believe it, it's my chicken *gotch-a-dor*," she said, her chicken cacciatore, one of our favorites. "They must have their own version in the French Caribbean."

Fort-de-France was as close as we'd come to Europe that year. It was more than some people got to do; that much we knew, but not nearly as much as others had; that much we didn't know. We didn't know those people.

My father endured months of losses the rest of the winter, the entire spring, and now the summer. My parents went to the annual New York Auto Show at the New York Coliseum to consider a replacement for the Gray Comet, which was gone forever. They came back, shaking their heads.

"Are we going to buy a new car?" I asked, excited, when they got home.

"Forget it," my mother said, "the prices."

"Telephone numbers," my father said.

So we wouldn't be buying a car. But we would go to Boston for a weekend, July Fourth, with the dual purpose of getting out of Co-op City and looking at a few universities for my sister. She would be entering her junior year but was working, and excelling, at such a level that she was due to finish high school in three years, maybe to help save my father a year's tuition. There would be more tuition, but my parents wanted to help her through the next step, the research of selecting a college—something they'd never been through.

No, Cambridge wasn't on the itinerary. My sister was as diligent as a student could be, and had the lack of any social life to prove it, but her SAT scores weren't high enough, we were told, and besides, why even bother to try. Harvard wasn't for people like us. Your parents had to go to Harvard, or at least to college. We were unpedigreed.

We were there to see Boston College and Boston University, some fireworks on the Fourth, and breathe fresh air. Compared to the Bronx, Boston had fresh air. BC had a nice campus but, my mother said, it was too Catholic. BU seemed to have no campus and was frenetic, almost like New York.

The day we checked out of the hotel, it was a big tower hotel, the Sheraton, I think, I remembered that this game was to take place, Italy vs. Brazil. In fact, being six hours behind, it had already taken place. Italy needed to win the game to progress to the semifinals, Brazil only needed a draw. My father bought the Boston papers that day, and in the sports section, there was a listing for Boston's equivalent of Sports Phone, which my father called incessantly for score updates in New York, no matter the season, no matter the time. Sometimes he had me call for him since he didn't hear well and the broadcasters spoke at a pace so fast Minnesota could sound, even to someone of normal hearing, like Oklahoma.

I found a bank of phone booths in a quiet corridor of this tower hotel, all empty conference rooms and white tablecloths piled haphazardly. I dialed the sports phone, which sounded remarkably like ours, fast, clipped, in cadences all its own. It went through a series of baseball scores at startling speed: boston4kansascity3minnesota5detroit3milwaukee10chicago4. . . . And I'm waiting for this soccer score. Do they even give soccer scores on this thing? Does anyone gamble on it? My father hadn't found a way, so maybe no one did, and weren't these phone lines only for gamblers and bookmakers? I waited. All these cities and numbers, stlouis6cincinnati5sandiego8montreal6sanfrancisco3philadeplhia1. . . . And then this: . . . andinworldcupsocceritaly3brazil2nextupdateintenminutes. staywithus.click.dial tone. Wha? Huh? I couldn't have heard that right, no. That or it was a mistake. So I called back, but after ten minutes, so that if it had been a mistake by then it would have been corrected. I waited through all the American League scores again, that Boston beat Kansas City 4–3, the Twins beat the Tigers 5–3, on and on through the National League and then: . . . andinworldcupsocceritaly3brazil2.nextup-dateintenminutes.staywithus.click. dial tone.

This was the beginning of an obsession—both with soccer and Italy—sometimes an unhealthy one, other times an exhaustive one, still other times a ridiculous one. Most times it was a lonely one, this pursuit of my missing side, a part of myself I hadn't known had been there.

I didn't know this when I hung up that phone in an empty corridor of the Boston hotel, when the recorded voice of the Sports Phone announcer set off before-unheard-of emotions. No, now it was pure excitement and joy. That night when we got home, PBS showed the day's World Cup games in a seamlessly edited hour-long version, as part of the *Soccer Made in Germany* telecast. The host for that Saturday morning program was a daft Briton named Toby Charles. The theme song was "Shame," the R&B classic that was often blasted in Co-op City, from home stereo, car radio, boom box.

When I watched the game on tape, I still expected the Italians to lose. I had called New York's Sports Phone when I got in—to triple check. They too announced, in that rapid-fire staccato, italy3brazil2. The game was in Barcelona, and from TV, it looked as if the fans, who all appeared shirtless, were pressed up against the fence in front of the field. The sun was bright, and there was this perpetual beat of drums and horns, from the Brazilian fans, I knew, because I had watched all of their previous games. I liked how that sounded. Paolo Rossi was the hero, with three goals. He had been involved in a match-fixing scandal and after the game he called his mother. "Mama," he told her, "the nightmare is over."

Over the next week, Italy would go on to win the semifinal and would meet the West Germans in the final.

So we gathered around our TV, as we often had, but this time without my father. He was happy for the Italians, wanted Italy, desperately, to win, but he still had no patience for the game of soccer. He simply couldn't watch it; he didn't really understand it or want to understand it. It was the only aspect of Italian culture he didn't have enthusiasm for. He would stay in his bedroom, his office, watch the Yankees, and keep track of the other baseball scores on Sports Phone. Before the game, he found out through his associates that Italy was the morning-line favorite. "It's on the board," he said, "but no one's called in to bet it."

My mother was convinced of defeat. "Look at these krauts, they look so confident," she said. And then, when the camera focused on the towering Hans-Peter Briegel, she said, "God, he looks like a Nazi." The game began. A key Italian player was carried off the field almost immediately. "This is a bad omen," she said.

Italy was awarded a penalty kick and missed. "See, I told you," my mother said. "They're gonna blow it." Every ten minutes my father would come in. "Anything happen?" To him, nothing ever happened in soccer. He couldn't change the channel on his bedroom TV, because it took me a while to balance the bow-tie antenna just so in order to get decent reception on WPIX for the Yankee games, then another way for WOR Channel 9 and the Mets. Each channel needed a different angle from the antenna, and a little love, so it was easier for him to leave it as is and run into the living room. A few minutes later he came in again. "What's happening?"

"They missed a goal," my mother said, referring to the penalty kick. "This jerk, what's his name?"

"Cabrini," I said. "Antonio Cabrini."

"They should call him Mother Cabrini—what a loser. Useless," she said.

"Relax, take it easy."

At halftime, the guest analyst was Giorgio Chinaglia of the New York Cosmos, who we only had a passing familiarity with, mainly from the sports highlights on the nightly news. He said the missed penalty kick and the injury weren't good signs for Italy.

"See, what did I tell you," my mother screamed. "Go in and tell your father what Giorgio said."

I decided it was best not to. Besides, I knew what my father would say: "What does he know." That, or "He wants Italy to lose."

A half hour later Italy was winning 2–0, another goal from Rossi and one by Tardelli who let out what was to be known as "the Scream." "I can't believe it," my mother said. My sister rushed in to tell my father—it was safe now, a two-goal lead. The final was 3–1. The crowd in Madrid appeared overjoyed—why were they for us? Giorgio Chinaglia seemed jealous and happy at the same time in the television studio. My father watched the ceremony, King Juan Carlos of Spain awarded the trophy. My father's face beamed. "This will be good for the country," he said. He remembered the bombing of the Bologna train station two summers before—was it the Red Brigade or neofascists? We remembered what the second cousins told us nine years earlier: "We may go Communist and never see you again." This was a splintered nation, it always was. Today, it had Rossi, Tardelli, Altobelli. Today, we had Gentile. The Italians were the good guys. And we had no money on it.

I went to my first soccer game just after the 1982 World Cup, in August. *The New York Times* ran an ad soon after the final for a special game at Giants Stadium. All-Stars from Europe vs. All-Stars from "the Rest of the World." Players from the World Cup, it promised, would be there. My father bought tickets immediately, the cheapest seats in the top of the upper deck, and took me to Giants Stadium, every seat sold, via bus from the Port Authority that was crammed with New Yorkers from every inch of the world, standing. The stars did show up, they all showed up. It was for Unicef, how could they not? Danny Kaye, a UNICEF ambassador now, gave a speech before the game. I think he told us all to yell. Where we sat, in the upper deck, section 336, row 26, seat 8, for eleven dollars, it was steep, and it frightened me. I wanted to run out and go home before the game started; this was worse than Leonard-Duran I. My father, as usual, seemed oblivious, as if there were more important things on his mind, numbers being scribbled in his head, subtotals, totals, what money he had coming in, what he owed. He always said he was claustrophobic—apparently never at sporting events. The European All-Stars won 3–2, a last-minute goal from Giancarlo Antognoni, a member of Italy's World Cup team, a shot that slipped through the hands of Thomas N'Kono, the goalkeeper from Cameroon. I loved our mammoth Britannica World Atlas, spent hours flipping through it, and now had all these new places to find—Kuwait, Cameroon, Honduras—all because of this new sport.

The game, and the sport, bored my father, I could tell. And he couldn't gamble on it, or take action from it. He was just there for me. All he kept saying was, "Madon', I'm starving." As soon as the bus arrived at the Port Authority, he said, "Ah, I know where we can go. Follow me." We walked through the muck of Forty-second Street and Seventh Avenue. I just wanted to go home; I wasn't hungry. He insisted. He took me to Tad's. "You're gonna love this," he said. "You get a steak, they cook it over the fire, a baked potato, and a salad." All for some ridiculously low price, $4.99 or $5.99, maybe $6.99 but not much more than that. He couldn't wait. He didn't mind all the fracas, ongoing, on Forty-second Street, the menace, the steaming filth, the stenches, or the frayed carpets of Tad's.

"Isn't this great," he said.

"It's okay," I said.

"How's your meat?"

"I don't know, it's kind of chewy," I said.

"Maybe they overcooked yours a little bit. Help yourself to some of mine."

"No, it's all right. I'm not that hungry anyway."

"One of these days, I'm going to take you to one of the great New York steakhouses. You've heard of Peter Luger's or Smith & Wollensky's?"

"No."

"Well these are like institutions," he said. "Maybe for your next birthday. We'll see who's playing and we'll do the Knicks or Rangers and have steak."

"Okay. But can we come back to see soccer?"

"Yeah, we can do that, but it's a little far, being we don't have the car. We have to come to the Port Authority. But then we can come back to Tad's."

When I got home, I showed my sister the game program. We pored over the photos and read the essay by Paul Gardner over and over until we memorized it. Later that summer, after Toby Charles's World Cup repeats, I went outside and played by myself, hour after hour, in the open, empty expanses of Co-op City. I was taught to play solo by a kid in my building, a special kid—Ahmad was his name. He was in my sister's grade and lived on the tenth floor in our building, which meant you could go months without seeing him. Ahmad had an aura around him. He lived with his sister and mother, who I never recall seeing or meeting. He was never in our inner circle when our group had still been together. He'd drift in and out. He wasn't a lone wolf, but never associated closely with anyone.

I always liked him and wished he was a fixture. I wondered why he wasn't. He had bright, intelligent eyes, was well spoken, friendly. He was black and had a quiet confidence and self-assurance that I don't remember anyone in Co-op City ever having, black or white. Ahmad, at a young age, was his own man.

"He's so impressive," my mother would say when she'd run into him in the lobby. "He calls me Mrs. Agovino. He asked about you. I wonder where he'll go to college. I bet he'll go to an Ivy League school."

It was no wonder then, that later in the summer of 1982, when I'd go outside a few steps from my building I'd see a lone figure, Ahmad, in the massive Truman High School athletic field—the one where you had to sneak in through a hole under the fence or climb the fifty-foot chain-link. He was either running laps or kicking a soccer ball all by himself. To me, this was the coolest thing. I asked if I could join. "Of course, Mike," he said. "I didn't know you liked soccer." Ahmad graduated I.S. 181 two years earlier. He was never going to Truman High School, he was far too polished and had too much potential, and I don't remember if he made Bronx High School of Science or Stuyvesant or one of Manhattan's music and art specialty schools. Either way, his mother sent him to a prestigious private high school in Connecticut. My sister went to New Rochelle Academy, a private high school. But this was ten minutes up I-95, twenty up Boston Post Road, in a converted house.

The school Ahmad went to was different. It was affluence and power. Other kids from Co-op City went to New Rochelle Academy, there were two black brothers from my building who were also friends of Ahmad's and three Puerto Rican sisters from the town house next to Calvin's, but no one from Co-op City went to boarding school in Connecticut. It added to the mystery of Ahmad. How did he get in? How did he and his mother even know about such a school? How much does it cost? Is he on a full scholarship? Does his father help? Who is his father?

My mother would ask me all these questions. When I didn't know and said, "Should I just ask him?" she'd quickly say, "No, don't you dare, it's none of our business." Ahmad wasn't one of the ill-bred kids who asked me if my father was in the mafia. When I told him I'd been to Europe, he'd respond with an engaging anecdote about whatever country I'd mentioned or about how'd he'd seen it on TV and would like to go himself. He was never jealous, just curious and interested. He'd be there soon himself, he seemed to know. In turn, I was never to put him on the spot; I was never to act like the common kids of Co-op City. So Ahmad remained close, at times, but most of all politely far away. That's how it was, and in the years to come I would see less and less of him. He found an entryway into a new world and that appealed to him more than the Bronx. "Could you blame him?" my mother said.

I only remember going up to his house once—it was one of those summers, '82 or '83. I was with Ravi. No one was home. His mother—this woman I never met—worked, and it was a weekday afternoon. I don't remember why we were there, for how long, or anything about the apartment, the furnishings, the smell, the particulars of his room. I only remember his high school yearbook, which he pulled out to show Ravi and me.

These kids in these photos weren't like kids I'd known. They didn't even look like the kids in my sister's New Rochelle Academy yearbook. They didn't seem like kids at all, but sophisticated young adults, entitled, confident. Ahmad pointed out one kid, a senior, who had been his friend. He had his own page and he sat on a chair with his legs crossed, hands folded up around his chin, a piercing stare, with an inscription that started off saying something like, "I'm staring right through your ass." My first thought was this: How could he use language like that, publicly, for anyone to read, especially his mother. I wasn't allowed to curse in my home, nor was I allowed to say words like "ass" or "sucks." If I invited kids to my house, I had to remind them that there was no cursing in my house. If they did, and for some nine-, ten-, eleven-year-olds it came naturally, they couldn't help themselves, my mother would tell me: "I don't want that kid back here."

Ahmad seemed enamored with this teenager in the yearbook; he was an athlete or class president or something. He was eighteen but looked like he was twenty-five or thirty, how could he be only two or three years older than me? Who was this guy? I hated him. How could Ahmad like him? Ravi, as usual, seemed unimpressed. I was immediately intimidated by this guy in the photo and was glad I didn't go to this strange school with all of these very white kids. Ahmad looked to be one of only a few blacks. For once, I was happy to be in Co-op City. I was happy Ravi and Calvin were my best friends. If my man Calvin met this white boy, when he wasn't working at Waldbaum's, angry that he was passed over for a twenty-five-cent raise—the boss didn't like him—he'd fuck him up, kick his ass back to Connecticut, teach him some respect, what he couldn't learn in private boarding school. And Ravi would be down with that.

WORCESTER, MASSACHUSETTS (OR MEXICO CITY), 1983

I don't remember the first eviction notice. My mother noticed it when the UPS deliveryman rang the bell. He had a package for my father from Notre Dame Press, a book, *Weber, The Ideal Type, and Contemporary Social History* by Susan J. Hekman. What else?

My mother noticed a big white form taped to the front door. The UPS guy was black, and blacks never asked nosy questions. He pretended he didn't see it. *What he must have been thinking?* He was the regular driver and he delivered to us often, university presses, Lord & Taylor, Bonwit Teller, Saks Fifth Avenue, Hammacher Schlemmer. And now an eviction notice.

She was mortified, embarrassed, humiliated. What if the neighbors saw it? Or maybe they did see it. Who knows how long it had been there. Minutes? Hours? She cursed this book in her hand, this box from Notre Dame Press. When my sister and I got home from school, she was in a fury.

"Him and these damn books, and he can't pay the rent, four months have gone by and he hasn't paid. First it was the bill collectors calling, then his check was garnished, my rings hocked, now eviction notices." She paused, raging. "He still hasn't paid New York Hospital for his surgery, how many years ago was that?'

"Six," one of us said, "nineteen seventy-seven."

"Six years. And that doctor was so gracious. A WASP gentleman. What he must think?"

"What happens when you get evicted?" we asked.

"They come in and remove all your furniture," she said. "They throw it and leave it right outside, in the street, for everyone to see, your clothes and everything."

"Are they going to evict us, Mom?" my sister asked, scared. I was too, but tried not to show it.

"I don't know, probably not."

She paused again. "I'm going to get a lawyer, this has gone too far."

A *what?*

"You mean you're going to leave Daddy?" I said.

"Don't leave Daddy," my sister said.

"He's driving me to it."

It was hard to tell how serious she was. For as long as I could re-member, she said, and he said, "I don't believe in all this divorce that's going on." I don't know what sounded more traumatic, divorce or eviction. When my father rang the doorbell, she told one of us to answer it. She still raged. He had his own set of keys, but for whatever reason, he always rang the doorbell for one of us to answer it, usually my mother, and they would kiss.

"What the hell is this?" she said, holding up the notice, with the masking tape still attached at the top.

My father didn't give a damn. "What the hell do I care," he yelled. "Let them go fuck themselves."

He tried not to curse in front of us, but he would say that—"let them go fuck themselves"—when bill collectors began calling inces-santly in 1980, '81, '82, maybe before. They called in the afternoon when he wasn't home. My mother answered, and she said, "I'll tell my husband." What else could she say? When she told him, he said, "Let them go fuck themselves." And she'd tell my sister and me: "That's what he goes and tells me? 'Let them go F themselves.' What kind of an answer is that?"

He yelled, at her, at the world, that they shouldn't be calling, that they were shakedown artists, lowlifes. He screamed that banks were the scum of the earth, that they preyed on people, that they were worse than the racket guys. *They're the scum of the earth!* All of Building 6 must have heard. *And what they must've thought.*

His check had been garnished, on and off, for years. He opened and closed bank accounts, on and off, for years. He bounced checks, on and off, mostly on, for years. Bill collectors had called, harassed, whatever you want to call it, on and off, for years. Credit card companies turned him down for years. And still we saw Yorkshire, the White Cliffs of Dover, The Tate, Den Hague, *The Night Watch*, El Moro Castle, repeatedly, The Netherlands Antilles, and did I mention Montreal and Quebec in '81, back to the Château Frontenac, back to my parents' honeymoon spot, when it felt as if they were in France then but now, in the hotel lounge, there were video games, Pac-Man and Asteroids. *What a disgrace, video games in the Château Frontenac.* We went to Charleston, South Carolina, the city of Spoleto. We still talked about the food at Poogan's Porch, *what incredible food.* We went to the Metropolitan Opera House in that time, to see *Carmen*, and to the Philharmonic. We went to the museums every few months. "It's important to get in these habits," my mother said, "to keep up."

And my father considered Chapter 11, on and off, for years. This was something to be ashamed of, embarrassed about, something you shouldn't consider unless you absolutely had to, something not to be discussed openly, unless it was with your twelve-year-old daughter. *"Do you think I should claim bankruptcy?"* "No, Daddy."

To him, to a generation, bankruptcy was an admission of failure, of giving up, of saying, as a once-great man said, "No mas, no mas." *He did what?*

My father always said to me, like all other fathers, "Never give up," only he put it this way: "You keep jabbing."

He thought about Chapter 11. Institutional debt was black and white. Unofficial debt, let's call it that, to Peter and Paul, was less exact. There's room to maneuver there, *and I need a little wiggle room.* But what of the potential danger, of borrowing from Petey and Paulie, Matty and Johnnie, the Apostles? The stress, the knots in the stomach, *as it is, I think I'm getting an ulcer,* the cold sweats, the panic if Joe D., one of the two Joe D.'s, didn't get the five grand by Thursday morning? *Never show you're afraid.* What of the sleepless nights? *Oh, don't mind him, he sleeps like a baby.*

Is it better to owe your life to a credit union, to Men in Positions of Power, *the scum of the earth*, or the twelve or so street Apostles, the interest rate being more or less the same?

During all this time, the ups, downs, mainly downs now, on the cusp of bankruptcy, he kept his day job. He kept his day job, his night-and-weekend job, the bookmaking, and his third job. His third job was seasonal, January through April. He did tax returns for his old friend Tommy, the kid he grew up with, who used to run the number bank and then started his own business, completely legit. He told some people in his office and one or two neighbors on our floor. Word got around, and soon he had a steady stream of clients every winter. And word got around because he didn't charge, he didn't have a set price. *Give me what you can give me.* This often meant a ten-dollar bill or something well below what H&R Block would charge. Often, it wasn't even that. It was a bottle of liquor. If he was lucky, it was a good bottle of wine, or two; he tried to make it known that he was a wine drinker. Other times, it was hard stuff, the kind we didn't go near. Canadian Club was one. He once brought home a bottle, said so-and-so gave it to him for doing the taxes, and my mother lost it.

"Canadian Club?" she yelled. "What in the hell—we don't drink this stuff. This stuff is poison. Couldn't it at least be a nice cognac or brandy? Jesus Christ."

He agreed, you could tell, by gesture and tone, but he said, sheepishly, "Well, just put it in the liquor cabinet. Maybe we'll find use for it."

"They're making a jerk out of you," my mother said.

"No one's making a jerk out of anybody," he'd say back. "They don't have much. I know, I do their taxes. What am I supposed to do, squeeze people? And what does it take me, an hour?"

"But what about that one down the hall?" she said. "You said they were loaded."

"Ouff, you wouldn't believe what they have stashed away," he said. "They dress all *shon-god*, but you wouldn't believe what they have in the bank. But that doesn't leave this table. What's said here, stays here." He looked at my sister and me to make sure that we understood. "That's their personal information. They trust me with that. Look, whatever they give, they give," he said. "It's pocket money for me." He paused and laughed. "So we can buy our Easter goodies at DiPalo's. Now, Brother Michael, put the phone back on the hook so I can get back to work." With that, he left the dinner table.

"How stupid," my mother said to us. "That's why your father never got ahead." *Whatever that means.*

We shrugged. What else could we do?

How do you act when you're bankrupt, officially or unofficially? Who do you tell, what do you say to the ones you decide to tell, to yourself? And what do you do? Do you drop out, take to drink, leave the wife and kids? Start over, someplace else?

No, you take the wife and kids to Mexico, to Mexico City—he loved reading about empires—and Acapulco. Maybe we could learn how to swim.

My mother was still livid. They would now go weeks and months without talking. We still ate, the four of us, around the dinner table, every night at five forty-five or six, earlier on Sunday, but with long silences. If they needed to communicate, they did it through my sister and me. If there was an event in the news that they wanted to discuss, they would look at one of us and say: "Those poor Marines in Beirut." Or, "What about this Korean plane shot down." Or, "Are we kidding, Grenada?"

Or if there was an article in *The New York Times* worth discussing, my father would say, "You should read this article today." By then,

I would read the *Times* every night when he brought it home. We had it delivered, but he would bring it with him and read it on the way to work in the morning and bring it back for us, along with the *New York Post* or the *Daily News*.

We talked about a long, long article, in the *Times Sunday Magazine*, on how Italian Americans had finally made it. My father couldn't believe it, he was so proud.

"Did you read the article on Italians?" he said to my sister and me, but especially wanting a response from my mother, who still wasn't talking to him.

My sister had, I hadn't, but said I would later. I preferred the dispatches from Central America in the main section. I thought this is something I might want to do, to be a foreign correspondent. *Which is why you should be studying Spanish—but no one listens to me.* My mother had started the article, but hadn't finished. She said to my sister and me at the table that she found it patronizing, that she stopped reading after a few paragraphs, after it cited Tommy Lasorda and Billy Martin. *Why do they go and mention that loon for?*

"Who wrote it?" my mother asked my sister. "Was he even Italian?"

My sister didn't know, and then asked my father. "Daddy, who wrote it?"

"It was a fella with an Anglo name, but his grandparents were from Italy. Excellent article. Don't throw it out, I'm going to keep it. We've been made fun of and put down for so long."

"Great," my mother said to my sister and me, "more piles of junk. We have no more room for this stuff. And more on the Italians. I like Tommy Lasorda, but is that success?"

My sister relayed this point. "Yes," she said, louder to my father so he could hear, "I wouldn't have mentioned the sports figures so much. I mean, isn't that Billy Martin guy kind of crazy?"

"Well, it wasn't about Billy Martin," my father said, "the writer just mentioned him." Then to me, but really to my mother, he said,

"You know Billy's half-Portuguese. He's from the Bay Area. His father abandoned him."

I nodded.

"The article," he said, "mainly talks about Cuomo, Lee Iacocca, Eleanor Cutri Smeal, Robert Venturi, people like this, not just sports figures."

"But Daddy," my sister said, "it also made the point that we aren't present in academia."

"That's true," he said, "but there's this man Giamatti, who's the president of Yale. And maybe you and Michael can go into those areas. The academic world would be wonderful."

My mother knew we shouldn't be going to Mexico, that we should save the money. "But he'll never save," she'd tell us, when he went back to his room after dinner to answer the phones.

"These trips are consolation prizes," she said. "We have to be practical. We don't have anything to show for it. We don't have a house. We don't have a pot to pee in."

The plan was to pay for the plane tickets, bring some traveler's checks for spending money, and worry about the two hotels later. *I'll pay by personal check.* Or maybe the tower hotel in Mexico City was prepaid, and Acapulco wasn't.

Acapulco was first. We knew it would be something; we had the brochure at home, my mother may have read about it in a travel magazine. It was called Las Brisas, and instead of conventional rooms, it had rooms built up and down a cliff, with every two sharing a small swimming pool. You got to your room by pink buggy that an attendant drove. When my sister mentioned that she was going to stay there, a rich classmate from Westchester, who oozed money, said, "You're staying where?"

"Las Brisas," she said.

"But I stayed there last year. You're going there?"

She didn't know what to say. She said, "Yes, with my family."

"You should've told him that it's open to everyone," my mother said after my sister told her the story. "Anyone can stay there, not just people like him. Where does he get off?"

You could see why he felt proprietary; Las Brisas was nicer in person. "Wow," we said when we got there.

But there was confusion, as soon as we checked in. How were we going to pay? Personal check? "But, *señor*, we don't accept personal checks," the nice woman at the desk said.

"What do you mean, you don't accept personal checks?" my father said.

"Sorry, *señor*, but we don't. I'm sure we told you over the phone."

"I'm hard of hearing," he said. "Maybe I misunderstood. Can you make an exception. I have two forms of identification."

"Let me check with my supervisor," she said, trying to help. She spoke in Spanish and then said to my father that they could take a personal check for only one night. "Sorry, *señor*. But you can pay by credit card, American Express, MasterCard, Diner's Club, or traveler's checks."

He paused. We watched. And then he said, "Okay, this is what we'll do. I'll call my personal secretary back in New York. . . ."

And that's when my mother put her two forefingers on her temple, lowered her chin, slowly turned around, and walked away to the other side of the hotel's reception area.

My sister and I followed her.

"His personal secretary?" my sister whispered. "He doesn't have a secretary."

"That's a new one," I said.

"You know, I'm not going to say I told you so," my mother said.

"You think they're going to kick us out?" my sister said, nervous and on edge, which was becoming part of her makeup now.

The embarrassment could have been worse; no one was in the lobby.

"I don't know. Let's see if he can talk his way out of this one."

After ten minutes of him talking, the concierge talking, her getting back on the phone, him laughing, her laughing, him saying, "Gracias, gracias," he came over with a big smile on his face. "Don't look so forlorn," he said. "I figured it out. Now let's enjoy ourselves."

What he did was this: Instead of spending four nights in Acapulco and three in Mexico City, the original plan, we'd spend three nights in Acapulco, one night he'd pay for with a personal check, whether it would clear or not, who knew, and the other two nights he'd pay with the traveler's checks he had intended for our spending money. Tomorrow morning, he'd call someone in New York, who he didn't know yet, maybe Albert, and have him wire money to Mexico City, to compensate for the traveler's checks he had to use now. While we were on the other side of the lobby, watching all of this—aggravated, embarrassed, guilty, proud—the nice woman at the concierge desk called ahead to the Mexico City hotel and asked if we would be able to check in a day earlier and could we pay the extra night by personal check. Yes, they said, to both.

"So we're all set," my father said. "Besides, Mexico City has more culture. It's better for us there. We'll see the ruins, the Museum of Anthropology, there are other museums. The famous muralists, Diego Rivera, Orozco, Siqueiros. We're not the swimming types anyway."

When we got to the Pyramid of the Sun in Teotihuacan, my sister and I made it to the top. It felt like the top of the world, even if it was only about as high as our twenty-second-floor apartment in Co-op City.

But the air. "How do the people breathe in this city?" my mother kept asking. "It's so polluted."

I said, "It seems unfair the way some people have to live."

"That's right," my father said. "We don't realize how lucky we have it in our country. And Reagan and his people, they don't give a damn about anyone but the fat cats." My father pronounced it REE-gan, he always pronounced it this way.

———————————

In the late summer, we took my sister to freshman year of college. Just before that, we managed a week in Vancouver in July. *Oh, what a city. Those parks.* . . . Chapter 11? My father said, not then, but at some point, I can't remember when exactly, but more than once: "Never let life defeat you." *What are you talking about, Daddy?*

My sister had always been smarter than I, and when she worked hard in that little high school, finished four years in three, she became the valedictorian. But she wasn't one of the popular kids; she studied all the time, she hated sports, and there were no social outlets in Co-op City for teenagers; just boys, badass boys, and trouble. So she wanted to leave home for college. At home, there were the fights, my father screaming at clients over the phone, slamming the phone down at midnight when he found out Fresno State didn't cover. Could you blame her?

We did the weekend in Boston the year before. I think she applied to BU and BC, even if it was too Catholic, too Irish. We did a weekend in Baltimore and toured Goucher and Johns Hopkins.

She chose Clark University in Worcester, Massachusetts. She had a good visit there, it was small, not too far from home, strong in the liberal arts, and they were generous with their financial aid and scholarship package. We took her by plane, a small plane from LaGuardia, to this little airport in Worcester. It was on top of a hill.

It couldn't have looked more New England. But we knew already, and were reminded by taxi drivers, that Worcester wasn't what it used to be. All those jobs in the shoe factories gone; options, limited; crime, now a problem.

The first person we met was my sister's roommate, a woman, apparently eighteen, but who seemed like a twenty-five-year-old. She was petite, like my sister, and had, I think, a short, boyish haircut. Already, her walls were covered with all things David Bowie, sometimes dressed like a woman. I could hear my father: *a debasement of our society.* To my parents, higher education, the kind they never had, meant higher culture, the classics, the Three Bs, not rock 'n' roll.

But it was clear the roommate was bright. She was verbal, extroverted, confident, and talked nonstop, preached, you can say, to my sister, me, my mother, and my fifty-six-year-old, Jimmie Lunceford–loving father about Bowie.

She asked questions, rapid-fire: Do you love David Bowie? Not really? How could you not love David Bowie? What do you mean you're not sure what his songs are? How could you not know who he is? "You, what about you?" she said to me. "Do you love David Bowie?"

I don't think I said anything. I'd heard of David Bowie, knew his big hit, "Let's Dance," but didn't particularly like it, and knew nothing else about him or about "early Bowie," as she kept saying. We tried changing the subject, I forgot to what, and I could hear my mother: *of all the roommates for my daughter to get stuck with*. Was she ready for this?

My mother knew I spent a lot of time listening to music with Ravi and Calvin, so later she asked me, "What's with this David Bowie?"

My parents still hadn't forgiven me for quitting the violin. I was assigned to violin at I.S. 181, "the Pablo Casals School," was our unofficial subtitle, and was good enough to play exclusively for the string orchestra, in seventh and eighth grade. We played compositions like the *1812 Overture* and *Hebraic Dance and Lament*. There was also a big brass brand—they played cooler songs like "The Hustle"—and a chorus for those, like my sister, who didn't show a talent for an instrument. They got to sing Roberta Flack and Donny Hathaway's "Where Is the Love."

My mother had been enthralled at the evening concert we gave for the parents at Truman's auditorium two years before. It was a spring ritual in Co-op City for us in I.S. 181, the string orchestra, the big brass band, and the chorus, to give a concert for our fellow students during the day and the parents at night. By eighth grade, with Afrika Bambaataa an ongoing sound track around the 181 basketball courts and my building, everywhere in Co-op it seemed, I found I had no use for the violin. It was the epitome of uncool; I no longer practiced, and told my parents I wasn't interested in pursuing any private lessons beyond what I.S. 181 offered in eighth grade. I wanted to be the first white member of Earth, Wind & Fire or the Brothers Johnson or the Gap Band or especially Grandmaster Flash and the Furious Five. I knew all the lyrics to "The Message," "The Message Part II," and "White Lines."

Calvin, Ravi, and I bought the cassette version of the album *The Message* at that small record store on Gun Hill Road where no one bought records. We played it on Ravi's box, or mine, over and over. I brought it to school, high school, I was at New Rochelle Academy now, to lend to a new friend, Julius, who was from Tanzania and lived in Mount Vernon. His father had run for president of his country, he said, and now worked for the United Nations. He lent me African and reggae mixed tapes—Third World, Jimmy Cliff, Peter Tosh, Yellowman, Dennis Brown, Eddy Grant—and I lent him what I had, the Gap Band, *Steve Arrington's Hall of Fame*, Marvin Gaye, my own reggae tapes I made from WBAI, and today, "The Message." One kid, and I have to admit an Italian, very popular, the girls liked him, would talk about music I had no idea about: Zeppelin, AC/DC, Maiden. *That shit's devil music, man.* He may have gone to the Who concert the previous year at Shea Stadium. I couldn't have imagined being allowed to go to Shea Stadium for anything besides a Mets game, and not to a rock concert where pot, and beer, were inhaled. This Italian kid looked at the cover of the cassette, with the Furious Five, corn-rowed, in the South Bronx, glaring at the camera, and said to me, "What's this?"

"Grandmaster Flash," I said. I mumbled this really; I knew what was coming.

"Huh?" was his response. And without looking at me, he said, "Nigger lover," and tossed the tape toward me and to the ground. The plastic case broke.

I didn't say anything. I picked up the four pieces it was now in and later gave it to Julius. I don't know if he saw what happened or heard what was said. I don't remember if I told him.

If my mother was disappointed in me rejecting the violin, she couldn't deny she liked Rick James. *Oh, he's hilarious, that Rick James.* When she'd prepare dinner every night, she would either play the classical station or the black stations, whistle or sing along with Smokey Robinson, Diana Ross, Luther, the Temptations, the Commodores. She loved the duet with Rick James and Teena Marie, "Fire and Desire"; she laughed hard as it reached its crescendo, with her squealing and him posturing.

Who didn't like Rick James. Next to Afrika Bambaataa and the Tom Tom Club—"What you gonna do when you get out of jail? I'm gonna have some fun"—that's all people played in Co-op: *Street Songs.* In I.S. 181, in eighth grade, we talked about what Teena Marie might look like.

"Yo, she's white, yo," Mike, another Mike, told us.

"She ain't white," one of the black kids said.

"I'm tellin' you, she's white. My pops has her record."

"There's no way anyone who sings like that can be white."

When I told my mother that one of the kids at school said Teena Marie was white, she said, "No, she can't be white."

So when my mother asked me about David Bowie, if my friends listened to him, I told the truth.

"No," I said. "No one listens to David Bowie." Someone, somewhere in Co-op City, must have listened to David Bowie, but no one I knew. To make sure, I asked Ravi: "Yo, do you like David Bowie?"

"Who?"

"David Bowie."

"Oh, that guy, the singer? Nah, I'm not down with that."

I asked Calvin. "Yo, Calvin, you like David Bowie?"

"Who?"

"David Bowie, the singer?"

"Who is he, some white boy? Mike, man, you know I don't listen to that shit."

Yes, I knew that. I knew he sang the lyrics to "Double Dutch Bus," by Frankie Smith when someone double-dribbled in one of our basketball games. I knew he sang "She's a Bad Mama Jama" by Carl Carlton just because. I knew that. I just wanted reassurance.

Things hadn't been going Calvin's way. He'd been to three high schools in four years. He'd been playing more varsity basketball and football at Kennedy his senior year, but not as much as he thought he should. The coaches didn't like him, he said. Playing college ball would be difficult now. I told my parents this.

"How could the coach not like him?" they said. "He's a nice kid."

"I don't know," I said.

He spent more time at Waldbaum's, the supermarket, to pick up more hours, and he hung out with his friends there more and more. He told Ravi and me that he wished he could quit, that he deserved a promotion, but knew he wouldn't get it; the new boss didn't like him. But now his sister had a kid with her boyfriend and he needed more money. He talked to us about his boys at the supermarket, funny stories, how they played football with a roll of toilet paper outside in the parking lot in a snowstorm, but one story was sad. One of his homies saw his father go into the motel just behind Waldbaum's on Rombouts Street with another woman. It was the same motel my mother took us ten years before, as little kids, to play in the swimming pool, the pool where my mother thought she saved the little girl's life, even if she didn't know how to swim. The motel had hourly rates, maybe they always did, but not for mothers and their kids anymore. This was one of many now near I-95 and it had a name, "The Hot Sheet Belt." It started in Queens, along the highways from the airports, and continued over the bridges to Boston Road in the Bronx. When Calvin heard his friend's story, he said, "Dag, man," and tried to console him.

We met his boys from the supermarket once. They were Calvin's age or older by a year or two, black and Puerto Rican. Some lived in

Co-op, others didn't. One of them said to Calvin, loud enough for me and Ravi to hear: "So, B., when are we going back to Hunts Point to get our dicks wet."

Calvin said, quietly, "Oh, I don't know, man," and changed the subject. He was embarrassed; he hadn't wanted me to hear this. He wanted to set a good example. He knew my parents, was always at my house, and felt an unspoken responsibility.

I knew he had had women before, but he didn't talk about it with me; I was too young. He might say to one of the other guys at the basketball courts, "Man, some of these girls be tryin' to get over." And then he'd sing from the song: "Over like a fat, over like fat, over like a fat rat."

Ravi also had new friends. He left Truman after one year and enrolled in a Catholic school, St. Nicholas of Tolentine. It was in the central Bronx, an extension of the South Bronx. To fit in, he bought a sheepskin coat. I don't know if they were made from the skin of sheep, but that's what they were called; they were all the rage in the Bronx. I can't remember seeing a white person in one, even if they were into this new thing called rap. It was like Onyx jeans, it was their thing, even to whites like me *down with the music, and down with the sneakers.*

But these coats would get stolen, right off people's backs, sometimes with a knife to the throat or a gun to the temple. You'd hear stories in the basketball courts, where the three of us still played. "Yo, that nigga got jumped and they stole his sheepskin. Yo, it's gettin' crazy out there, yo."

We heard other things. Our neighbor Ricardo told my mother that he heard that someone was scaling the sides of the buildings in Co-op City and breaking into apartments. "Keep those windows closed," he told my mother.

When she told me, I said, "That's crazy, impossible, some kind of urban legend."

"I believe it," she said. "I don't put it past anyone. This place is a dump."

What was rumor and what was real? You couldn't trust the *Co-op*

City Times, one of the two newspapers. Tenants thought of it as a public relations sheet. Only the other paper, the *City News*, told it like it was, and they had crime reports every week now. It had one report that said someone was held up in Co-op City and told: "Run your jewels."

Ravi wasn't going to have this happen to him. He ushered me into his room one afternoon when no one was home, and beneath the posters of Hindu deities, he pulled out an Adidas box from under his bed, unwrapped something, and said, "Mike, come here, check this out."

"Ravi, Jesus, what the hell is this, man?" I said.

"It's a twenty-two-caliber," he said.

"Is it real?" I asked. I had never seen a gun before.

"Of course it's real. Here, hold it. It's not loaded."

"Are you sure?" I said.

"Of course I'm sure."

He laid it on his bed, and I held the small gun in my hand, for four or five seconds, then set it down gently.

"Man, you're crazy, Ravi," I said. "Does Calvin know?"

"Yeah, I showed him."

"What did he say?"

"Nothing. Make sure you don't tell anyone, not my sisters, not my mother, not your mother."

"You know I won't say anything," I said.

"Don't worry, Mike, I ain't gonna use it," he said. "It's just for protection."

Calvin had news for us, for me and Ravi. He said: "Guess what, fellas? I'm joining the Marines."

"You're doing what?"

"That's right, next year I'm going to be a devil dog."

"A what?"

"That's what they call Marines, devil dogs."

I didn't know whether to say sorry or to congratulate him.

"That's great, Calvin," I said. "What are we gonna do without you?"

When I told my mother, she said, "Oh, no, I hope a war doesn't break out."

"He'll be a good Marine," my father said. "He's a good kid. He's loyal."

They wanted to say good-bye to him, and when he came up, they poured him a drink. "You're old enough to drink, aren't you, Calvin?"

He said, yes, he was, and we all drank a shot of something, brandy or cognac.

When Calvin cleaned out his room, he said he had something for me. It was a record, my first vinyl record. He knew I was planning to get a turntable to connect to my JVC box, it would be a Technics turntable, at Ravi's urging, and I might get it for my sixteenth birthday. So he gave this to me, it had been his father's or mother's, but they didn't want it anymore. It was old, an Earth, Wind & Fire double album from 1975, a famous album with a simple cover, all-white and in script lettering on the front, the title: *Gratitude*.

FRANCE, 1984

Out of the train station came the hordes. Us among them. It didn't matter that we didn't speak French and didn't know, exactly, where the palace was. This organic wave of tourists would simply bring us there. And it didn't matter that it was August, the bourgeois time to travel, or that there were tour buses everywhere, from every spot on the globe, red and white flags from Denmark, Switzerland, Japan, Austria, Canada. We were here, and that's all that mattered. First Paris, now this, Versailles.

We approached the palatial grounds with the sound of the crunching pebbles, the kind only present in old European gardens, beneath our collective, urgent step. In the sensory overload, the sprawling palace, the great, verdant pathways, the ornate fountains, the undulating droves, the clicking cameras, we began to recognize something, something implausible but somehow becoming clearer. It was three people, a man, a woman, and a grown boy. Which one of us noticed first, I don't remember. My father, maybe? "Those people there, they look like those people in our building."

"Huh?"

"Over there—standing. Are they the ones from our building in Co-op City."

"Who?"

"The kid Michael used to play ball with under the building."

"Oh yeah, Sherman Frank. Yeah, it does look like him, with his parents."

"No, it couldn't be, not here."

We got closer.

"I think it is."

"It is—it's them, Sherman and his parents."

"Oh my God. Here? In France?"

"What should we do?" my mothered wondered out loud.

"Do we even know Sherman's parents' names?" We've lived in the same building as them for fifteen years but didn't know their names, and they probably didn't know ours.

"I can't believe this."

"Let's say hello," my father said.

"No, wait," my mother said. In all the trips we had, we never ran into anyone we knew, much less anyone from Co-op City, the place we couldn't wait to escape, the shame we left behind, the place we didn't want to be from, the place we dreaded going back to. The place we didn't even like to say, those two alliterative words that sounded so downscale, like everything wrong with life. And here, why here, during a monthlong respite, where there was still grandeur and possibility and hope. In our dream, we ran into ourselves. So we thought about one thing: saving us, and them—the perennially sulking Sherman, a Charlie Brown kind of kid, and his parents whose names we didn't know—from embarrassment.

But before we could do otherwise, to walk the other way, get lost in the swirling crowds, head straight to the palace, my father closed in. Then they saw us. And there, in Versailles, we ended up hugging these people, and they us, in front of everyone, the Danes, the Japanese, the Canadians, whoever else, in a triumphant reunion, them not knowing our names and we not knowing theirs, just knowing they were from Co-op City, from Building 6, exchanging "ohmygods" with these people, not really our neighbors, not really strangers. Them from the fourteenth floor, we from the twenty-second floor. Eight floors apart meant you could go weeks, months, or longer without seeing them.

"How embarrassing," my mother said, as we made our way to the château.

"What embarrassed? What are you always embarrassed about?" my father said. "You're too self-conscious."

She said: "We came all the way here and we run into Co-op City."

We were in France for a month—Paris, Chartres, the Loire Valley, Lyon, Strasbourg, Nice, Aix, Monaco, Carcassonne, Rouen—because of Marcus Allen, and that run in the Super Bowl, seven months before. It was the Raiders, and all the residual checks that came in the next weeks and months, but it was also the games no one can remember, the college basketball games on a Tuesday in February, games from the West Coast that my father couldn't even watch, and wouldn't learn the result until the next morning, when he added and subtracted the figures.

It was a good half a year, and even then we had no business being in the Louvre. There were bills, piling. Clark University, my high school, New York Hospital still. Buy why, why pay those when you have a chance to get to France, to at least get there, and worry about how you'll pay for the rest later.

Maybe—maybe—we could have afforded a week in Paris, but why go all the way there and not see the cathedral in Chartres, and the châteaus in the Loire Valley, and Provence. How can you not? So let's just get there *and if worse comes to worse. . . .*

This dream, like the ones before it, the trip to Italy and the others, began in Queens, at the airport, but JFK wasn't what it was. This wasn't the TWA terminal, Eero Saarinen. Departure was from a dilapidated humdrum hall more like the grime of a bus station than any architecture of imagination. We got there by the notoriously unreliable Co-op City Cab, which once had its entire fleet of cars painted in olive green, the official, or maybe it was unofficial, color of Co-op City. Now it had abandoned this and allowed its drivers to use their own cars, often more disheveled than the actual taxis, usually with a smell of tobacco.

All the drivers needed to do was put a handmade sign in the front windshield or the side window, often in Magic Marker that said CO-OP or CO-OP CAB, and have a CB radio put in, or something that looked like a CB radio. Whatever it was, it worked remarkably well, and nearly all the drivers kept the talking piece attached to the visor, which they kept flap-down, whether it was sunny or not. And they often kept the volume on so they, and the passenger, could hear the dispatcher, who knew he had an audience. It often felt as if the dispatcher was performing. One-liners, witty retorts, in thick Bronx accents, about some poor old lady who didn't show up for a fare.

This was the first thing I wanted to be when I grew up, a driver for Co-op Cab. Now that our car was gone, we relied on Co-op Cab, when my mother took me to Burke Avenue, to Dr. Prinz's office, with earaches, coughs, once with walking pneumonia, and each time he said to my mother, "Don't worry, he'll grow out of it." Co-op Cab took my mother to jury duty, no matter how terrified she was of the Bronx County Courthouse, deep in the South Bronx.

These cabdrivers were chatty. You'd say to them, "How are ya?" And they'd say, "Eh, another day, another half a dolla," and then go on a soliloquy of the street. After my mother absolutely had to report to jury duty in person, after deferring and deferring and deferring, she got in a Co-op Cab. When she told the driver, a middle-aged Puerto Rican man, that she was going to the courthouse, to make conversation, he said, "What, jury duty?"

"Yes," she said. "I'm dreading it. I hope I don't get chosen."

"Don't go," he said.

"Well, I have to," she said, "I've already postponed."

"Nah," he said, "don't go. No one I know goes."

"Well, how can I get out of it?" she asked.

"Rip it up," the driver said.

"Rip what up?"

"The notice," he said.

"What do you mean?"

"You just rip it up and say you never got it in the mail."

"But that must be illegal," she said.

"What illegal?" he laughed. "Everyone does it. What's a nice lady like you gonna do at the County Courthouse. You'll be a target."

"Oh, God, you think?"

"Of course," he said. "They mug people in the hallways of the courthouse. It's no place for good people."

"Well—"

"I'm telling you, rip it up."

"But—"

"You want me to do it for you?"

"But—"

"Here, give it to me," the driver said. "What are they gonna do, put someone like you in jail. Please, c'mon. Say you never got it." By now he was amid the din of Gun Hill Road, triple-parked cars, boom boxes, kids piling into Evander Childs High School.

"No, I shouldn't," she said.

"C'mon, give it to me," he said. By now he's driving with his left hand and reaching back to the backseat with his right hand, waiting for my mother to hand him the jury duty summons, ready to rip it up.

She started to laugh, when she said, "No, with my luck, they will arrest me. I'll just stick it out. But thank you."

That night at the dinner table, she told us the story, relieved now that she had been dismissed on the first day.

We all laughed. "Here, gimme, he said, I'll rip it up," she reiterated. "Would you believe that?"

"He meant well," my father said. "But you have to do your civic duty. It's the law."

And then to us, under her breath, she said, "Yeah, right, the law."

When the Co-op Cab drivers weren't laughing at the dispatcher's quips, or talking your ear off, they were listening to music, 92 KTU or BLS 107.5. The day we left for Paris-Orly, there was a Puerto Rican cab-driver and a friend of his, a black man, in the front seat. He scooted to the middle, my father squeezed in, and kept his right arm leaning out the window. My mother, sister, and I sat in the back. No one wore seat belts, front or back. Did the car even have seat belts? They had BLS on and for some reason, I remember this song playing: "Just a Touch of Love," by Steve Arrington's Hall of Fame. I don't know why I remember this. Was that it was so incongruous a picture, with my bifocaled father in the front seat, his sport coat sleeve hanging out the window, on his way, finally, to see the Art Treasures of France, like the title of his book on Uncle Pep's shelf, while a funk song played by the former front man of Slave? Did my father even hear the song? Or did the New England Thruway to the Whitestone to the Grand Central to the Van Wyck, with all the windows open, drown out the bass line and the backbeat? Or did he choose not to hear it?

I had my first beer in a bar, in Lyon, with my father. It was still early evening, still light out, and my mother and sister were getting ready for dinner after a long day of sightseeing. We tired of waiting and said we'd meet them in the hotel lobby at 8:00. We didn't know where to go. My father said, "Let's get a drink." So we went to a bar, sat on the stool, and he ordered two beers. He didn't speak French, none of us did, but he managed. "Bonjour, monsieur. Deux Kronenbourg, s'il vous plaît."

We touched glasses. "Always toast before the first sip and look the other person in the eye," he said. "It's polite." Then he said, "*Salud*," and we sipped the beer. Alcohol was never taboo around my father, as long as it was in moderation and with food. An eight-ounce beer with a sandwich on Saturday afternoon while watching college basketball or wine with my mother's cooking or a splash of cognac in the strawberries after dinner or a shot of sambuca in the espresso was more than allowed, even if I was sixteen.

He explained that Kronenbourg sounded German but was actually French, from Strasbourg, Alsace-Lorraine, where we were the other day. He explained that it was a disputed territory up until the end of the war. He talked about the war.

He said, "You know your uncle, my oldest brother, was a war hero, you know that, don't you?"

I nodded yes, I knew that he was wounded in the Pacific theater, earned six or seven battle stars.

He said if the war lasted another few months, who knows where he would've been. "Thank God it ended."

He talked about the French resistance, the mythology of it. "Yes, it existed, of course, but not how it has been romanticized." He said that I should study it in college. He said that he wished he had gone to college, just to study history.

"Why didn't you?" I asked.

"Eh, who knows? I qualified for Colgate, but, well, whattaya-gonna do?"

There's nothing more wonderful than history, he said, and music and art, but history could be manipulated. Nixon was a scoundrel, he said, but in a hundred years' time, who knows how he might look. It might depend on who's writing the history, what they emphasize and what they don't. "You know Nixon hated Italians, don't you? And he hated the Jews."

He asked me if I liked history. I said yes.

"Is it something you might want to pursue in college?" he asked.

Again, I said yes.

"Do you have any idea where you might want to go to college?"

This time I said, "No."

"Well, don't worry about the money," he said. "It's tight, but I'll get you to college, just keep up with your studies. And just do me one favor, learn how to think. Don't let anyone teach you what to think, especially these university professors. Always question them."

I nodded that I would, when the time came. But enough with ideals, I thought, what about practicality? "How are we doing, money-wise, for the rest of the trip?" I asked, emboldened for the rare moment. Maybe it was the beer.

"We shouldn't even be here," he said, not seeming surprised. "I'll need to call New York to have some money wired for later in the trip, but don't worry about it. That's for me to worry about. I had to see France, like I had to see Italy. Your mother's right, it's an education."

I changed the subject back to something safe. We talked about the Mets, that after all these years, they were winning, that they had a chance to win the East, it didn't seem real. That was the only bad thing about being in France; we'd miss the Mets for a month. We'd watch them, more than the Yankees, our eyes glued on Keith Hernandez play first base. "He's some ball player, this fella," he said. "As good as any of the old-timers. What a glove." We bought the *Herald Tribune* every day and followed the scores, to see if they could keep up with the Cubs. "And besides, it's an excellent newspaper."

He asked me what magazines I bought earlier that day.

I showed him. They were soccer magazines, one called *Mondial*, the other *Onze*, both in praise of France, the brand-new European Soccer Champions, and its captain, Michel Platini. I had watched it all live on the Spanish channel in New York, enthralled again like I was two years before. I told him that my goal was to collect soccer magazines from all around the world, everywhere I went, why hadn't I done it sooner. Last year in Vancouver, I found two British magazines called *Match* and *Shoot*. This was the start of something.

"That's a good idea," he said. "Well you see all the magazines I collect, the *Times Magazine*, Buckley's magazine, and *Daedalus*. You're old enough where you can start reading them now."

I shrugged, maybe, and now it was eight o'clock. We had to meet my mother and sister. We toasted, a second time, *salud*, and we took the last sip of Kronenbourg.

Before Lyon we went to Strasbourg. We had a drink in the late afternoon, in a courtyard. There was a woman there, a blond woman of middle age, who drank, by herself, and stared into the sunset. We imagined what she was thinking or who she was or what life she had led. We took the train down to Nice. Who knew they made pizza so well? *We're close to Italy, that's why.* The same in Aix, but why was there dog shit on every block? In Carcassonne, the medieval walled city in the southwest, my father stood with me on a bluff in the new city, facing south. "Those are the Pyrenees," he said. *Do you see them, and beyond that, Spain, if only the sky was a little clearer?*

We took an overnight train, without beds, way up north, to Rouen, the bane of Joan of Arc, then back to Paris, as perfect as we'd left it three and a half weeks before, when we first arrived. We stayed at the same American-style hotel, not because we liked it but because it was the best deal we could find. We stayed in smaller hotels in the other cities, but here we had no choice, even if the exchange rate was in our favor, seven francs to the dollar.

The next morning my father left for a bank near the Champs-Élysées. He had made a collect call in Carcassonne, after he taught me to look over the Pyrenees, to always look deeper and further, to always challenge myself to see and do things, and learn things, after he told me, like he had over and over, that life didn't owe me anything, after he wrote a bum check at the cute inn, just inside the thirteenth-century fortified wall. The collect call was to remind Ray, his bookmaking associate and fellow colleague at the Department of Welfare, the man with the tinted glasses and fedora he met doing all the paperwork after the 1977 blackout. He'd become an unofficial partner in this very unofficial business of theirs, the unofficial business of balance and chance. He spoke slowly, Ray did, and it annoyed my father. Nor did he like how Ray handled clients who they owed money to. There was a way to talk to them, to reassure, but to also create wiggle room, to be straightforward, but to charm when necessary, to buy time. "You told them we'll pay when?" we'd hear my father yell from his bedroom after dinner. "What the hell are you doing, Ray? I can't come up with it by then. Don't you know how to handle yourself with these guys yet?"

But he never disparaged Ray, publicly, or even to us. *He drives me up a wall sometimes, but he's a good man, he means well.*

So when my father called him in Carcassonne, before we even got on that overnight train to Rouen, he said, "Raymond, I need a favor." He told him that in three days' time, we would be back in Paris, and needed him to wire a bunch of money to such and such a bank there. *I don't have money to eat over here.* The amount, who can remember? The tower hotel was prepaid before we left but we needed money for daily expenses, food, transportation, museum admissions, we wanted to go back to the Louvre, maybe buy a few souvenirs for the people back home. Ray said he would, slowly and reluctantly.

That first morning back in Paris, my father left the hotel early. He told us to take a taxi and meet him at the top of the Champs-Élysées at eleven. So we did.

When the taxi pulled up, my mother saw my father, and said to us, "The money didn't come in."

"How do you know?" my sister said.

"I can just tell," she said.

She was right. When he saw us walking toward him, he made an Italian hand gesture with his forefinger and thumb, turning it side to side meaning "no luck."

"What are we gonna do?" my mother said. "We still have four more days in Paris."

"We'll have to eat a late breakfast in the hotel and try to last until dinner," he said. "We can eat dinner in the hotel. There I can pay for additional meals with a personal check."

"I'll stash some extra croissants and rolls from the breakfast room," my sister said. "I'll put them in my bag, if we're hungry in the afternoon." *We laugh about it now, but at the time it wasn't funny.*

My parents had hoped for at least one great meal in a notable Parisian brasserie. They had talked about new restaurants that they read about, in *The New York Times* or *New York* magazine, but it was usually just that, talk. Talk as in: "I wonder if this Odeon place is any good," my father said about the converted diner near where he worked on 60 Hudson Street, the Art Deco landmark.

"Who goes there?" my mother asked.

"It's all these live-wire types," he said. "None of the people from my office. You don't hear none of the social service people talk about it."

"Maybe we should go?" she said.

"Well, I used to go there when it was what it was," he said. "Before these young English fellas took it over a couple of years ago. It was plain inside. Yeah maybe we can go."

They never did go to Odeon. They'd make up for it in Paris.

When it was three o'clock our time, my father called Ray in New York. "What the hell happened?"

"I had trouble getting the money," he said. He had to call this one, that one, the other one, to get the cash.

"What did he say?" my mother asked my father.

"It'll be here tomorrow."

"Tomorrow, tomorrow, and tomorrow," she said. Then under her breath, "That's the story of my life."

That day we did as little, and as much, as possible, trying to see Paris without spending money, and knowing we might never get here again, that we'd have to make the most of these last days. We went to the Tuileries, the Luxembourg Gardens, we walked along the Seine. We walked and walked. We said this was the best trip ever, even if money was tight. We said we wished we lived in Paris, how nice it would be to live here. We said how we dreaded going back to Co-op City, *ugh, just the thought of it, just saying it*. We talked about the upcoming football season, and whether it would bring luck, like it used to, or would it bring more losses. *Let's hope for the best.*

"They must think we're a bunch of philistines eating in the hotel with all these nice restaurants," my mother said. "As if we don't know how to eat. That we're ugly Americans. They don't know it's because we ran out of money."

"What do I care what they think," my father said.

Tomorrow the money came.

CONFOEDERATIO HELVETICA (OR SMITHTOWN, LONG ISLAND), 1985

Or maybe this chapter should be, "The Harvard Club, 1985," because my father said this: "Guess where I was today, you wouldn't believe it. The Harvard Club."

"The Harvard Club, what?" my mother said, incredulous.

"Yeah, Rusty took me."

Rusty had been one of my father's customers since the late 1970s, but in the last few years was more and more involved. Meaning, he brought in other clients, and often lost large sums of money—and won large sums of money. He also became more than a client. Not a friend exactly; clients could never really become close friends. *Daddy, who's your best friend? You are. Not Vito or Stan or Albert? No, you are.*

But after he placed his bets, they might chat for a few minutes about a book or politics or music. If the other extension rang, my father often ignored it so he could continue the conversation with Rusty. *They'll call back.* It was about more than over/unders, two-time teasers, UNLV fifty times, and how Buffalo performed away from home, on natural grass.

He was a big shot in insurance. And his father before him, who was the insurance agent of Tyrone Power. My father thought Rusty was giving him a line at first. *Tyrone Power? C'mon.* But he was telling the truth. His father's obituary was in *The New York Times.*

Was it Rusty who sent the writer my father's way? A young writer, *a young Jewish fella, nice fella, big guy,* came by recommendation, placed a few bets, small ones, and asked my father if he could write about him, about moonlighting as a bookmaker. My father said, yes, as long as you don't use my name. It was published somewhere, a small publication, *for the life of me I can't find it. It was titled "The Gentleman Bookmaker," something like that.*

Yes, the writer may have come through Rusty. Rusty was a Harvard man, six-foot-two or six-three, *with baby blues,* married to a Swede, lived in Tuxedo Park, New York, *swanky,* and kept a pied-à-terre opposite the Metropolitan Museum. It came out that he had a Swiss bank account. *A Swiss bank account?* He came to my father through a recommendation from one of the regulars, possibly through Leonard, a longtime customer, a high roller, or Ned, a professional gambler, the best my father ever dealt with, who had relationships with bookmakers all over the country, freelancers like my dad but also with wise guys. He was a Jew, Ned, but an Italophile.

At the dinner table, my father never discussed business, rarely brought up his associates, but one night told us: "I spoke to Ned today. He just came back from Italy again and he said, "Hugo, I want to die there!" On another visit, Ned brought back a gold menorah. My father owed him money—he was always winning, Ned, *he played the middle*—and went to drop it off at his East Side high-rise.

"Ned, this is a work of art, this menorah," my father said. "You mind if I ask—"

"No, not at all, mid-five figures," he said.

"It's really something else."

"Thanks, Hugo."

Ned had once testified against a famous mobster years before—the mobster was trying to extort money from him—and he had a bodyguard, a fellow Jew, a quiet, small, apparently lethal man. My father would see him with Ned but only had one dealing with him. He had to deliver an envelope with three or four hundred in cash to Ned. It was a few days before Christmas and my father said to the bodyguard, "Will you tell Ned I was here and give this to him?"

"Don't worry about it," the bodyguard said.

"Yeah, but I owe this to him."

"I'll handle him," he said. "I'll tell him you paid. Now get out of here."

I bust out laughing.

Rusty had as much money but wasn't a pro like Ned. The insurance business always came first, gambling was a hobby. One of many. He was also a tenor, a real Irish tenor, and sang in a chorus at a Manhattan Episcopal church. *He's Catholic, mind you,* but they sang in churches all around the city.

Rusty called my father one afternoon and said, "Hugo, I need to see you."

"Is everything all right?" my father asked.

"Yeah, but you speak Italian, right?"

"Sure."

"And your people are from Naples."

"Yeah, my parents are from outside of Naples. Sarno, it's called."

"Perfect," Rusty said. "How about I buy you dinner and you help me with some pronunciations. My chorus will be singing some of the famous Neapolitan songs, and I'm going to have some solo parts."

"Okay," my father said, "let me check with my wife."

My father thinks he got him to roll the R. The check came and, of course, Rusty paid, but with his company card. *See these wealthy guys, guys born into it, they're taught don't spend your own money, spend someone else's money.*

But my father liked him. If Rusty lost, he paid, eventually. Some of his friends weren't the same. He sent someone my father's way, a colleague in insurance, from Alexander & Alexander, *you ever heard of Alexander & Alexander, they're one of the biggest heavyweights in insurance, on Park Avenue.* The guy loses $880 on a Sunday afternoon, meets my father with Rusty, and hands him a check for $440. He found out my father was hard of hearing; *he tried pulling a fast one.* My father told him that no, it was $880. Do you make a scene? You value Rusty as a client, bordering on friend, so what do you do? You let it go, no yelling, no screaming, no threats, not there, out in public, with Rusty.

When the Alexander & Alexander guy called back the following Sunday afternoon, my father said, "No, please take your business elsewhere." And he told Rusty, *with all due respect* . . . , and Rusty was fine with that, may have even apologized on behalf of the guy, and remained a customer.

Later, months, years, probably, my father was in a bind—again—and Rusty owed him money. My mother also liked Rusty. She never met him, but when he called, she would sometimes answer. He was well-spoken, *I mean, he went to Harvard after all*, and polite, but when my father told her, as he often did, "Rusty owes me a chunk of money," my mother exploded. "For Chrissakes, he lives in Tuxedo Park, he has a Swiss bank account, and he can't pay you?"

"He's always good for it," my father said. "I've made a ton of money on him."

"And he has it," she said. "To spare. I'm sure his house is paid for. He's not gambling the mortgage. This is sport to him. And all these guys. For us, it's our rent."

"He'll pay," my father said.

This time the chunk he owed my father was $3,400. My father called him and said, "Rusty, I'm really in a pinch. Can you get me that money you owe me?"

"Yes," he said. "Come meet me up at the Harvard Club."

Rusty said to him that it might take a couple of hours, but that he needed to play some backgammon, that Hugo should be patient, have a drink, there's plenty to read, chat people up.

Rusty, in addition to being a big shot in insurance and an Irish tenor with a house in Tuxedo Park and a pied-à-terre opposite the Met, was a well-known high-stakes backgammon player. My father called home, said we should go on and eat without him. It was one of the few times he wasn't home for dinner. That and when he taught Rusty the Italian pronunciations.

So he has a brandy, flips through some magazines, and watches Rusty win, right there at the backgammon table, the $3,400, even a little more. Enough to take my father to Gallagher's for steak. "Thanks for waiting there," Rusty tells him. And he picks up the check again, this time with his own money.

"Now let me give you a ride home," he said.

Should I accept? my father thought. *What will he say, or think, when he sees Co-op City?* Rusty knew my father lived "up the Bronx," but not where exactly. *But what do I have to hide? There are good people in Co-op City.* There always were. So my father said yes, sure. Rusty drove him, over the Willis Avenue Bridge, *this way you don't pay the toll*, past the massive Newport sign that declared, in flashing lights, ALIVE . . . WITH . . . PLEASURE, with the time and temperature, perhaps a local sports score, onto the Bruckner Expressway, careful not to make a wrong turn or you might end up in someone's novel, past the burned-out buildings, mile after mile—does it matter that it's dark, that you can't see them?—to the interchange where it joins with I-95, the New England Thruway, past Pelham Bay Park, *God, this place is far*, into, finally, Co-op City.

He didn't say to my father, "This is where you live?" He didn't say, "What am I doing with someone like you, who lives in a place like this?"

My father thought this to himself: "He's well-bred. What these people have is breeding, whether they're hypocrites or not, whether they mean what they say or not, there's surface mannerism. They aren't volatile, like us, Italians. Maybe less honest, but there's artifice."

My father appreciated it.

Guess where I was today, you wouldn't believe it.

In the late spring and early summer, my parents fought again. Not about the usual. When my sister came home from college in Worcester, for holidays, breaks, she'd ask me this, as soon as she saw me: "Fights?"

I'd shrug, *yeah, I guess.*

"About what?" she'd ask.

"The usual."

The usual meant money; eviction notices, which now came hand-delivered by the U.S. Marshal; the future; the question of our own safety net. A fight about the Catholic Church would be refreshing. But these latest fights weren't about money. They were about Greece or Yugoslavia, which was most affordable, which had the most to teach, which had the most rewards. The "every three years, we'll go to Europe" commandment lasted nine years and ended in 1982, but regained traction last year in '84, with the monthlong dream trip to France. As much as my father was losing, as much as he owed, he always had potential to earn. He had a lot of action on Big East college basketball. One of his clients gave us tickets four years in a row to the tournament at the Garden. Earlier that year, my father let his heart get the best of him, and he bet heavily, outside his bookmaking, on Villanova. They weren't the best team in the country, they weren't the best team in the Big East, but he liked how they battled. It helped that their coach, Rollie Massimino, was a *paisan*, but so was the St. John's coach, Lou Carnesecca, and from East Harlem.

Maybe it was this new client of his, a young guy, twenties, early thirties maybe, who was a Villanova alum. That's all he talked about. My father liked him. *He's a Polish kid, nice kid, good kid.* I met him at the Big East games and he was exactly that. He asked me where I intended to apply for college and said I should consider Villanova, that he could answer any questions, introduce me to people, show me the place. My father appreciated that. His clients, the ones I might speak to when I happened to answer the phone or the ones I'd meet in person when my father gave me an envelope of cash to deliver to an arriving car downstairs, were nice to me, but never offered anything in the way of constructive advice. Maybe they'd say, "Stay outta trouble, kid," and slip me a dollar.

So my father got this Villanova bug. No, the Polish kid didn't bet the numbers Rusty did, or Ned, or Leonard. He was small by comparison, but he had buddies and generated some volume. And he planted that idea of Villanova in my father's head. What more can you ask for than a good, timely idea.

I don't have to tell you what happened in the early spring of 1985. Villanova goes to the Final Four and wins the NCAAs, beating the feared Georgetown on 78 percent shooting. My father bet the feisty underdogs. Money came in, money went right back out—he owed so much—but more was still due in. Some customers took their time in paying—*I was never the pay-or-die type*. They took advantage. But eventually it would come, and we should plan on going somewhere, he told my mother. What great culture in Europe hadn't we seen, that was a must? Greece. It's where everything came from. *It would be great for the kids, a great education.*

But my mother seemed enamored with Yugoslavia. She never especially liked sports. She indulged my father and me, and she knew it had financial significance, but on her own, she would never watch it. But the 1984 Winter Olympics were different, and she was more and more curious about Sarajevo and Yugoslavia.

About this, they argued. "I'm not saying there's anything wrong with Yugoslavia," my father said, "but because of its history, it's really several countries in one. It'll be a hard country to grasp." Then he turned to me and said, "You ever heard the word 'balkanized'? That's where it comes from." Now Greece, that was the provenance of so much, government, literature, the poem, the tragedy, the comedy, philosophy, and most important to him, written history itself, Herodotus.

Then they came to a conclusion. Why not do both? *What the hell, we have nothing anyway.* The trip to France the year before was the best of many, and they were still on that high. She was admitting defeat long term, but still thinking big in the short term.

She started doing her research, getting brochures, looking through magazines, making phone calls. *What this will cost? Ouch.* The weeks went by, payments hadn't come in as expected, that or more money was lost in the time in between, and my father gave the bad news: "We won't be able to swing it." He was sorry, said he shouldn't have brought it up, that he had a good first quarter—not sure if he used that term—got carried away, paid some of the money he owed, was wowed by the thought of Greece, but this was out of reach. You never know, though, maybe something will come up. *Keep jabbing.*

It came together all very last minute. The end of summer was already in sight, and we'd have to make up our minds soon or not go anywhere. My father had cash on hand, not enough *to put a down payment or something*, but enough for four round-trip plane tickets to Europe. My mother thought, as she had in the past, might as well take the trip, otherwise the money will go to pay God knows who.

So we booked nine days in Geneva, Switzerland. It wasn't Yugoslavia or Greece, or both, but it was French, and might come close to last year's experience of croissants, great coffee, baguettes, and delicious wines for next to nothing. Even pizza the French did well.

We stayed in a nice, modest hotel, The Hotel California it was called, and took advantage of the country's smallness, taking the train one day to Bern, to Zermatt, to Zurich, to Lausanne, Montreux. The other days we stayed in Geneva. *The lake is to die for.* We got to use the few words of French we learned the summer before.

My father announced, beside the lake, "This is the Confoederatio Helvetica, that's the Latin name for Switzerland. It's the oldest democracy in the world. Do you know when it was established?" he asked my sister and me. Neither of us did.

"The year 1291," he said. "You haven't learned that?"

We both shook our heads no.

"What are they teaching you in that Clark University?" he said. "What is it, all non-Western studies? They're too leftist, these universities. They hate Europe."

When we went to Montreux, he said to me, "They have a famous jazz festival here, you know that, don't you?"

This time I was prepared. "Yes," I said, "I know all about it." Which was true. I was always searching for music that no one listened to—or that wasn't popular. The R & B wasn't what it was ten or five or even three years before. It seemed to lose its soul, by chance, when

I left public school in 1982. Reggae and African took its place for a couple of years, Julius helped with that, but then I saw Miles Davis on TV. Was it on Carson? He was playing from his album *Star People*. That was it. This was the coolest man on the planet. I got Jeff, another high school friend, interested in it, slowly. We traded records; my early Earth, Wind & Fire, pre–"That's the Way of the World," for his early Santana; my Miles for his Hendrix, Band of Gypsies first, then the Experience. We found out they were supposed to collaborate, Jimi and Miles. We spent hours talking about what it might've sounded like.

From *Star People* and *We Want Miles* and *Decoy* we started buying the older albums, *Kind of Blue*, *Sketches of Spain*, *Miles Smiles*, anything and everything. Then Coltrane, Monk, McCoy Tyner, Herbie Hancock. We spent hours in the jazz section at Tower Records, Jeff and me, the one on Sixty-sixth and Broadway. We'd go on Saturday afternoons or on a Friday night. My mother allowed it because she liked Jeff and she considered jazz, even if she didn't love it, an art form, something worth learning. "It absolutely is," my father agreed. "Just be careful up there around Amsterdam and Columbus avenues. It can get dangerous there at night."

With Jeff I saw Miles Davis twice: In 1985, with a fifteen-dollar upper-deck ticket at Avery Fisher Hall, that was stamped in red PARTIAL VIEW, and the next year at the Miller Time Concerts on the Pier, at Forty-third Street and Eleventh Avenue, worst seat in the house, almost in the Hudson River. We couldn't believe we were really seeing Miles. My mother told the story again and again, and probably to Jeff: She almost met Miles Davis—and Sonny Rollins. How Gladys, the woman she worked with in Brooklyn, had them in the house once in a while in the early '60s. Her husband knew them and they'd come for dinner, sometimes play. "She'd say, 'Yeah, Sonny came over Saturday night, he brought Miles Davis. They started playin'. Cora, you gotta come over sometime.' "

Why didn't you?

My father thought electronic instruments were junk, that they transformed jazz into rock and pop, *an abomination*. But for a fifteen- or sixteen-year-old, maybe it was a good way to get into the serious stuff. When I begged for a saxophone, he found the six hundred dollars and took me to West Forty-eighth Street, to International Woodwinds. I want to say he paid cash, but it might have been on the installment plan. It was a lot for my parents, the horn, an alto, and lessons on Gun Hill Road, at one of two music schools that were popular with kids in Co-op who wanted to continue their music education.

It was past the bowling alley we used to go to, near Evander Childs High School, not a good area, but on Saturday afternoons, it felt placid, so I would walk home with my saxophone case. I didn't tell my mother. *Are you crazy, you'll get robbed. That horn cost your father a lot of money.* But I liked going to the mysterious record store, to buy an album, any of the newer Miles records or Grover Washington or the Crusaders, who played in Kinshasa with James Brown and the Spinners at the Ali-Foreman fight ten years before. The Crusaders were the first nonclassical concert I saw live. It was at Avery Fisher Hall, on a bill with David Sanborn, earlier that summer at the Kool Jazz Festival. We went as a family of four.

"Oh, you're down with Grover," the one or two people who worked in the record store said to me.

"Yeah," I'd say. "Grover's my man. I play alto."

"Word?" They didn't charge me tax.

One afternoon, near the record store on Gun Hill Road, a black man with dreadlocks approached me, looked me up and down, and looked at my case. I thought: Oh shit.

"Yo, brother."

"Me?" I said.

"Yeah. You play alto?"

"Yeah, how'd you know?"

"The size of the case. I'm a musician. Who are you into?"

"Grover, Sanborn, my teacher is trying to get me into Charlie Parker."

"Good, good, you're learning right. What about Fela, you heard of him?"

"Nah."

"You should check him out. He's an African brother. Big sound. Plays alto and tenor. Hey, I'm looking for a horn section for a band I'm starting. You interested?"

"Well, I still suck. I can't play anything yet. I'm learning the scales, C major right now."

"That's good. Learn those scales, play them over and over. Has he taught you the blues scale yet?"

"Nah."

"Here," he said, "let me write it down for you on my card. When you feel you're ready, call me."

"Okay," I said. "Thanks man." We clasped hands, the black way.

So Montreux I knew.

My mother sat beside Lake Geneva, in Montreux or Lausanne, and began her ritual of writing postcards. She wrote them to the people back home, family, friends, neighbors, former neighbors, sometimes out of obligation, other times because she legitimately liked the person and wanted to convey her thoughts, however impressionistic, about a place, and felt they would appreciate it.

This time she made sure she didn't send a postcard to two people: her own parents. Why? We didn't know, but she wanted to make a point. We were there, at the Smithtown house, on Memorial Day weekend. There were no histrionics, no airing out of dirty laundry or grievances, past or present, not even a sharp exchange that I can remember. Maybe my grandfather, Jimmy, told my grandmother to "shut up" if she started to cough. This is something he'd done in the past, *the miserable bastard.*

I spent most of the time in the tiny guest room, the one I loved staying in when I'd visit over the summer or when my father had his operation. Smithtown may have been suburban sprawl, but for me, it seemed like the country. That weekend, I had work to do, racing desperately to finish my fifty-page term paper for eleventh-grade American history. Mine was on jazz, and I only came up for air during mealtime.

They talked about the old neighborhood, Bushwick, all the old characters, the ruin it had become. There was always a story, this time about Dr. Sal's father, their old landlord on Jefferson Street. Sal, the best doctor Lillian ever had, was dead, but the father was still alive, self-sufficient at ninety-nine. And then they killed him. Someone snuck through the window, robbed him, and bashed his head in. My mother asked her mother, "What was he still doing in Bushwick?" My grandmother said that he was advised to move, was told it was a ghetto, that for his own safety he should get out. And he responded to anyone who told him that with: "What am I gonna do, go to Forest Hills?"

"What a shame," they said together.

What else was said, or not said, I don't know. There was no drama, no name-calling. I would've heard, it wasn't that big a house. But when we came home on the Long Island Railroad—we never did buy another car—my mother said, "That's it, I'm never going back."

People say things, things they don't mean, things they don't follow up on, things they don't remember they said. She meant it. My sister and I asked why; we didn't get a straight answer. My father said it would blow over.

The only thing my parents agreed on was psychotherapy, what a sham it was, *a racket*. No, they agreed on other things: how Southern Italian food was better than Northern, how art was good for the soul, that divorce was brutal on the kids, how they were old-fashioned but believed in any and all New Waves. They agreed on *Days of Heaven*. But when they discussed therapy at the dinner table, they said, over and over: *People are looking for answers; sometimes in life there are no answers*. This was one of those times.

There were just no more visits to my grandparents, us to them, them to us, which had stopped anyway since my grandfather hated

Co-op City. There were no more phone calls, us to them, them to us, or Christmas cards. But first there was no postcard of Lake Geneva or of Grossmünster in Zurich.

We almost never got out of Geneva. What happens when you can't pay the hotel bill? Do they call the consulate, the embassy, work out a deal? It happened again, something about the personal check. *But I have two forms of identification. . . . I must have misunderstood, I'm hard of hearing, you see.*

"Sorry, monsieur." He was so nice, the man at the desk. There weren't traveler's checks this time; it was the end of the trip. And then my father said: "My secretary back in New York . . ." And we quietly walked away.

MADISON SQUARE GARDEN, 1986

The public address announcer had a gentle voice, a New York voice, insouciant but with authority. It was the voice I loved hearing when I came here. His voice meant you were with adults. My father said that the man was an Irishman from the old school. "Condon is his name," my father said. Nothing flashy, not like a ring announcer's, the lights didn't dim, spotlights didn't swirl when he spoke. They didn't have to; when you heard this voice, it was time to listen. It was game time.

The voice said: "Good evening, ladies and gentlemen, welcome to Madison Square Garden, the world's most famous arena, for the Big East semifinals." And we, the crowd, erupted.

The first time I went to Madison Square Garden, I don't remember much. I should have, it was only twelve years before, in 1974. The Rangers played the St. Louis Blues. We went with my cousin and uncle, who were Rangers fans. My father didn't especially like hockey and didn't get much business on it. *Only from the Irishmen.* It seemed like it was another century, 1974. All I remember was that we sat far from the ice. I can't remember who won.

Maybe the first time wasn't the Rangers but the circus. Yes, what am I talking about, it was the circus. The four of us went, my parents and sister and I. It was fun the first time. They cut off all the lights inside, and we all had to twirl our pocket flashlights in the air. When we went back a second time, whenever it was, it began to feel square. In the Garden lobby, they had wallet-size schedules for the Knicks and, on the other side, the Rangers. Seeing a man with long hair glide around in ice skates or a man in an Afro would be better than this kids' stuff. That's what I told my sister, that I would be back for the Knicks and Rangers.

In 1978, we went together again, to our first Knicks game. These were better seats—in the orange ring. The seats closest to the court were red, then orange, then yellow, then green, then above that, in a separate deck, blue. We got there early and saw the players warm up. The Knicks played the Seattle Supersonics. Almost all the men were black and music blared on the P.A.—"Flash Light," by Parliament. The Sonics had a tall white man, with blond hair: number 43, Jack Sikma. Their coach was a black man, Lenny Wilkens. "Did I ever tell you about the time Lenny Wilkens got hot in the NIT tournament?" my father said. "Oh, boy, did I lose a ton of money."

The court glowed bright, with the lanes painted a deep blue. The Sonics looked iridescent in their green and yellow, the Knicks, regal and crisp in the home whites. This was a rare thing, to see the Knicks in their home uniforms. They played on TV but always on the road, in blue. It seemed as if the Knicks always played away on Friday nights, on Channel 9, WOR, and home on Saturday nights, available only to those lucky people in the city who had Manhattan Cable, whoever those people were. Instead, the Rangers were on TV most Saturday nights, also on WOR, and home Sunday nights. Friday night was the voice of Marv Albert and Cal Ramsey.

The Sonics game was a weeknight. Somewhere the rich people in Manhattan were watching us on the exclusive Manhattan Cable.

Before the players went back to their locker rooms before tip-off, one of the Sonics, a young, stocky guy, not that tall, stayed on to sign autographs. Soon a few people, not that many, crowded around.

"Look," my mother said, "that guy is signing autographs. Why don't you go down, Michael?"

I hesitated. I was shy, sometimes paralyzingly shy. This was one of those times. So I just watched.

"I think that's this young fella Johnson," my father said.

"He looks nice, Michael, go ahead, have him sign the book," my mother said again. They had just bought me the Knicks' '77–'78 Yearbook. Willis Reed, now the coach, was on the cover.

"Hugo, would you take him down, he's too shy," my mother said.

"No, it's okay," I said. "I like the Knicks better." I was rationalizing. I did want Dennis Johnson's autograph.

"Michael, don't be bashful," he said to me. "He'll sign for you."

"Hugo, will you just walk the kid down."

"What, I got my hot dog here. What am I gonna go down for? He doesn't need me. Just go, we'll watch you."

Finally, my sister said, "I'll take him."

"Atta girl," my father said.

She grabbed me by the arm, with the Knicks yearbook in her other hand, and began escorting me down the steps, toward this bright, shining court. I thought for sure one of these older men in gray hair and red MSG sport coats would yell at us. But no one did. As we marched down the steps of the red seats, Dennis Johnson, suddenly, was gone, coolly jogging back to the tunnel, a dozen or so happy fans staring down at their program or yearbook or whatever he signed.

"You see that," my mother said.

The next year, it was the Knicks against the Washington Bullets, just my father and me this time, red seats, and get this, second row, not behind the benches, the opposite side, but still. Wes Unseld looked larger than life itself. Earl the Pearl, Ray Williams, Michael Ray Richardson.

My father was indifferent when it came to the Knicks and pro basketball. It bored him. He was only here for me, and because one of his clients came through with these tickets. The only Knick he liked was Red Holzman, the former coach. He was from the old school. To me, Red just seemed old, gray. My father raved about him. "He was an excellent basketball coach, very thorough, very professional. Good dresser."

In a way, Red reminded me of my father. Thinning gray hair, serious, not flashy, no entourage, his own man. The Knicks lost that night.

I mean, they must have. Washington was very good, and the Knicks weren't. Still, I loved them, all the Knicks, from Lonnie Shelton to Bob McAdoo to Glen Gondrezick.

Did we go the next year? I don't remember. In '80, we might have, no, in fact we did. He had a new client who was losing money and knew my father had a kid who loved the Knicks and Rangers. At the beginning of the season, my father would tell me, "We'll get two Ranger games, two Knick games—how does that sound?" He'd pull out one of those wallet-sized schedules. I was supposed to choose games that were on or near my birthday in March. We always saw the Indiana Pacers, the Milwaukee Bucks, or the Cleveland Cavaliers.

"Milwaukee again, Daddy?" I'd say.

"They're one of the premier teams in basketball, whattaya you talkin' about," he'd say, and he was right, better than Indiana or the Cavs, but they were boring. I couldn't complain, these were good seats the client had, not second row, but about ten or fifteen rows behind the Knicks bench, solidly in the red seats. Close enough to hear coach Hubie Brown scream.

"Watch this fella Sidney Moncrief," he told me. "He's a superb player—like a coach on the court."

"But he doesn't dunk," I said.

"Dunking is for show-offs—learn the game the right way."

That voice from the PA system, the same man, I'd hear every few seconds: "That was Sidney Moncrief, Milwaukee leads 6–0; that was Sidney Moncrief, Milwaukee leads 22–14; that was Terry Cummings, Milwaukee leads 48–34; that was Sidney Moncrief, Milwaukee leads 88–67; that was Terry Cummings. . . ."

In these years, my love for the Knicks grew. I liked them in '78, I studied them in '79, I loved them in '80, I was devoted in '81. So when they played the Pacers one night, one of those years, and my father needed the Pacers, laying the points, I took it personally. He didn't tell me he needed the Pacers; I could just tell. I knew. He was my father. It was the same feeling I had, earlier that year, or later that year, or the year before or year after, when the Rangers played the Winnipeg Jets.

He might not have gotten action on the NHL, but that night, of all nights, he needed Winnipeg.

The Garden was quiet for the Pacers game, maybe half full. It was midwinter, freezing out, the Knicks weren't very good, the Pacers were worse. In a seat nearby was a white guy, my father swore he was Irish, all by himself, surrounded by empty red seats. He was no Pacers fan, but I understood. I was surrounded by empty red seats and the only two people in the Garden rooting for Indiana.

Each time the Pacers as much as took a charge, the Irishman would urge them on. He was especially keen on "Wayman." "Yeah, Wayman"; "Shoot it Wayman"; "You're my man, Wayman." He was very loud, and he was happy; Wayman was dominating the game.

My father knew I loved the Knicks so he rooted silently. At one point he leaned over to me and asked, "Who's this fella Tisdale? He's somethin' else."

He didn't hear well, but he even heard the voice in the half-empty Garden. *That was Wayman Tisdale, Indiana leads 64–48.* I came home upset.

The whole ride back, we didn't say a word to each other, my father and I. After the bus made its last stop, at Eighty-seventh Street and Third Avenue, the driver would turn off the lights. I stared out the window, angry not so much that the Knicks lost, but because I couldn't root for them.

When my mother opened the door, she could tell something was wrong. When I was seven and eight, ten and eleven, even twelve, I would cry when it came to sports. Finally that stopped. Now I sulked.

"What's the matter?" she said.

"I couldn't root for the Knicks," I said. "Daddy needed the other team."

"Hugo, you weren't supposed to tell him!" she said. "You know he likes the Knicks."

"I didn't tell him anything," he said, sheepishly.

But we had September 16, 1981. We cheered together. There were no teams that night, just two men, 147 pounds each. Sugar Ray Leonard versus Thomas Hearns for the Welterweight Championship of the world. It was in Las Vegas, but in Madison Square Garden, packed for the closed-circuit telecast, it seemed live, right before us.

I'd sworn off these closed-circuit boxing events after Leonard-Duran I. But that was more than a year ago. I was in eighth grade, a senior in junior high, listening to Kurtis Blow and Fonda Rae, Denroy Morgan and Jimmy Ross, playing handball around characters who wore gun holsters as fashion accessories and blasted the Tom Tom Club. I was ready to go back to see boxing. I'd also left Leonard behind; I was for Hearns now. Maybe because he was skinny like me; maybe my father was having an influence. My father liked him because he reminded him of some of the old-timers—skinny arms with deceptive power. "This Hearns, he hits like a mule," he said.

So when I told kids in my new eighth grade class that I was going to the fight, they said, "Aw, man, word?" and then, "Who do you like?"

"Hearns," I said. "He's my boy."

Some agreed. "Word, Hearns is chill. The Motor City Cobra. The Hitman."

Others were for Leonard. "I'm down with Sugar Ray."

Calvin still was for Leonard; Ravi still thought it was a waste of money. *What if one of them quits again?*

My father and I were united this time. We didn't have to worry about the Indiana Pacers or Winnipeg Jets getting in the way of filial piety. We had the Hitman.

I met my father after school in Manhattan. I took the express bus from Co-op City and was told to stay on until the last stop, Twenty-third Street, between Broadway and Madison, where my father would be waiting. I'd done this before, when we'd meet for other events. "If he's not there," my mother said, "just wait and call me from a phone booth." He was always there. And each time he met me at the last stop, maybe to take me to Paragon Sporting Goods, he'd motion across the street and say, "This is Madison Square," where the original Garden was, not the one I'm always talking about. That was on Fiftieth Street and Eighth Avenue. I practically lived there.

"You know the first time I was there?" he went on. *College basketball, triple-headers, I know, I know.*

"I was there, believe it or not, for the something called the six-day bike race," he said. "You never heard of this, have you?"

No, I was about to say.

"No," he answered himself. "It became obsolete, but it was quite popular. Packed houses. It was a boisterous event. They raced all night, teams of riders. My uncle Neal took me. He liked cycling from the old country."

I nodded.

"Anyway, this was the original Madison Square Garden, there were two, right here, across the street on the other side of the park. Now it's a den of iniquity. If I'm ever late, just wait where the Co-op City bus stops. Never cross the street and go in the park. Your mother told you that, right?"

"Yeah," I said. "She said it was Needle Park." She'd been paranoid of something happening to me and my sister for the last two years, since 1979, when a boy disappeared from a Greenwich Village Street. He was about my age, *he even looks like you.* His name was Etan Patz. "God help that boy," she said. "And his poor parents. What this city has come to." *And God, after all these years, they never found that boy.*

"Needle Park," my father repeated. "It's good she told you that."

We walked east and south for dinner at Paul & Jimmy's on Irving Place. It was a place my family came back to, sometimes for Columbus Day, sometimes for Good Friday, after the fast. Or my parents would come by themselves, after or before a movie. *What happened to the movies? There are no good ones. Only* Raging Bull. *He was really like that, Jake. He was like an animal, subhuman. But was he tough.*

While we ate—I ordered the bistecca—my father said, as he had before, "One of these nights, I'll take you to one of the New York steakhouses, one of the famous ones."

"It's okay," I said, "Paul & Jimmy's is good, too."

"You're a good kid, Michael," he said. "We didn't spoil you. Remember what I always say: Life doesn't owe you anything, the world doesn't owe you anything. A lot of people think they've got something coming to them, like the world owes them something. The world doesn't owe anyone anything."

I shrugged and mumbled, "I dunno. I guess."

"I know, no lectures, tonight. So who's gonna win? Give me your prediction."

"The Hitman," I said. "Within seven."

"Let's hope you're right—I have a lotta wood on him. I've been looking forward to this for weeks."

Hearns lost. It didn't matter how much we yelled—*stay up, Tommy, stay up*—to just hang on, that you're ahead on points, just keep your legs and keep jabbing. It didn't matter how loudly we shouted, standing up by now, in the fourteenth round. *Leonard caught him one.* Hearns leaned way back on the ropes, all punchy, and the referee stopped it. *No! No! Let 'em fight!*

We lost, our guy lost, my father lost. How much, I didn't ask, but we won. We had this night. This was our night. Who else had that?

The closed-circuit fights, Fresno State vs. DePaul, the Cosmos vs. San Diego Sockers, Italy vs. U.S., Fiorentina vs. São Paulo, the Jets on *Monday Night Football*, a few Yankee games, all those Met games, the Chinese National Team vs. Internacional of Porto Alegre, Brazil, in Vancouver, the Knicks and Rangers every year, and now this, my father's favorite, the college doubleheader, the Big East semis, 1986.

After the games, two of his clients, Lenny from Corona, Queens, sweet guy, big Mets fan, chatty, and Joe D. II, tall, dark, and silent, who looked like Michael Madsen, both Italians, said to my father and me, "Who's starving? Let's go down Arturo's." We got in one of their cars and were off to Houston Street. It was a cramped, disheveled place, this restaurant, with a piano player who hammed it up. It was Friday night. Joe D. II didn't say much. His friend Lenny did all the talking and ordered for the table, everything: pizzas, pastas, salads, carafes of wine.

Lenny kept eyeing the waitress, in her snug T-shirt. Then he said: "Would you check out the lungs on this one? Unbelievable."

I knew what he meant, but didn't say anything. Neither did Joe D. II, maybe he smiled. And neither did my father. I realized, then for some reason, for the first time, that he never looked at waitresses like that, never looked at women like that, never made comments like that. He could have, as a way to bond with his son or his friends or to prance. We had our time together, at these games or when we went to get our haircuts on Saturday mornings, which we still did, even as I got older. But he never took a second look at a woman. Even in their months of silences, which were the rule more than the exception now, he'd say, "Your mother is the most beautiful woman" sometimes followed by, "she just needs to understand that this is a business, that we can't do what we do on my salary." But sometimes not. Sometimes he would just say it, like that: "Your mother is the most beautiful woman."

After Lenny paid the check—*guys like that always pick up the check, always*—he pulled out two tickets for the next night's final: St. John's vs. Syracuse. "Hey, thanks, Lenny," I said.

When we got home, my father said, "Why don't you bring your friend from school." I'd just turned eighteen—maybe he wanted to give me more autonomy. He was talking about my friend Jeff, the music fan who also loved basketball. Jeff's father had died when he was young.

"You sure?" I said.

"Yeah, I'll watch it from home. You go. Let's just hope St. John's pulls it out."

PLAYLAND, RYE, N.Y. (OR NYU), 1987

His name was Billy Dee. That was his street name. His real name, they said, was Curtis. He wore a Donny Hathaway–style cap, with the brim to the side, a pencil stuck inside it, had a gold tooth, and always had a toothpick in his mouth. That or smoking his Newports.

He was a black man of maybe thirty-five and lived with many kids and, it was said, two wives, in Port Chester, a town on the Long Island Sound between Rye to the south, the kind of place my mother always wanted to live, and Greenwich, Connecticut, to the north, both affluent. Port Chester, I was told, wasn't for some reason, even if it was surrounded by wealth.

Not that I knew. I'd never been there. I was only in Rye to work, summer work, for one of the oldest amusement parks in the country, Playland. People came from everywhere to be at this park, decade after decade, and they were still coming.

The park closed on or around Labor Day but stayed open for some private company events on the adjacent beach or in the parking lot well into September. I was working for one of these events, a weekday, mid-September, 1986, on the boardwalk. Only a few of us were there—either managers or high school dropouts—and me and Billy Dee, driving the forklift. That's what he did, he delivered food from the warehouse under the Dragon Coaster to the various food stands around the park—boxes of hamburger and hot dog buns, beer kegs, CO_2 tanks for the soda, frozen patties, condiments.

When he saw me on this weekday morning two weeks into the new school year, he looked stunned. He walked over to me and pulled me to the side. He lowered his voice and said, in the gravest tone, "Mike, shouldn't you be in school?"

"My school hasn't start yet," I said, touched. "I graduated high school in June and start college next week. It starts later than most schools."

"Oh, good," he said. "That's good. You should be in school. What college are you going to?"

"NYU," I said.

"I've heard of that," he said. "Where is it again?"

"In Manhattan," I said. "Greenwich Village."

"That's right, I've heard of it. Well, good luck with that. I guess we won't see you back next summer."

Julius, my Tanzanian friend from high school, started work at Playland a few months before graduation to earn spending money for Howard University, where he would soon be off to. He told me to come up to Rye and work with him, that it paid four-and-a-quarter an hour and that there was all the overtime you could get with double time after forty hours.

"Sure," I said, and thanked him. I was desperate for money before my freshman year and needed a job, any job. NYU guaranteed me work—that was part of my financial aid package, that I had to hold down a job—but that wouldn't be until the semester began.

My father was tapped out in 1986—it took him months to pay the hotel in Geneva—and it wasn't clear yet how he would come up with the first tuition payments by September. NYU was generous, like Clark was with my sister. They gave me a partial scholarship, the opportunity for a job, and various loan options. I was grateful. But NYU was expensive, damn was it expensive, even with me saving on board by commuting two and a half to three hours a day, depending on connections. I needed to earn.

I started looking for summer work in April and May while still in high school. My father said, "You've got to pound the pavement," so that's what I did. I'd go to Manhattan on Saturday mornings and fill out applications at Barnes & Noble, B. Dalton, and Doubleday book-stores, both Tower Records, Paragon, Crazy Eddie's, the Wiz, Her-man's, Modell's, various Duane Reades. Nothing. Not one phone call. My father knew of a friend, a gambling acquaintance, who worked, or knew someone, at Glen Island Casino in New Rochelle, and told him they might need some kids to work in the kitchen. They did Italian catering-style food, I think. My mother loved this idea. The food busi-ness was practical, *everyone has to eat*, it bought her father his first Chrysler then the house in Smithtown, and it would be worth learning the intricacies of it. But you needed to drive to get to Glen Island. We didn't have a car, and I didn't have a license.

With Julius and Playland, that wasn't an obstacle. He said, *no problem, Mike,* that he'd come pick me up with his father's old Peu-geot, and if I'd get my learner's permit, he'd teach me how to drive.

We worked for the food service, disgusting, overpriced fast food. The staff was almost all black—from the Bronx, Mount Vernon, New Rochelle, and Port Chester—and mostly teenaged. They called me "Nigga Mike" or "Mike Nice." We flipped burgers, boiled hot dogs, fried chicken, and mopped greasy floors for sixty hours a week, some-times seventy, twelve hours a day, six days a week.

When I showed my mother my paychecks, three or four hundred dollars a week, sometimes more, her mouth opened.

"What?" she said. "I think that might be close to what your father gets." Then she paused, and changed her tone. "But I've never seen his paycheck."

I almost didn't get to NYU, or any college.

During my senior year, I had no idea where to go to school. I spoke to a kind, open-minded recruiter from Beloit College in Wisconsin. She was engaging and smart—she seemed to know about everything, even jazz—she almost convinced me to come out for a visit. I would be close to Minnesota and maybe could go to Vikings games. But Wisconsin seemed so far. I promised her that I would apply.

My grades were good, not great, not as good as my sister's, so I couldn't pick and choose. I thought about Clark; it was known for its geography department, and I loved that Britannica Atlas. But studying an atlas, learning the capital cities of unpronounceable countries, wasn't geography. Geography was science and science was mathematical and anything mathematical wasn't going to happen for me. English, history, the arts, music, maybe. Math and science, why bother?

I decided this much: I wanted to stay close to home. I couldn't imagine being away from my parents. My first thought was always this: What would I eat if my mother didn't make it? My mother always liked the thought of Fordham University, first for my sister, who didn't want it, and now for me. My mother didn't like the idea of Catholic education, but for Fordham, she made the exception. *They have good kids who go to Fordham, not these uppity Catholics.* It wasn't all about the drinking, the partying, the fraternities.

My father also liked Fordham. He considered going there after the service, that's what he told us, after he decided to turn down Colgate. *Did Daddy really get into Colgate?* Even now, he gave money to Fordham's radio station, WFUV. They had a swing jazz program once a week and my father would go to his room and turn up the volume, extra loud because of his hearing. He was in heaven. My mother would say, "God dammit, would he lower that, all that screeching. And he talks about rock music?" During and after the radio program, his friend Vito would call, and they would praise, debate, but usually curse the DJ's big-band selections, especially Vito, who some nights flew into a rage. "How could he choose that recording or that version? I'm going to write a letter to the station—better yet, I'll call." He wanted this poor man's head.

"Calm down, Vito," my father said. "And when are you going to come up for dinner? Cora and the kids want to see you." *Why do you still ask, he's never going to come.*

I also listened to the Fordham radio station. Late, every Saturday and Sunday night, they had a sports call-in talk show. *Who ever thought of such a thing?* It was called *One on One*, and two commentators, Fordham students, would discuss the week in sports and take calls from listeners. I never called; I was too nervous.

It ran from eleven at night until two in the morning. My mother thought I was too sports obsessed, she blamed my father for that, but liked that this was on late at night. *They sound like nice fellas, these radio hosts.* It kept me home and in my room, listening. Outside, not that she'd allow me out, there was nothing but trouble. At best, there were guys playing basketball in the wee hours, under the orange strobe over the I.S. 181 basketball courts. Or kids having dance contests in Dreiser Loop, with a boom box on the hood of a car, them practicing their moves, and what moves, moves I hadn't even seen on *Soul Train*, late into the night. That was best case.

I told my parents, "Maybe if I go to Fordham, I might be able to be one of the hosts on the show."

Well, apply there, see what happens, they said. My sister thought it was too close to home. "Don't you want to branch out?" she said, now in an off-campus apartment in Worcester.

I was set to apply to other schools, Rutgers was another, but my first choice was NYU. It was a good school, expensive, but I could take the subway, the QBX1 bus, to the number 6 train, and save on the room and board. Sherman, the Jewish teenager in my building, the one who we ran into at Versailles, *of all places*, went to NYU. He told us, in front of the palace that summer day in 1984, that he was about to start in September. He was so excited. If he could manage it, maybe I could.

There were other schools, some I can't remember, maybe eight in all. But these applications never went out. My father owed my high school back tuition. This was a pattern, from when my sister started there in 1980, through when I graduated in 1986. He always owed them money, he always bounced checks, he was always warned. He never thought they—the headmaster, that's what he called himself, and his wife, *what delusions of grandeur they have, those two*—would do anything vindictive, like expel us, just like he never thought we would ever really get evicted from Co-op City. *I know what I'm doing.*

My mother said to my father, "You better be careful, they may not let Michael graduate."

"They're educators," my father yelled back at her. "They care about educating young people. And I've always paid them. They know that. They'll get their money. I'm not trying to beat anyone."

He was wrong. They didn't expel me, but they said to him, "If we don't get the money by this date, we won't mail out Michael's college applications."

My father thought they were calling his bluff. He'd been through this before, with other potential consequences. *Don't worry about it.* But this time, they weren't bluffing. When my father began to realize this, he had one last option. He turned to Mrs. McIlheney.

Mrs. McIlheney oversaw the school's bookkeeping. If your tuition was late you would get a letter, or a call, from Mrs. McIlheney. My father then had many dealings, and always pleasant ones, with Mrs. McIlheney. She was a middle-aged woman, *from the old school*, who wore conservative skirts and blouses buttoned up to the top. She wore a lot of green. She was very Irish, and, my father found out from these repeated dealings over the years, very Catholic.

My father told my sister and I that when we would see Mrs. McIlheney at school, to be sure to be gracious to her, that she always treated him with dignity, no matter how much he owed or how late his payments were.

When my mother would ask my father, again and again, about how he was going to pay the late tuition, he would say, "Don't worry about it, I spoke to Mrs. McIlheney. It's taken care of."

This time, in his latest fix, I don't know what he said to Mrs. McIlheney. He wouldn't have raised his voice to her, but two of my college applications somehow went out the night before the deadline: NYU and Rutgers; the others, Fordham's, Clark's, Beloit's, didn't.

My father said, "Well at least that. If you don't get in, we'll cross that bridge later. If worse comes to worst, I'll call Fordham myself and tell them it was a money situation that stopped you from applying."

Cross that bridge later?! I thought. *Call Fordham?!* I was upset, worried, but I knew he was upset, that he only wanted the best for me. To kick and scream might make him feel worse. That and maybe provoke another yelling match between my parents, something I was always out to avoid. By now, kicking and screaming weren't even in my nature. I'd learned to live with all this. This was our life.

And it never came to that, the crossing the bridge later. I was accepted to NYU.

I went from Playland one day, from Billy Dee, kids from Mount Vernon High School singing Eric B. and Rakim lyrics, over and over, *I'm not a regular competitor, first-rhyme editor, melody arranger, poet, etcetera,* to NYU the next. Like that.

I felt alone. These NYU students seemed impossible to get to know. Did I even want to get to know them? They seemed older, adult, aloof. Friends were hard to find. There was a guy at the bookstore, where I was assigned for my work-study job, a West Indian full-timer from the Bronx named Jim, who worked in the basement with me unloading the cartons of books. There was the hot-dog-stand guy on the southeast corner of Washington Square Park who was from Romania. We talked about soccer and he snuck me free hot dogs; he couldn't believe anyone, an American, had heard of Steaua Bucharest. And there were three guys in Spanish class. I would study Spanish in college, like my sister. One was an Indian from Queens, another was a Greek from Queens, the other was from the West Side, a WASP who I could've sworn was Jewish. We bonded, for the time being, a little before class, a little after, and then we all had to go home, our separate ways.

My mother told me Sherman, from our building, had left NYU. She ran into him by the elevators and, all excited, said, "Hey guess what? Michael just started NYU. Maybe you'll see him at school." He looked so depressed, she said, not like the excited kid we ran into in

Versailles two years ago. He told her he wasn't there anymore, that he couldn't afford it. She felt for him, told him there were plenty of other good schools. "Too bad," she said to me, "you could've had a friend right there. You could've gone downtown together instead of taking that subway alone."

I felt lost and exhausted. I was at the bookstore twenty hours a week, sometimes more, and that commute. It felt as if all my time was on the subway. *Can't you read on the subway?* Yeah, you could, but you could also fall asleep, right there with Thucydides on your lap. And was it even advisable? You didn't want to look like a book-worm on the subway, especially after twelve noon, when it was empty and no longer ran express from Parkchester to 125th Street. This was the southeast Bronx, Hunts Point, still the days of Fort Apache.

Sometimes I ran into Danny on the QBX1 bus to Pelham Bay Station. He'd say, loudly on the bus, or sometimes in the subway car, "Yo Mike, sup, man?" He was one of the nicest kids in I.S. 181, a good student, an especially good illustrator—he drew superheroes for us—and was interested in the military. In fact, he'd be joining the paratroopers next year. He couldn't wait. Until then, he was taking classes in Manhattan.

It wasn't likely that anyone would bother Danny on the subway. He may have been a sweet kid, but he was big and athletic. He was the fastest runner in our grade. That said a lot, because a lot of us were fast. I was fast, but some of these kids were another kind of fast. About Danny, they said, "Man, that nigga can book." His brother played for the Co-op City Rams, a football team, the only club team in the area. They had the same uniforms as the Los Angeles Rams and if you wore one of the Rams jackets around Co-op City, it meant you were a member, past or present, of the team, that you were a badass. My friend Calvin had played for a year or two, cornerback. Ravi and I went to one of the games at a worn-out field in Mount Vernon. But he didn't play much; he said the coach didn't like him.

Danny would ask me on the subway, "So who do you see from 181?"

No one, I said. A couple of years ago, I told him, when I spent the summers practicing soccer in the Truman High School field by myself, I'd see three kids from our grade, all classmates at one time or another in junior high: Duncan, Ray, and Julio. They all were members of the Truman football team, and they started practice, in pads, in August. When I saw them for the first time every summer, we hugged. *Yo, what up, Mike?* We were all in sixth grade together, laughed in swimming class together, and had gym together.

Ray's mother worked for the rental office in Co-op City. My father often had to speak to her over the phone, or in person, to buy more time to pay the rent. "It's all taken care of—she's a very dignified lady," he'd come back and say. When he would send me to drop off a check, she'd ask, "How's your daddy?"

"He's good," I'd say. "And how's Ray Ray? Tell him I said, 'What's up.' "

"He's good. I will, honey."

Ray knew we were late with the rent every month, he must've, but he never said anything about it in school, in front of anyone, or to me alone. He pretended he didn't know.

On the field, after their practice, we joked about how hot it was, that they were sweating in pads and I was in soccer shorts, and who of the boys from Section 5 had I seen. "None really," I said. "I don't go to five anymore." Section 5 was the worst part of Co-op City and wasn't getting any better.

"Word," they said, and handed me the garden hose that they drank out of.

Then they told me they were headed to the Marines after graduation.

"Word?" I said. "That's good, but be careful. My boy Calvin went in two years ago, but his drill instructor didn't like him. They might not like guys from New York."

They said they would be careful, and that they'd see me around Co-op City, after boot camp, around by the supermarket.

During my first year of college, '86–'87, I had no more friends in Co-op City. Calvin was out of the Marines and out of touch. He wrote letters at the beginning, in envelopes that said UNITED STATES MARINE CORPS with an illustration of the Iwo Jima scene, return address, Parris Island, South Carolina. I kept those letters. Right away he became a sharpshooter, he wrote, hitting targets with M-16s from hundreds of yards away.

On his first visit back, he said, "Here, I have something for you," and he handed me his thick Marine guidebook, in olive green camouflage, with his name written on the inside cover in black Magic Marker. It gave directions on how to take apart and put together an M-16, how to do proper sit-ups, how to use your gas mask.

"Oh, wow," I said. "You serious?"

"Yeah, man, I want you to have it."

"Yo, thanks, man." I kept his letters inside that book. He said next time he came back he'd try to bring me a shelf.

"What's a shelf?"

"That's what we call hats in the Marines." He showed me his tattoo, his first, of a devil dog. And he told me stories about how he was the best in his platoon but still wasn't promoted to private first class, how pissed off he was.

He visited one more time in the early months of 1985. I think he just rang our intercom from the lobby. We had just finished eating dinner. My mother said, "Hey, come on up."

We all gave him a big hello. My father said, "Sit down, let's have a drink." He poured us all a brandy and we toasted. Calvin had a car with him, and said, "C'mon, Mike, let's go for a drive, to the movies or something."

So we did, we drove around with nowhere to go. It was snowing, and we ended up at The Whitestone Cinemas in the east Bronx, next to Saint Raymond's Cemetery, where my father's father was buried. It used to be a drive-in movie theater and now was a generic multiplex. It was between a comedy, I can't remember which one, and *The Killing Fields*. I said, "Let's see *The Killing Fields*, it's kind of a war movie."

Calvin slept through the whole thing, and when he drove me home, that was the last time I saw him.

Months later, I saw Ravi by the elevators. We weren't close anymore but would still chat when we saw each other.

"Any word from Calvin?" I asked

"Oh, I guess he never told you?"

"Tell me what?"

"He was discharged from the Marines. He mentioned to me that he came up to your house and your parents were there, and he was too embarrassed to tell you."

"Really?" I said. "Shit. That's too bad. Why? I mean why was he discharged?"

"He didn't really say, but said he was having problems with alcohol." Ravi paused. "Yeah, and he said, your father gave him a drink that night, and that he wasn't supposed to take it."

"Man," I said. "Well, where is he now?"

"I'm not sure," Ravi said. "He said he might move to D.C."

When freshman year of NYU ended, I wasn't sure what to make of it. My grades weren't very good, my bookstore job paid for books and carfare and McDonald's, but not much else. I'd gotten locked out of classes in the spring '87 semester since my father couldn't pay on time. Registration, late registration, was a long nightmare, going from one line to the next, being told that they had to have at least this amount, and that no we will no longer accept a personal check from your father, too many had bounced.

I was angry at him. This was embarrassing, and enervating, but I also felt guilty. I wasn't producing, I wasn't keeping up. I was so tired, I was sleeping on the subway in the morning. Maybe this was a mistake coming to school here.

He knew I was upset, but said, "Look, I'm sorry, but work with me here. Don't be angry with me."

I just nodded. He didn't have to apologize, I thought. He still got me here. And I knew life was getting harder for him. The '86 Mets, a miracle for everyone else in the city, was a disaster for him. He needed the Red Sox. Game Six for us was like a funeral, rock bottom. Our stock-market crash. My childhood team, the team I happily cheered all those losing years, became a powerhouse and I couldn't root for them. They weren't lovable losers anymore but cocky, my father thought insufferable, my mother thought arrogant, *and there's nothing I can't stand more than arrogance.* And they were arrogant, cocky, and insufferable, but they were still my team, and now I couldn't support them. I couldn't go against my father. The Mets weren't going to pay the rent or NYU or the phone, which would be turned off every few months. *What if there's an emergency, what the hell are we supposed to do?*

But it wasn't just Game Six. The whole year leading up to the pennant and World Series, my father would yell more and more over the phone, at the top of his lungs, sometimes: "Ned, I said I can't pay! I don't have it!" That we'd heard before, but then we heard him yell this: "Oh yeah? Then do what you gotta do!" I'd come out of my bedroom, where I was studying, worried. Was a threat made? My mother would be standing there, as worried as I was.

"Close your door," she said. "Otherwise the neighbors might hear." She paused. "God, things are getting worse."

"What can I do?" I asked.

"There's nothing you can do."

During the summer of '87, I had no options. And I had to make as much money as possible. Julius wouldn't be going back to Rye Playland. He was transferring from Howard University to a college in Dar es Salaam, his home country.

But my boss from the amusement park called me. He was a nervous Italian guy, always on edge, early forties, with beard and glasses who only went out with black women, and made a point of telling everyone. He hated his job, and worse, was in constant fear of losing it. He wondered out loud what went wrong in his life that he was supervising teenagers deep-frying five different types of food. The only good thing about it was that there were young, pretty black women who worked there.

He asked me if I would come back to the park as a supervisor, it would be something like $5.50 an hour, all kinds of overtime. He said the Forresters would be back, four Jamaican brothers who managed to be both conscientious and funny, and a guy a few years older than I whom he referred to as Mr. Glenn, a brilliant student at SUNY-Purchase who quoted Kant and was one of the few other whites who worked for the food service.

He asked me if I drove yet. I said no, I didn't have a car. He said I shouldn't worry, that he or one of the Forresters would come get me every day.

I said yes, and thanked him.

"Playland—again," my sister said. "You should've tried for an internship somewhere. Rye Playland, yeah, the money might be good, but what are you learning? A lot of college kids, even sophomores now, they get internships and build their résumés."

My sister had been out in the world. She had done an unpaid internship in Costa Rica for a reforestation program after she graduated Clark University. She learned Spanish, double-majored in Spanish and government, and had studied abroad for a semester in Segovia, Spain. She wrote that I must do this, study abroad, when the time came.

I said okay, but where was I supposed to intern? And the money, yeah, I needed money. We needed money.

What I didn't tell her is that I was learning something: I was learning how to drive. I was a supervisor this second summer; I wasn't tied down to one food stand. I roamed from stand to stand, made sure all was running properly, collected cash from the register, and deposited it into the safe. And I'd go to the warehouse, sometimes to pick up supplies or just to talk to the guys.

Billy Dee said, "Sup, Mike. I'm surprised. You're back."

When it wasn't busy, they let me drive the forklift. Billy taught me and so did a guy named Juan, a Puerto Rican guy, bright, salt-of-the-earth, from the Bronx. My boss, he didn't mind that I didn't have a license. "Who's gonna know?"

I asked them, "If I can drive a forklift, do you think I could pass a road test?" They said yes, if you can drive this, it means you know the basics, and you'll probably pass a road test. That alone made it worth it.

My last two memories of Playland weren't even at Playland. The 1987 summer season had ended. It was in those weeks after Labor Day and before the NYU semester began, when I was still able to work at the park for special catered events.

My boss called me on the phone, excited and panicked one weekday afternoon.

"Mike," he said, "what are you doing tonight?"

"Ah, nothing," I said. "I'll be home. Everything all right?"

"Yeah—say, you wanna help me out tonight and make some money?"

"Yeah, I guess. What did you have in mind?"

"I don't know if I ever told you this, but our company is also responsible for the food service at Jones Beach Theater. You ever been there?"

"No."

"Doesn't matter. Anyway, they have an event tonight, a concert. You like James Brown?"

"James Brown? You mean *the* James Brown?"

"That's right, the Godfather of Soul James Brown."

"Yeah, I like James Brown."

"Well my boss, the regional director, needs three people—me to supervise, a guy to work the beer tap, and a guy to sell hot dogs. And, this is the best, you'll get a hundred bucks for the night, probably for three hours' work."

"Well, can I do the beer?"

"Can't. For this, I need someone older. But, Mike, all you have to do is stand there and put hot dogs in the water, take 'em out, and put them in the buns. You'll have one of the umbrellas, like a hot dog stand. Whattaya say? C'mon Mike, I really need you. And it's for the Godfather of Soul."

"Yeah, okay."

"Great, Mike, I'll be in Co-op in two hours, be in front of your building."

And there he was, his beard trimmed, with a clean white collared shirt, pressed, with a sport jacket. He had a co-worker of ours, a few years older than I, in the front seat. They both started howling like James Brown.

"Look at you," I said to my boss. "You look good. Why—I mean—"

"You mean why do I look presentable tonight," he said.

"No, no, that's not what I meant, I meant—"

"It's okay, Mike. But you should know why."

"I don't know, are you going to try to meet James Brown?" I said.

"No," he said, "they won't let us near him. We're only the food service. We won't even see most of the concert. Think, Mike."

"I give up."

"Black women," he said. "There'll be hundreds, thousands, of beautiful black women at this concert."

"Oh, right. But won't you be too busy?" I said.

"You never know," he said. "It can't hurt to look nice."

When we got there, something didn't seem right; there were no black people.

"I didn't know all these white people liked James Brown," he said.

"Yeah, everyone likes James Brown," I said. "My mother likes James Brown."

"Yeah, but—"

"We're early," I said. "Most people won't get here for a while."

Then we saw a sign. TONIGHT: JAMES TAYLOR, 8:00 P.M.

"James Taylor?" my boss said.

"But I thought you said—"

"Yeah, yeah, it's supposed to be James Brown," he said.

He asked one of the parking attendants who was performing that night.

"James Taylor."

"No!" said my boss. "You mean James Brown, right?"

"No, James *Taylor*."

"Who told you it was going it be James Brown?" I asked.

"My boss," he said. "The regional director. You mean I volunteered to come all the way out here—"

"Well, at least you'll get the night's pay," I said, trying to console him.

"No, you guys get the night's pay, I'm on salary." Then he cursed his life, his luckless life, and disappeared into an amphitheater of James Taylor fans, not a black woman in sight.

To me, they couldn't have been nicer. They bought overpriced hot dogs, thanked me, and even tipped. Then I felt two feet tall. Standing on my line was someone I knew: my twelfth-grade high school English teacher.

I'd never been any teacher's pet, for whatever reason, except maybe for two, my eleventh- and twelfth-grade English teachers. The first came from Harvard, like our "headmaster." She taught as if she was from a different planet, with great verve, compassion, and generosity. She forced us to think. Our tenth-grade English teacher gave us Agatha Christie mysteries—and told us not to tell anyone.

Now this new teacher had us reading *The Catcher in the Rye*. I told her this was the greatest book I'd ever read. She said I had good taste. She asked us to interpret lyrics to a song, "though some would say it's a poem," she said. "You might know it." I didn't recognize it. Why couldn't it be "Winter in America." I found out later it was "The Sound of Silence."

She taught us *The Great Gatsby* and gave us an assignment, an odd one we thought, to write a dialogue between Daisy and Gatsby where Fitzgerald ended chapter five, with the two of them alone. Some students wrote things, like "I love you, Daisy" or "But I love you, Gatsby." I didn't write any dialogue, but continued the silence and wrote of glance and gesture, and left it at that. When I finished, the room was quiet and finally she said, "Michael, that is the silence of admiration." I'd never received such a compliment, before or since.

Then, like that, she announced she was leaving the school, that it was a pleasure teaching us but she could not work for him, "the headmaster," and she was so sorry to abandon us like that, in the middle of the school year. It was devastating. She was like no teacher I'd ever had; it felt as if my father's money, the money he didn't have, was being well spent. Now she was gone.

Her replacement was a pretty young woman, who we eventually warmed up to. She challenged us and brought great depth to her subject, classical drama: *Antigone, Oedipus Rex, Oedipus at Colonus.* At graduation, she gave me a gift, in front of everyone, a framed picture of a trombone; she knew I liked jazz. I was deeply embarrassed.

"Wow," my friends Julius and Jeff said. "What's that about?"

"I dunno, man," I said. "How should I know?"

And there she was on line to buy a hot dog from me, under my umbrella, before the James Taylor concert. She had told me at graduation that NYU was a good choice for me, that downtown New York would be, too. I wasn't so convinced, but she assured me. Now, here I was, fifteen months later, hawking hot dogs under an umbrella, with a primary-colored fast-food polo shirt. As I smeared mustard on a frankfurter and thanked another genteel James Taylor fan, I looked out from the corner of my eye and saw her dart away from the line. She must have seen me. She had nothing to be embarrassed about; she was only there for James Taylor. She was embarrassed, I knew, for me. The hundred bucks, plus the tips, wasn't worth it.

My last memory of Playland was really one of Co-op City. It was my last day in the park, and Juan from the warehouse offered to drive me home. He lived deeper in the Bronx, and Co-op City was on his way. He looked tough but was pleasant, intelligent, easy to talk to. We chatted and promised to keep in touch. Playland wasn't going to be his future. When he pulled up to De Kruif Place, he slowed down, looked up at three buildings in the loop, and said to me, "Okay, Mike, where should I stop? Which one is your project?"

I was stunned, and paused. *Project? You mean my mother was right?* "This one right here," I said, "on the right."

CO-OP CITY (RIGHT DOWNSTAIRS), 1988

They were just hanging out, doing nothing. That's what one of the friends, if you could call them that, told the district attorney. "Everybody was just hanging out, pretty much doing nothing." They played music. They drank beer or Bacardi. "I was high, on my way to get loose," one said. And they played dice. They were twenty, twenty-one, twenty-two years old, my age more or less.

And here came Rodney. He strolled over from Building 12, arm and arm with a woman, not the mother of his child, but his latest woman, Lauren, one they didn't all recognize, his boom box slung across his body with a strap, like a messenger bag. He had intense eyes, a strong, compact body, trendy acid-wash jeans, and heavy boots, even if the night had an early September balm to it.

She had a bad day; he, a perfectly fine one. He worked in Co-op City, for the cable company. He took drugs, everything except heroin, his boy said, but was sober. She wanted to go out for a walk, to clear her head. He didn't want her to go alone, Co-op being what it was, so he met her downstairs at ten-thirty and they ended up here, in the back of Building 6, my building.

She was black. He was black—light-skinned—but sounded white. Most of the crowd was white, and Puerto Rican, but some wanted to be black. That, or they weren't quite sure anymore.

She didn't know his real name, she told the police, just his street name: Ticky. He was the one with the dice, two red, one green, and showed them all, the twelve or fifteen of them, how to play a game called "high-lo." She said she knew Ticky from the street, as one of Rod's friends, that he was always there, hanging out. That he was into his beer and that's about it. She said: "He's your present-day hippie."

Rod greeted everyone and then went about the job of doing nothing with the gathered acquaintances. After forty-five minutes of nothingness, he snapped. Ticky was buzzed and unsteady and nearly toppled on Rod's girlfriend. Maybe you should watch it, Ticky might have said to her—no one could quite hear exactly what he said. Something like that.

"With Rod, and his being a man, and his pride, he just didn't feel like what was said about me was correct. But I don't know what was said—I have no idea what was said."

Maybe you should never talk to a woman of mine like that ever again, Rod said back. Then a powerful punch was thrown to Ticky's head. He collapsed to the ground, head banging on a small square of all of the famous Co-op City concrete.

Ticky was unconscious and helpless. They tried pulling Rod off, grabbed him by the strap of his boom box, but he pushed them away, flailing, raging. They thought they were next. His friend Marc tried to grab him. He said, "Yo, this is Marc, cool out. What are you doing?" Rodney said, "Get the fuck out of my face." He punched Ticky again and again in his head—loud punches, said Hector, like a punching bag. And then he delivered a final blow: a powerful kick to the head, so powerful, the prosecutor said, that it dislocated his head from his body, that it ruptured a vein in his neck.

"He, like . . . he just, like, bugged out."

Lauren saw the kick coming, the woman the others hardly knew. "I was, like, screaming. I probably woke up Co-op City."

Johnny Carson was on, and I heard a scream. It didn't wake me up; I was already up, my mother was, too. We watched *The Tonight Show* on separate TVs, me in my room, which overlooked the scene at an obtuse angle, twenty-two stories above, and my mother in the living room. I'd just finished the summer working for the same boss, this time for the food concessions at the Jacob Javits Convention Center. It wasn't a fun job, like Rye Playland. We weren't all teenagers, with all the overtime we could get, still with a future. At the Javits food service the people were older, twenties, thirties, forties, fifties, working for minimum wage or close to it, and only when there were events. They seemed angry—*could you blame them*. I would come home depressed.

My junior year of NYU was just beginning—and I was glad. I was going to force myself to try out for that student newspaper, no matter how much it intimidated me. This night in September, I was home reading, with *The Tonight Show* on in the background. In the room next to mine, within the same earshot, my father was sleeping. Even if he wasn't sleeping, and hadn't been hard of hearing, he would've chosen not to hear. If there were screaming or sirens or Run-DMC pumping or what sounded like the occasional gunshot (*was that a gunshot?*), he'd learned to block it out. My mother said he used his hearing problem, his handicap, to his advantage.

All this was happening down the left-field line, straight below my window, the square concrete-and-dirt plot that we transformed into our punchball field. It had a wall, just for left field, that was about 70 feet from home base. Most of the kids in 1975 could punch the ball—we used a "super pinky," the Spaldine of my father's generation mostly passé by then—over the wall for a home run, so much so that we often stationed an extra outfielder in the grass patch above the wall, where Ticky was now being pummeled, to negate easy home runs.

Hitting the super pinky over the wall was a big moment for anyone in our group. When the day finally came for my first home run, it took me years, my arms were so skinny, I was lifted on someone's shoulders around the bases, the happiest day of my life then. That was 1977.

After the scream, and the kick, Rod said to everyone, to those he had pleasantly greeted earlier: "When he wakes up, just tell him don't nobody say anything like that to my girl again or I'll kill him. And you tell him that Rod did this to him." Then he stormed under my building and its maze of pillars—our "slap ball" and "running bases" court all those years ago—out toward the vast open space of the Greenway, to Building 16, Building 18, then home eventually.

Photos of the crime scene showed this: A crumpled-up box of Marlboro Reds; an empty forty-ounce bottle lying gently on the grass; the dice; the bottle of Bacardi; a puddle of blood; and a pair of white leather Pumas with a blue strip. Other than that, it looked like the word most often used to describe Co-op City—quiet. Here, in this patch of green, above the wall, we played another game called British Bulldog, where one kid would have to tackle as many of the others as possible to convert them to his team, until there remained only one, the victor. Some kids called it British Bullshit. When I was sick, and couldn't come down—*can little Mike come down? No, he's sick today*—sometimes I could hear them yell, "British Bulldog!" *British Bullshit!* If my fever wasn't too high, I'd watch from my window.

At Jacobi Hospital, they worked on Ticky for three hours. But the laceration of the aorta, of the lungs, everything else, the fracture to the left eye, the crushed trachea, the acute subarachnoid hemorrhage, the subluxation of the anthro-occipital joint—nothing could be done.

A rumor circulated: Someone, someone from outside Co-op City, just walked up to Ticky and beat him. "Whoever said that is a big liar from the Jump Street," Lauren told the police. "Everyone that hangs out in Co-op City is usually from Co-op City. That was something to give Rod time to get himself together and leave town."

Rod's friend Melvin wasn't there that night; he stayed home and watched a movie. "Man, what happened?" he said to Rodney. "Ticky is dead. The cops are going to be looking for you—you better run, get out of town." Rod said: "Where am I going to go? I don't have any money."

I had met Rod before. Nearly in the same spot. In the back of my building, Building 6. Someone I went to high school with, who lived several buildings away, seemingly a different world away, couldn't make sense of the music I listened to. "You must listen to what Rod listens to," he said. "You should meet him." So there was an introduction, after one of my high school soccer games. I saw his intense, maybe diabolical, eyes, his disconcerting gaze. He didn't sound like the other black kids I was surrounded with in Co-op, ones who I tried to sound like. He sounded like the son of a Harlem schoolteacher he was.

"Allan Holdsworth," he said to me, "you must like Allan Holdsworth."

"Nah, never heard of him," I said. "More into the 'seventies Miles stuff these days. *Agharta. Pangea.*"

"Oh," he said, "you got to check out Holdsworth. I can lend you some albums."

I said, "Okay, yeah, let's do that, but, man, I'm beat right now—I just had a game. I need a shower and my bed."

He said, "Okay, I'll see you again."

That was a year before he would slash an off-duty cop with a knife—a four-inch gash—because of a woman, and a year before he dangled outside the side of his building, outside the twelfth-story balcony, like Spiderman, manipulating one of Co-op City's skyscrapers, and was sent to the psychiatric ward at Jacobi Hospital. *Keep those windows closed.* And three years before now, pounding the life out of someone.

My sister knew Ticky, but she never knew him by this name. She just knew him as John, a classmate, from K through 8 at P.S. 178 and I.S. 181. They were the same age, in the same grade, sometimes in the same class, in which case I'd see him in the annual class picture, always a shaggy-haired kid, nice enough. He never picked on my sister, she said. He had a brother, maybe a year apart. They looked like twins.

When we learned who'd been beaten to death, we couldn't believe it. *Was that the kid who was in your class? Or was that the brother?* I knew that I knew the killer but didn't say, not to my mother. *How come it wasn't bigger news? How come no one was talking about it?* Or maybe they were. Did anyone talk in Co-op City anymore? Or did they just pretend bad things didn't happen? Or did they live on the other side of our massive thirty-three-story building and face the other direction—the Greenway, Buildings 16, 18, on and on—and just hadn't heard the screaming, her screaming, his raging?

And when the sirens arrived from the Forty-fifth Precinct, the Co-op City Security patrol cars, the ambulance bound for Jacobi, the streets of Dreiser Loop and Defoe Place and the patch of grass with a sandbox where we played British Bulldog and punchball lit up in white and blue and red light, swirling. My mother looked down from our balcony. She said: "We've gotta get out of here. But where're we going to go? We've got no money, no nothing."

So much for Utopia.

ATLANTIC CITY, 1989

We took the bus to Atlantic City. "This is the first time I've been out of Manhattan or the Bronx in four years," my mother said. "Since we went to Switzerland." We went for Mother's Day. Why, I'm not sure. Because we'd never been, to spend an afternoon away, maybe enjoy its garishness. It was Sunday, but it was easier for my father to take the afternoon off these days. His bookmaking business was dwindling; the phones didn't ring like they used to. He had claimed Chapter 11, finally. There wasn't the cloak of shame surrounding it that there once was. But it was his street credit, or lack of it, that kept his business stagnant. He'd lost good customers because he didn't have the ready cash to pay them within a reasonable amount of time—and didn't have the associates anymore who could lend him that money. His talent for juggling money, juggling debt, had abandoned him. And there was still another year of NYU to pay—even if it was just a percentage, it was more than he could afford.

We'd heard about Atlantic City so often, neighbors in Co-op City raved about it. Except for my father, in another lifetime, on the way back from a prizefight in Philadelphia—Joey Giardello vs. Sugar Ray Robinson, now *abunam'* Sugar Ray Robinson since he'd just passed away—we'd only seen it on TV. And the movies. My parents loved *Atlantic City* with Burt Lancaster and Susan Sarandon. *Look at that, it took a Frenchman to make a great film about America.*

There wasn't much to do there, unless you liked the tables, and none of us did, not even my father. Oh, he tried. *You never know.* But he didn't like gambling dens, except La Concha, in San Juan, and that was more out of obligation with his gambling clients, the closest my father came to a business trip. But it had been seven years since he last went. Here, like there, he went to the blackjack tables—just for a laugh. The three of us, with the few bucks we had and what the bus company gave us, went to the slots. I should have had more courage and learned one of the casino games; it's what guys are supposed to do. But why tempt addiction. I took the easy way out and gave my coins to the slots. I lost; it was quick and painless. The same for my mother and sister. "Just my luck," my mother said.

"Where's Daddy?" my sister asked.

"Maybe he got lucky," I said.

"Yeah, right," my mother said.

Then we saw him, with a big smile on his face. "You wouldn't believe it," he said. He was up, he got hot, what a streak he had, where were we, we should've seen it. Then he lost it. He said he should've quit while he was ahead.

"The story of his life," my mother said to us quietly.

"But then I won a few hands, enough for dinner. We'll drink a good Bordeaux tonight."

That afternoon in Atlantic City was the only place we went that year, or any year since 1985. No Europe, no Caribbean, no Canada, not even Smithtown. "Never again," my mother had said, and she meant it.

To get some air one warm afternoon, my mother took a walk to shopping center number two, in another section of Co-op City. She took the walking and bicycle path. It was always said Co-op City was quiet. But at what point too quiet? No one was around. Some black teenagers, two or three of them, they didn't surround her, but they followed. *They were up to no good.* She got scared. Then she heard one of them say, "Hey, white bitch." Now she was really scared. A few months earlier a woman was brutally raped and left for dead in Central Park by a gang of teenagers. It was the story of the year in the City, so far. "Wilding," the press called it. My mother talked about the case with our neighbor, Beverly, who was black. She said to my mother: "What was this white girl doing jogging in Central Park anyway? Everyone knows it's not safe."

My mother didn't know what to say. She herself hadn't been to Central Park since the late '60s or early '70s. She had what seemed to me an irrational fear of Central Park and used to tell me, "Never go into Central Park, you'll get killed." And I listened. I didn't go into the park. But she also thought people should be able to use the park, *like when I was courting your father.* And apparently people were trying to use it, people did jog there, even if my mother wouldn't dream of it. So my mother said to our neighbor, "Yeah, but still," and she left it at that. How, she thought, could anyone make excuses for those kids.

Now, someone appeared out of the quietness of the Co-op City Greenway, where political candidates—mayors, governors—would land every four years via helicopter, then fly out an hour later. Whoever this person was, they were enough of a presence, and close enough, to get my mother to the next building where there was more activity. When she turned around the teenagers were gone.

When my father got home, she told him. She was still shaken. He said for the first time, "We have to get out of here," and meant it. *But where?*

In August, we read this in our *New York Times*: "Co-op City: A Haven Marred as Drugs Enter." It said all these things, most that we knew, some that we didn't want to believe. It said the obvious, "Carrying charges have increased and construction defects in the massive apartment complex have multiplied."

Our building, like so many of the others, had trenches dug out all around it to repair pipes. *That's what you get when you build on landfill.* This had been ongoing for ten years. I may have seen Ravi only by the elevators these days, but my main memory of him, of all things, was not the gun, not walking onto the bus through the back entrance, not our trips to Fordham Road for sneakers, but he and I with buckets and pots stuffed inside our mothers' shopping carts, going downstairs and waiting on a line fifty or a hundred yards long on De Kruif Place, in our loop, to get water from the fire hydrant. This was seven or eight years before. There was no water, hot or cold. We were told it was because of the repair work and that this was the only way to get water.

My mother refused to go down; it was too humiliating to wait on line for water from a fire hydrant. My mother looked from the window, saw this serrated human line, and said, "Would you look at this, it's like the Soviet Union." Ravi's mother must have felt the same way.

So about repairs we knew. We knew about the parquet floors, how they would buckle from condensation leaks in the central air-conditioning system, how unsightly that looked.

We kept reading the *Times* article. It quoted our congressman, Eliot Engel: "The people who live in Co-op City are the backbone of American society." I remember seeing Engel every morning. He lived in another section in Co-op City, but when my school bus to New Rochelle Academy, the half school bus we were so embarrassed to be seen in, made its rounds, one stop we made was for Eliot Engel's daughter. He was in the State Assembly, and he put her on the bus every morning. For whatever reason, he didn't want to send his daughter to school with the backbone of American society.

He said in the article that the people of Co-op City "get up in the morning, go to work, and do the same thing the next day." Maybe we were the backbone of American society, but he didn't say that we didn't count to New York society. He didn't say that we didn't matter, that we were beside the point. Except when they wanted votes.

The article quoted the president of the Black Forum of Co-op City, a residents civic group, who said he saw dozens of crack vials outside his building. "I stopped counting at thirty-two," he said.

It said Jesse Jackson won nearly 50 percent of the vote in Co-op City the year before in the Democratic primary. It quoted a young, thirty-two-year-old black father, who had three cars stolen in four years—out of the garages. He had an eleven-month-old and said, "Because of her, I'm considering leaving New York. It's just no place to raise a kid these days."

And it quoted the inscription from a man's T-shirt, a seventy-two-year-old postal worker's. He was white; it had his picture. His T-shirt read: LIFE MAY NOT BE THE PARTY WE HOPED FOR, BUT WHILE WE'RE HERE, WE SHOULD DANCE.

Dance? I'll take Paris. Or Amsterdam.

Two weeks later, we heard the news, like everyone else in the city, on TV, one of the local eleven o'clock newscasts. A black teenager had been shot to death in Brooklyn, Bensonhurst. He was there to buy a used car; a gang of whites thought he was someone else, the new boyfriend of a neighborhood girl. Her ex, half-Italian, half-Jewish on the mother's side—had anyone reported that?—rounded up twenty-five guys and the black kid was shot to death. An innocent kid was dead and the media was loving it. The circus was back in town.

"Oh, Madon'," my father said, "not again." Something similar had happened three years before in Howard Beach, Queens.

Then he said, "Let's hope they're not Italian kids."

The kids arrested were Italian American.

"You know what this is going to do?" my mother said. "It's going to cost Giuliani the election." The Democratic primary was in a few weeks, the mayoral election soon after. My mother liked Giuliani. "The city could use him," she said. "He's practical and he's tough." *But he'll never get in.*

My father liked him, too—thought he was smart, competent—but not without ambivalence. When Rudy Giuliani was a U.S. attorney, he put away Fat Tony Salerno, the boss from East Harlem. *Not to make excuses for these guys*, but Fat Tony had done my father a favor a few years before. He owed money, my father did, *nineteen big*, to shylocks under Fat Tony's jurisdiction. He couldn't go to Fat Tony personally but he still knew Fish, Fat's close associate. My father knew Fish from the neighborhood since the 1940s, when he was just a teenager. He liked Fish. *Believe me when I tell you, he wasn't a pay-or-die type. You could reason with him.* He went to East Harlem, asked around, and found him. It wasn't hard. He explained the situation to Fish, who was understanding and said he'd talk to Fat Tony. He secured him an audience with the boss.

My father once saw him on the street, in the mid-1970s, walking alone by chance, outside Max's Kansas City, the rock club on Park Avenue South and Seventeenth Street. My father didn't know what to do; he knew of him, but didn't know him. So he nodded. Fat Tony nodded back.

Now, for his meeting, my father spent just a few minutes with him, *he wouldn't have even remembered, it was insignificant to him*, and was absolved, not of the principal, but of the massive, accumulated interest. He wouldn't be touched. End of story.

When Fish turned state's evidence against his boss, Giuliani took over. Fat Tony was sent away, and Fish disappeared into Witness Protection. But how do you not forget a favor like that? *This Giuliani, he's by the book, boy. He's ambitious.*

The media couldn't get enough of Bensonhurst. We, the four of us, not even my father, had ever been there, but we somehow felt, not responsible, definitely not responsible, but both kinship and embarrassment. Shouldn't someone in the media circus contextualize this? If not a TV reporter, then a writer? Did we even have a respected writer at a respected publication?

My mother didn't like Italian neighborhoods, only her own, Bushwick, from the '40s and '50s. And even then it was love-hate. When my father used to tell my sister and me stories of the old days—of East Harlem and *abunam'* Bence and his famous saying, "All you need is a thousand a week," though now it would be two thousand—he'd say, especially to me, "Oh, you would have loved my neighborhood. It was a wonderful experience, a cauldron of life." My mother would sneer, and say, "Those Neapolitans in East Harlem, they were street urchins."

She could say it, the way he could say the Brooklyn Sicilian wise guys were depraved, without the acumen, without the vision of the Neapolitans uptown. Only brute force.

My mother could say, about this, now unfolding before us in Bensonhurst: "This is why Italians never get ahead. Where were their parents? Don't they supervise their kids." My father could agree: "What were they doing out in the street, marauding."

They could say it, in front of us, in our house, but it was different when someone else said it. Not the media, not this circus of hypocrisy and double standards.

A few nights later, my father brought home the newspapers, the *Times* and *Post*, as he always had, and said, "Would you get a load of this?" It was a column in the *New York Post* titled: "The Lesson of Howard Beach Was Lost on the Punks of Guidoville."

We read it aloud at the dinner table, taking turns:

"The Guido decides early that homework is for jerks. So is work. . . . Go to a library? Read a book? Finish high school? Go to a university? Figget abo't it! Om gonna go work construkshun, eight bills an hour!"

"Oh, God, that's vicious," my mother said.

There was more: "Ey, wah, ming, mah. . . . I like to get some a dat. . . . Whassamatta wit you, Joonyuh. . . . I truckin' tole huh, I says to huh, I says, I dough wan no truckin' backtawk, and den I slap huh in da truckin' mout', I mean, in the mout', cause dat's all a trucking broad respects, a rap in da mout. . . . Huh mudthuh tells huh to be home oirly, says to huh, Who you truckin' gonna listen ta, ya truckin' mudthuh aw me? Mah. . . ."

"Is that really in print?" my mother asked.

My father said: "I don't believe he wrote that. Or that they published it. I don't believe it."

These were the words of Pete Hamill. My parents liked Pete Hamill. He was a real New Yorker, like them, Brooklyn, kept a trace of his accent, *no one gave him anything on the arm*, an Irish Catholic, perhaps a little lapsed, but who among us wasn't? They liked his writing, his sense of place, his outlook. So from him it hurt even more. It wasn't some young up-and-comer who was trying to make a name for himself or some rabble-rouser. It was Pete Hamill, one of us. So what if he mentioned Lennie Tristano?

My parents were somewhere between devastated, almost in tears, then apoplectic. "Hamill, that son of a bitch," they said. "What about people like us?"

They had always said that the word *guido* was a new, accepted way of saying *guinea* or *dago*, that it shouldn't be tolerated. It didn't matter what they thought. The word was now part of the vernacular; what could we say? If we didn't like it, too bad for us.

This was 1989. Billy Martin died on Christmas Day.

PENNSYLVANIA STATION

PART IV

THE 1990s

If you want to know what God thinks of money, just look at the people he gave it to.

—Dorothy Parker

NEW YORK, N.Y., 1992

In January 1991, on the eve of war, I had to look for a job. My father said, as he had before: "You've got to get out there and pound the pavement."

"Daddy, nobody pounds the pavement anymore," my sister said. "It's through connections, networking. Pounding the pavement, that was the old days."

"Never mind," he said. "He's got to go out and hustle."

My sister was right. I ended up at a magazine, a famous one, a good one, sometimes a great one, because I knew someone. I made a connection.

I finished NYU a semester late, December 1990. Slowly, I began to enjoy it there. My high school English teacher was right: It was a good place for me. I couldn't have imagined going anywhere else. It changed, slowly, with a sophomore writing instructor, a young woman, a graduate student, a few years older than us, who said I was good at something. Mazzola was the last name, but she said to us, "Just call me Liz." She entered something I wrote into a writing contest. *Who me?* She took us to see Earth Room in a SoHo gallery. *Now write about it.* My parents took me to museums, all over the world, but this was my first time in a SoHo gallery. She had us read this recent novel called *Bright Lights, Big City*, my new favorite book, with Odeon on the cover, the Odeon that my father worked a couple of blocks from, that he always talked about, but never entered. This expository writing teacher, a graduate student, started it.

If a *New York* magazine writer who taught in the journalism school, who everyone was eager to impress, didn't know who I was or referred to me as "Gideon," another adjunct was there to say, "You should major in this."

Major—but would I finish? Would we pay? Could we pay?

My father barely came up with the tuition money at the last hour of the last day of late registration, two weeks into the semester. I didn't tell anyone. Who was there to tell? I hardly had a friend yet. What was there to say? He'd meet me on Greene Street with a bank check in hand—no more personal checks—sweat dripping from his face.

I thought he might get a heart attack, or a stroke, right there, around the corner from the Bottom Line. "Daddy, where'd you get the money from?" I was twenty-one now, twenty-two, not a little kid holding his hand at Shea Stadium.

"Don't worry about it," he said. "That's not your concern." Maybe it was from a sister, maybe from loan sharks from East Harlem, maybe from a friend/client, maybe a combination of sources. But all this, was it killing him? He'd always had high blood pressure—was I making everything worse?

One of those semesters when it looked as if we wouldn't be able to pay, my father told me to go to class anyway, deal with the professors personally. "Just tell them it's a money issue, and your father will straighten it out with the bursar," he said. "No professor would lock you out of a class. I fail to believe that. These are intellectuals we're talking about here. I read these academic books. They're above that."

"No one's above money," my mother said to me.

The extra semester came out of my own pocket. NYU said they would defer the entire semester's payment to me, interest free, and I could pay, upon graduation, in installments, small installments. I was grateful. I'd worry about it later. The journalism school had a good internship program, and I ended up as a fact-checker at a prominent magazine my last semester for twenty hours a week. I was still heavily involved in the student newspaper, helping to convert it from a biweekly to a daily, often working until two, three in the morning, sometimes taking a taxi back home—if they would go to Co-op City. Experience, that's what was most important now.

I wouldn't be invited to graduation in Washington Square Park the following May, because of the arrears, nor would I be given my diploma. Still, this didn't bother me. The school gave me a copy of my transcript, verifying that I completed all of my credits, and said they would confirm that if any potential employers contacted them.

And graduation, maybe it was nice, but I had already gotten a full-time job, in an unofficial recession, at the same magazine where I interned. Again, I was grateful.

Who were these magazine people? I wondered. When I finally settled in with a group of friends at NYU, at the newspaper, they were mainly locals, from Brooklyn, Queens, Long Island, New Jersey.

Here, almost no one was from New York, and not the New York of one-hour-and-twenty-minute commutes. There were no black people and there was only one Hispanic, who did the photocopying, nothing more. I told my parents. My father said, "Oh, God, isn't that against the law?" My mother said, "Figures. And I bet they're all good liberals. What hypocrites." *Never trust a liberal.*

Two young editors there showed me things. They talked to me. One was from a small town in Texas, the other from a small town in Pennsylvania. They were a few years older than I, but they seemed so much smarter. They invited me out for a beer when no one else did, after work when I had nothing to do except take the long subway ride back to the Bronx. They were good to me; they didn't have to be. There was nothing I could do for them, they had nothing to gain.

It was because of them that I even got the full-time job. I interned for them and when something opened in another department, they threw my name in the hat, sang my praises. When I had to meet the editor in chief for the final interview, they prepped me.

"Try to steer the conversation to the outdoors," they said. "He's really into that."

"But I don't know the outdoors," I said. "I can't even swim."

"Okay, you don't want to advertise that," one said.

"What about fishing," the other said. "Did your father ever take you fishing, hunting, that kind of stuff?"

"No, never."

"Cars? Are you into cars?"

"Not really. I never owned one. My parents' car was stolen and we never bought another one. I have a license, but only got it two years ago. I haven't driven since." I didn't say that my father couldn't drive.

"Okay, so don't bring up cars. Oh, he likes alternative rock. He might bring up Jane's Addiction. You can talk about that."

"Who?" I said.

"You don't know them—Perry Farrell?"

"Never heard of them."

"No? Well, make it up as you go along," they said, finally.

I was hired.

My mother said: "We should invite those two boys over. They've been good to you. I could make a lasagna."

"But then they'd have to come to Co-op," I said. "Maybe that's not the best idea."

"Yeah, who knows what they might think?"

"What if there's urine in the elevator or something happens to them?" I asked.

"God, you better not."

And we never did.

We had beers, one of these young editors and I, after work. He asked me about my background, my family, the Bronx, what it was like. Slowly, I told him about my father, the bookmaking, the phones, the trips, all of it. "But don't tell anyone," I said.

"Wow," he said. "You've got to write about it."

"What do you mean?" I said.

"You should write a book," he said.

"A book? I can't write a book," I said.

"Why can't you?"

"I don't know," I said. "I just can't. It seems impossible."

"Start small," he said. "Write that story you just told me, and send it to *The New York Times Magazine*. They have a column called 'About Men.' This would be perfect for them."

"Yeah, right," I said.

"No, I'm being serious," he said.

"Well, I can't anyway," I said. "It's a secret."

When I told my mother that I told this very smart young editor about Daddy, the Super Bowls, the phones, the trips, she said, "What are you crazy? What are you telling people that for?"

"He won't say anything," I said.

"Yeah, but what he might think now."

"He thinks I should write about it," I said.

"What? Write about what, for who?"

"About Daddy, the gambling, what we saw. He even said I should write a book."

"Book?" she said. "What book? You can't write a book."

This was the first time I met people from Harvard, Princeton, Brown, Penn, Duke, Cornell, Barnard. They were hyperarticulate, hyper-ironic.

I was asked questions I'd never been asked before.

I was asked what I thought of Kurt. *I hate that music.*

I was asked which dorm I lived in at NYU—or did I live off-campus in the East Village? It was inconceivable that I commuted and I was asked why. And why did I still live with my parents.

I was asked what my parents did and where they went to school. I was asked what high school I went to.

I was asked, "Where do you live again?" The Bronx wasn't a

conceivable answer, but when it was the only answer, I was asked again—no, told—"you must live in that Little Italy up there, right?"

I heard someone say they didn't like Italian food, unless it was Northern.

I heard someone else say that her boyfriend's family was a typical Italian American family: That they watched TV and ate junk food. *Junk food? We don't eat junk food! Tell them we don't eat junk food.*

I read a page proof for the magazine, the magazine I worked for, the very smart, sophisticated magazine, that said this: "Worst New Trend: Retro Italian American restaurants with names like Carmine's and Vinny's that serve the kind of dago-red glop that once made Brioschi an Italian hero." I wanted to say something, but sensed it would be held against me. *You're lucky to be here.* I was there, but only as an entry-level copy editor; I was there to question whether *dago* should be uppercase or lowercase. It was taken out, but how did it even make it to the page-proof stage. I photocopied it; I knew no one would believe me.

I heard for the first time, the term "guinea-T." *(Guinea, uppercase or lower?)* When I went home I asked my mother what she called those tank-top undershirts. She said, "I don't know, just undershirts. White, ribbed tank-tops. Why?" I told her at work they called them guinea-Ts.

She said, "What? No. Who said that? Don't tell your father."

I didn't tell her about the dago-red glop reference, even if I had a copy. I didn't tell her that my nickname at work was Mickey the Squid, that it was my "mafia" name, that it was joke, that I think it was a joke. There was always something to get. It was psychological, intellectual hazing. Maybe. I think. This would have crushed her, and my father. After Clark University, NYU, and the travels, trips that they saw as an additional education, the Prado, the Louvre, the Rijksmuseum, all that money it cost them, money they didn't have, their son was given a mafia nickname.

And I was expected to laugh. *Don't think you're better than you are.*

There were others, there was always someone who made me want to stay. An editor from the South invited me to watch college basketball with his wife and him. They said, "Don't worry if you don't know Anthony Kiedis, you know Gil Scott-Heron, that's all that counts." They said, "Don't worry if you don't fish, or fly-fish, you have that sweet twenty-foot jumper."

Another editor recognized the photograph of the Maracana, in Rio, on my desk and immediately took me to a soccer game, ex-Cosmos players vs. the 1982 Italians. Rossi and Gentile signed my World Cup book. *Wait till I show my sister.* He said he remembered Rossi, that he was there, with his father that day, in Barcelona, in the stadium, for Italy-Brazil, 3–2. *Really?!*

They were nice to me. They didn't have to be.

At this new job, everyone called me Michael. Maybe because that's what was listed in the masthead. Before that, in Co-op City, Rye Playland, even in college, I was always Mike. So when I heard someone call out my name—Mike Agovino!—I thought this could be someone from my deep past. It was. It was Ahmad. I smiled. *Yo, sup, man?*

I had just joined a gym to finally try to build up my skin-and-bones frame, and one evening there he was. It was good to see him. I thought he'd become a doctor or lawyer, maybe go into politics, run for office, but he was working as a TV producer for a famous African-American broadcaster. He asked me what I was up to, how my family was. Then he asked, "What about Calvin?"

"I don't know," I said. "I just hope he's okay, wherever he is."

"I thought of him during the Gulf War," he said.

"Yeah, so did I—and I knew three other guys from 181 who joined the Marines. But Ravi had told me that Calvin was discharged. I don't think he was over there."

"Oh, I didn't know that," he said. "And how's Ravi?"

"Don't know," I said. "He told me that ages ago. I can't remember the last time I saw him. I think he left Co-op. I'm not really in touch with anyone there these days."

"Yeah, me either," Ahmad said. "I live in the city now."

"Really?" I said. "So do I." I might have said I had my own place.

We hugged—or did we shake hands?—and promised to keep in touch.

My place—*I didn't really call it that, did I?*—came by way of an occasional co-worker at the magazine. Not a co-worker, really, but a writer, only a few years older, but who seemed to me like a world-wise correspondent. He was fluent in French. He told someone in the office, who told me, that he had this apartment, a small studio. He had the lease for years, then passed it on to his sister, then they sublet it. Now he had it back, but was moving on to something bigger. "Do you want to look at it? It's in Manhattan, in Yorkville, off First Avenue."

"Sure," I said. "Thanks, man."

It was on the top floor of a five-story walk-up. It was cheap, but my starting salary at the magazine was only $20,500. I'd barely be able to afford it. It was that or the company's 401(k) program. I chose the rental. It was time.

"It's time to get out of the Bronx." My friend at the magazine said that to me. I came in for the second time in a month and said, "You won't believe what happened to me on the subway this morning."

I'd never been a victim of a crime. I was lucky, all those years. Then, like that, there were two incidents, both on the way to work. I was on the 6 train as always. I was in the last car, it was nearly empty. The commute always had me exhausted so I closed my eyes and tried to sleep. I did this all through college and nothing ever happened. Then I felt something. The doors were open and it was the 116th Street stop in Manhattan, my father's old neighborhood. Something felt different. I recently needed eyeglasses for the first time in my life, and realized that they were no longer on my face. Someone just took them, either as a joke and just because. I never liked the glasses—I thought they made me look like a nerd, possibly a target—but they were nice tortoiseshell frames, not cheap, and they were just stolen right off my face.

I had another second before the doors would close or it would be too late. I jumped out of the subway car, the door closed behind me, the train pulled out of the station, and it was just me and them, two thugs that I couldn't even see well, probably my age, maybe younger, at the end of an empty platform on 116th. I should have stayed on the subway and pretended I was still asleep.

This was the stupidest thing I'd ever done. I was still groggy from sleep. I said this: "Yo, gimme my glasses back."

They turned around and looked surprised. They got on the balls of their feet, in a fighting position, and said, "Yeah, you want your glasses back?" I thought if they pull a gun or a knife, I'm dead. And people, a lot of people, got killed in New York for less.

I put my hands away from my sides, palms facing them, and said, "I just want the glasses back." *Never be intimidated; never show you're afraid.*

"Yeah, you want them back?" they said again.

"That's all," I said. "I don't want no trouble, fellas."

"Yeah? Here," they said, and tossed them toward me on the platform, and walked away, looking back at me every few steps.

I slowly picked them up and hoped they would keep moving toward the exit. And they did. I looked down the tunnel and saw the headlights coming from the next train. I was lucky. *You wouldn't believe what happened to me just now on the subway.*

Three weeks later, I was on the same train, crowded this time. I had to stand. A black man suddenly was in my face, mumbling, making no sense.

"What?" I said. People looked.

He was nose to nose with me, and I realized he was either out of his mind or high, and because of that even more dangerous—with less to lose—than I could probably imagine.

At different times in my life, I had been the only white person in a public school classroom, the only white person in a packed elevator, in a school yard playing basketball, on city buses in the Bronx, the only white person walking on Gun Hill Road, the only white person on a subway car, in a kitchen deep in the bowels of the Jacob Javits Convention Center, and I hadn't been afraid. Maybe once or twice or three times, but not usually. There was no reason to be. I noticed if I was the only white person, but I wasn't afraid. Often, I preferred being the only white. Usually, I was completely at ease. *What, you sleep on the subway?* This was something else. I'd never seen a look like this in anyone's eyes, and so close.

"Yo, chill," I said to him. The whole crowded subway car was watching now.

Then I felt his hands trying to get in my pockets.

As scared as I was, I tried not to show it. I had to do something fast. I pushed my arms hard into his chest and mumbled something like "Yo, what the fuck?" to try to sound tough. I realized I wasn't street tough nor was I an ironic, brainiac nerd. So where did that leave me? He backed into someone else, people began scurrying out of the way, and he started back at me. *People had gotten killed for less in New York.*

The subway came to its next stop, 125th Street. I put up my arms and prepared to push back again, but before I could, someone, a big Puerto Rican, came from my left and grabbed him in a bear hug and threw him out of the subway car and onto the platform. A woman screamed, people piled out of the car, others in, oblivious to what was happening. I stood next to the Puerto Rican in case the insane, drugged black man came back in the car. But he disappeared into the confusion.

"Hey, thanks, man," I said. "You okay?"

"Yeah, no problem," he said. "I'm just sick of these people, what they're doing to this city." And then he said it again, louder, for the whole subway car to hear: "I'm sick of these fuckin' people!" *Time to get out of the Bronx.*

I thought I'd be in Co-op City forever. Now I was leaving. The lease on the studio apartment was mine now. The new landlord owned a few buildings in the area from what I could gather and just asked me a few questions over the phone. That was it. He sounded old, though I never met him.

The move wasn't one day, or one weekend. It wasn't big hugs and good-byes and waves from U-Hauls. I had no friends here anymore, just people I might nod to while waiting for the elevator—that and people I wish I hadn't recognized. It wasn't triumphant; I couldn't help feeling I was abandoning my family.

I did it all in stages. I brought the bare essentials little by little—clothes, books, records, a bow-tie antenna, the Technics turntable, the JVC box that still served as my stereo—picked out a futon with my parents, and lugged a TV up the four flights with a college friend. My sister gave me two pots and a bowl she used when she lived off campus in Worcester. Someone else I worked with gave me her old couch, a TV stand, some cutlery.

Even when I moved in, I went home on weekends. It was still required that I be there for Sunday dinner.

"It's not the same without you," my sister said.

And then they asked: "What's it like living in Manhattan?"

My last picture of Co-op City wasn't of boxes or masking tape or suitcases or moving vans. It was from a few months before, in the spring. It was during the Los Angeles riots, three thousand miles away, after the Rodney King verdict. I opened the terrace door one of those days, leaned my forearms on the concrete wall, and with the Bronx fanned out before me, just gazed, as we often did. *We had a nice view, I'll say that.*

As usual, it was windy. It was always windy in Co-op, so much so that we used to walk backward to P.S. 178 and I.S. 181, to keep the gust out of our faces. To my left, on the immense chevron monolith that was Building 3, I saw something flapping in the wind from a top-floor terrace. It was the American flag. *But why now?* It wasn't something you saw very much of here. And the Fourth wasn't until July Fourth, Memorial Day another month away. This was late April. Then I looked again. The flag was flying upside down.

PENNSYLVANIA STATION (OR SOUTH TOWARD HOME), 1993

We crowded, the four of us, into my Manhattan studio apartment for one night, another night, and one more after that. It was the tightest of tight squeezes, my parents sharing the futon, my older sister on the couch, in a fetal position to fit, and me on the floor, with a comforter to cushion my bones from the unforgiving hardwood.

It was an extended layover for them, from point A to permanent point B, one lease expiring, another one commencing. A three-day difference. The interim they would spend with me in the apartment I'd been renting the past six months. They were moving, after all these years.

It was an interminable three days. It was May, early May 1993—the Derby went off that Saturday—and warm. Me on the top floor of an unremarkable walk-up, four flights, the heat rising with each one. We were, as my mother might have said, like sardines, sharing the one room, the bathroom, and the kitchen, which only held one to begin with.

We'd been crammed like this before, in surer times. Ten and fifteen and twenty years before in our travels. A younger family of four, a husband, wife, and their two little kids, usually in two rooms but sometimes, for whatever reason, packed into one, until we were onto the next city—to Palermo or Casablanca or Fort-de-France or Strasbourg.

Now my mother and father were living in Manhattan, for just three days, but didn't it feel different not to have to take a subway or bus back to the Bronx at dusk? On the Upper East Side no less—Yorkville, formerly Germantown. At least it was close to a home turf.

They would talk, yell eventually, the walls encroaching, over a meal—my mother could always make something out of nothing, even in my kitchenette. He'd say, as if we needed reminding, that he was raised thirty blocks from here, *a hun' fifteenth*. She'd say, louder to keep up, that she twice gave birth at New York Hospital, fifteen blocks the other direction. He would say: "Where they took out my gallstones, don't forget, in 'seventy-seven." And we said: "And was paid for when?" and laughed.

As Day Three came and went—*God, I can't believe we're leaving*—my mother, father, sister repacked their last bags and got a taxi to Pennsylvania Station. I wasn't there—I put the bags in the trunk of the taxi, and hugged them curbside on my block—but my mother said this, I know she did: "Look at this Penn Station, how filthy it's gotten. And to think what it was." From there they boarded an Amtrak train, direction south, to their new home.

Did I say home? I meant to say apartment—bad habit. They heard about this city in the New South, in the paper, by word of mouth, that it was up-and-coming and affordable. They made two short trips and decided to make the move. It was that quick. "The air smelled of gardenia," my mother said. Co-op City wasn't getting any better—and they'd been there all that time. *If we don't like it, we'll move* turned into twenty-three years. The goal was to leave, for the last five, ten years, for my mother the last twenty, and it was finally happening. My mother never cried. But what happened when she taped the last boxes, with all those Christmas ornaments, everyone loved our Christmas tree, or stood on the terrace for the last time and remembered when the streets of Co-op City weren't even paved yet, or went into the kitchen, where she spent so much of her time, and looked up at the corner windows of the twenty-fourth floor, where the Cohns used to live? Or when she opened the front door, she could see Ricardo cheerfully wave his cane sword, *How's Mikey?* Or the last ride into the city, on the express bus, how they were so much more comfortable than the subways, even if the kids in the South Bronx occasionally threw rocks at them? I never asked her.

They didn't want to leave New York. They hated it, *this city's going to pot*, but they still loved it. It's the only place they belonged. *But where do you go?* Their last date in Manhattan, when they were still living in Co-op, was the Matisse show at MoMA and the movie *We the Living.*

My father's business, his bookmaking, whittled to nothing. His credit—formal credit, street credit—was shot. He couldn't gather new investors, he wouldn't be able to pay his clients. He thought if he could make one more go of it, have a windfall, a streak, even if only for a month or two, thirty-five, forty Gs, *maybe for a down payment or something.* It never happened. The business, slowly, quietly, folded. The phones, the two lines we had, once alive, *ringing off the hook*, were quiet now. A call here, another one there, the bets once a hundred, or two hundred times, became five times and then nothing. His gambling, the addiction—*was that addiction?*—ended. He simply stopped.

He retired, after forty years of service, from the Department of Welfare, now known as the Department of Social Services, two years before, in 1991. He was given a luncheon and a plaque. Everyone came, his boss for the last six years, the best boss he ever had, a black woman who came to his mother's funeral, who treated him with dignity, who knew of his side business, but never made it an issue, who didn't judge, who wasn't petty, who let him be, as long as he kept it out of the workplace, which he did.

Leon was there, his colleague from the 1950s, and so was the playwright Loften Mitchell. They talked about Romare Bearden, how he would've been there if he hadn't passed on three years ago. They talked about Bearden's farewell luncheon from the department, one like this, when my father was one of a few people to say a few words about the artist.

The forty years gave him memories—Romey, the Non-Residence Center, the blackout of 1977—and a pension, a viable one. At least that. And Social Security to come.

But now what? Where to go, where to live? What do you do if you don't have five, six, seven figures in a 401(k), IRA, or savings? What if life didn't work out like that, neat and tidy? Where do you go when you can't afford a home? When you can't afford your home, your city? When your city, even now, in May 1993, after it's gone to hell in a hand-basket, is still the place to be, still the place for strivers from Indiana, by way of the Sorbonne, who couldn't care less that you're from here, that you're rooted here, that you helped make it what it was, in your own small way. What would those people say? *That's not my problem. You have the money or you don't. You don't, well whose fault is that?*

For what they paid in Co-op City they would rent a nice apartment in a town house complex in the New South, across the street—a wide six-lane street—from a bookstore, a movie theater, and a great big super-market. It wasn't a dream house, it wasn't Westchester, it wasn't even a house, it wasn't ownership, but it was a new beginning. *We'll give it a shot.*

If this very new place didn't have the cans of imported tomatoes we used, the imported olive oil, the veal cutlet pounded paper thin, just wait, they were told, this is a boomtown. You don't drive? Well, it's not normal down here but you can manage—maybe. The mall is not far.

My sister was with them. Her plan was this: She would accompany my parents, help them settle in, and head for Seoul, South Korea, to teach English as a second language. She'd heard there was opportunity there. After a year or two there, perhaps Taiwan. She hadn't been to Asia before and wanted to go—not for a week or two, or a month, but to be there. *You won't believe this, but some of it looks like Co-op City.*

She had been back with us in the Bronx, after Clark University and after her internship in Central America. She worked for the Manhattan District Attorney's Office, *that's Morgenthau's office*, as a paralegal, the kind of paralegal where you didn't need a certificate or advanced degree. In other words, a low-paying paralegal.

She thought about law school, or some postgraduate work, which seemed natural for her; she'd always been studious. But this wasn't an option, not now, probably not ever. As generous as Clark was, she was still deep in student-loan debt, six years later.

But her job was a respectable one. It was in the news in those years, not so much because it was Robert Morgenthau's office—yes that— but because John F. Kennedy Jr. began work there.

When my sister told people where she worked, she answered the question before they asked it. "No, I haven't seen him yet."

Then finally, sometime in 1990, she came home and said, "I saw him today."

"Really," my mother said. "Where?"

"In the elevator," my sister said. "He held it open for me."

"What? Really?" my mother said, excited.

"It was no big deal," my sister said.

"What did he say? He seems so nice."

"Nothing, he just held it open."

"And what did you say?"

"Just thank you," my sister said.

"And what did he say?"

"Nothing, he kept going."

"Wow. You'll probably run into him again," my mother said.

"What difference does it make?" my sister said. "I'm not in his league. Nowhere near."

"You never know."

"Please, Mom."

_____

Two months later, July 1993, I went to their new home, their new apartment, for the first time. When I walked in, I saw the flight of steps, and ran up the steps and then down the steps, up again, then down.

The apartment was smaller than the one in Co-op City, only two bedrooms, not three—I'd be sleeping on the couch—still no den, and room only for one bookcase, not all three. Most of the books, and my father was still ordering them, austere books, *those damn books—Chivalry* by Maurice Keen; *The Dark Brain of Piranesi and Other Essays* by Marguerite Yourcenar; *Suleiman the Magnificent* by Anthony Bridge; *Robert The Bruce: King of Scots* by Ronald McNair Scott; *Ciardi Himself; Fatal Decision: Anzio and the Battle for Rome* by Carlo d'Este; *The War in Italy: 1943–1945: A Brutal Story* by Richard Lamb—would have to be put into storage.

But we had steps, and we never had steps before, and I said, "Wow, it's like our own house."

I liked it there. I liked the bookstore across the street; I was astounded by the supermarket, with its soda aisles forty yards long, even if we didn't drink soda. "So far, so good," my mother said, though she was worried about fitting in, *the South is a different culture*, that maybe we stood out, looked different, looked too ethnic. She told me to wear a baseball cap to blend in.

"I don't wear baseball hats," I said. "But next time I'll bring an old-style New York baseball Giants hat I have." *I ever tell you the story when I went up the Polo Grounds and saw Warren Spahn?*

"No," she said. "Nothing with an N.Y. on the front. I get the sense they don't like New York down here."

"Oh, would you stop it," my father said.

"They probably take us for Jews and they don't like Jews in the South. And they like us less."

"Cut it out," he said. "That was when we were growing up. Times have changed. This is 1993. Don't give him a complex." *You wanted to move here.*

After a week, I had to get back—back home. To my job, my respectable and low-paying one. *And you're lucky to have it.*

Later that year, I was asked this, a simple-enough question from a co-worker: "Are you going home for Christmas?" No, I said, I was going South, to see my parents.

As if I was being sarcastic, she said, "Ah, so you *are* going home Christmas."

"No," I said, "my home is here. New York is my home." *This is where I'm from, where my parents are from. My father's from Harlem, East Harlem—you ever heard of Pleasant Avenue? My mother's from Bushwick, in Brooklyn. My mother's parents, they were from Brooklyn, Flatbush. I was born in Manhattan, grew up in the Bronx, twenty-four years, the northeast Bronx, in a place that used to be called Freedomland, that they made into the largest housing complex in the country, maybe the world, though my mother always called it a project, a glorified project. It's called Co-op City, do you know it?*

EPILOGUE

I will have spent my life trying to understand the function of remembering, which is not the opposite of forgetting, but rather its lining. We do not remember, we rewrite memory much as history is rewritten. How can one remember thirst?

—*Chris Marker*

ROME, 1995

My father was endlessly curious about my job. I mailed him every issue of the magazine. He asked me, over the phone, if they talked about Isaiah Berlin in the office. He envisioned a place of political, artistic grappling, and that his books, now in storage, would provide my entryway. There was back-and-forth, but not how he envisioned it.

"No," I said, "they talk about Nirvana and *The Simpsons*."

"The what?"

I wasn't sure if he couldn't hear me, so often the case, or he didn't know who and what *The Simpsons* were."

"*The Simpsons*," I said. "It's a cartoon. They talk about pop culture."

"Cartoons? What are you talkin' about, cartoons? I thought you said these are highly educated people."

"They are, more than me, but they have original takes on pop culture, they look at it from different perspectives, with distance, irony."

"But it's still pop culture."

"I guess, but—"

"Never mind," he said. "Read Isaiah Berlin. And Meyer Berger, do they talk about Meyer Berger? He was a great writer, Meyer Berger."

"Who?"

After three years, I wanted to try to write. I was awed by some of what I read in the magazine. Even fashion captions and three-hundred-word articles were packed with erudition and wit. One writer, just two years older than me, described Stomp—the music, dance, and performance-art troupe that incorporated found objects—as "dada with a face." Wow, I thought, what a line, how did he come up with that? Someone else wrote that Bernd and Hilla Becher's photographs "not only serve as memento mori of the fading industrial era, they imbue the most unlovely, unloved of objects with a fragile and poetic might. They are, perhaps, the last picture show." *Damn!* That's how I wanted to write. But there was little opportunity at the magazine. *Is it just me, man?* You were expected to pay your dues, but it had been three years of dues and dues only.

Then I surprised even myself: I got something published in *The New York Times*, the Styles section. *What,* The New York Times*?! Are you kidding?* That was my mother.

"Well, it's not that big a deal. It's short."

"Still, it's *The New York Times*. How'd you do that?"

I explained to her that if you mailed them a letter, wrote it well, as if you were writing the article, they would consider it. In this case, I wrote the proposal letter to the nephew of a famous writer.

My parents couldn't believe it. "What was he like?"

"He was nice."

"And he's some writer that kid. We read his byline all the time."

The article wasn't a big deal. It was on the history of the World Cup poster. I cited Joan Miró, Antoni Tapies, and Annie Leibovitz.

"Well, you're not Clement Greenberg yet, but it's very well done," my father said. "I commend you." *You're familiar with Clement Greenberg, aren't you?*

It was so not a big deal that no one at my job saw it.

My mother said: "Did people at work say anything?"

"No," I said.

"Why not?"

"I don't know? Maybe they didn't see it."

"Oh, please," she said, "they don't read the Sunday *New York Times*? Of course they do. Everyone reads the Sunday *Times*. I read the Sunday *Times*."

I wrote a few more articles—small pieces on Romare Bearden, those small football gambling slips, and Gil Scott-Heron. *Write what you know.* My father couldn't have been prouder. Then I wrote a longer profile on Gianni Amelio, an Italian film director from Calabria, and another on Albert Murray, the Harlem intellectual, who was close friends with Bearden; he had original Beardens in his foyer! *Did you tell him I knew Romey?*

Still, I couldn't get even a blurb at the magazine I worked for.

"What should I do?" I asked my mother over the phone.

"I don't know what advice to give you," she said. "I don't know that world. Talk to your father."

The year before when I told him I was fed up and wasn't going to go to the office Christmas party, he told me: "No, you go. You put on a coat and tie, you have a scotch, seek out the editor, give a firm handshake, offer to buy him a drink, and you thank him for the good year."

"That's it?"

"Well, he's Irish, he'll have a drink, won't he?"

"Yeah, I guess, but that's not the point," I said. "Besides, he's from out West."

"So?"

"Daddy, he's not like the Irish guys you know," I said. "He's not like the New York Irish."

"Never mind," my father said. "You give him a firm handshake. He'll appreciate that."

I didn't say anything back; I just exhaled. I don't know if he heard my exasperation over the phone. *Don't make out you're getting angry.*

Then he said: "You're good, you're quality. Be sincere. Always be honest. Write with honesty. Keep jabbing."

"What? Keep jabbing? Be sincere?" I said, annoyed out loud this time. *That's it? Nothing about building alliances, strategizing, reading Machiavelli, knowing whose rear end to kiss, keeping your friends close, your enemies closer?*

"Sincerity is out," I said.

"What's that?" he said. "I didn't hear you."

"Nothing," I said.

And then he said: "Don't ever let anyone define you."

"I'm going to Rome," I told my parents over the phone. This was 1995. It would just be for a week, but I needed to be away—somewhere else, far. I was frustrated, still. We had a new editor, and I knew I wasn't going anywhere with him. He looked not through me, but past me. I didn't exist. He was from New York, but there wasn't even small talk, about the Knicks or Giuliani or Mike Tyson or Pete Hamill, how my parents forgave him and hoped I would get a chance to meet him now that he was writing for the magazine. *Though if you do get the opportunity, ask Hamill nicely why he wrote that vicious column that time.* No, not a word from this editor.

The previous editor, I did give him a firm handshake at that Christmas party. Did he appreciate it? Maybe, maybe not. It probably didn't even register. But at least he said hello.

I didn't have the money to go to Rome, but I had a credit card, something my father hadn't had since the early 1980s. Maybe my money should have gone to Fannie Mae or to NYU but it had been a dream of mine to go to the city of Bernini, Rossellini, Bruno Conti. I had been there before, but who could remember? I would charge it and worry about it later. It was off-season. I left on Halloween night.

"Take pictures," my mother said, excited. "Take lots of pictures. And write. Send postcards." They reminded me of all the things I had to see, the churches, Santa Maria Maggiore for sure, this and that piazza, the hills, the light—"the light in Rome is famous," my mother said—and see the Sistine Chapel. *We missed it that time.*

I left from the Eero Saarinen TWA building, the same terminal we left from in 1973, when things were surer. The glamour was faded now; there was talk of closing it. But then I remembered: the TWA flight bag, me chewing on the strap, frightened, my first flight, then falling asleep on my father's arm.

This was my first trip without my parents, the first time by myself. When I got out of the subway in Rome, I stopped a passerby for directions to my hotel. "Scusa, dove Via Germanico," I said, pronouncing it *German-ico*, as in Puerto Rico. He corrected me: "Via Ger-manico." I couldn't speak, even pronounce, the language of my grandparents from Campania, my great-grandparents from western Sicily.

I bought postcards, something of Bernini, something of the Forum, something of E.U.R., where Antonioni filmed, and sat down to write them. I didn't know what to say. That it's not the same without you, that the food isn't as good, the breakfast room not as fun, that it's not as alive. No, I couldn't write that. How silly. And they wouldn't want to hear that. *Would they?*

I couldn't say to my mother, "Sorry about your father, that he died, while I was here in Rome." I couldn't write that because I didn't know. None of us did until seven years later, when I did an Internet search.

Instead, I wrote them: "I'll have to come back, there's so much more to see. And you were right about the light. Why is that?"

When I visited my parents for Christmas, with my five rolls of photographs, I decided to rent a car. I hadn't done any driving since I got my license in 1988 and thought if I didn't reacclimate myself soon to being behind the wheel, I might not drive again.

I rented a subcompact, a white Geo Metro, the cheapest one, for a week. I didn't feel altogether comfortable behind the wheel, I never had, but especially not now, and asked my father to accompany me, to destinations unknown, just to practice.

"How much did this run you?" he asked me in the car.

I told him whatever price it was.

"Not cheap," he said. "Like abuman' Bence used to say." He knew I knew the rest. *Would it be three thousand dollars a week by now?*

"Daddy, how did Bence die?"

"Oh, I never told you that story?"

"No."

"I must have."

"No, I would've remembered."

"He was in the hospital, up the Bronx, and one day he just pulled everything out, all the tubes, everything. He didn't want to live no more."

"Oh."

He changed the subject. He thanked me for the pastries I brought. They had asked me to go to Ferrara's or Veniero's to pick up sfogliatelle, pastacroce, and pastachiotto, four of each, and a small struffoli. I complained—that they might turn bad or get crushed on the plane.

"Please," my mother said over the phone. "We miss that stuff so much."

"C'mon, Michael," my father said, "can't you do us the favor?"

So I did, reluctantly. I went to Veniero's.

As soon as my mother bit into the pastacroce, she said, "Oh, Veniero's went down. This isn't what it used to be."

This led to an argument, that I schlepped all the way down to Veniero's, dragged this stuff on the plane, and that's the thanks I got.

My father tried to calm us down. "Who do they have working there now?" he asked. "Any old-timers?"

"No," I said. "Young kids."

"Are they Italian?"

"No, they don't look it," I said.

In the car now, one fast-food restaurant after the next, some landscaped just so, he told me that the pastries weren't bad, that my mother overreacted. But that Veniero's was probably better in the days when Louie I, the racketeer from his old neighborhood, was working there. "He wasn't a baker of course, it was just a place to hang his hat, but he knew quality food."

"They tasted fine to me," I said.

"Next time you come," he said, "we'll need you to get us a new maganette." He was talking about the old-fashioned Neapolitan stove-top espresso maker. "You know where you get them, in Little Italy, on the corner there. It's an old dusty shop. An old lady runs it. You re-member? We used to go there on Good Friday, after DiPalo's. She sells all kinds of things, odds and ends, and she has the maganette. Four-cup, six-cup, eight-cup. We need a four-cup."

"I think I remember," I said. "Is it still there?"

"Sure it's still there. We only left what, three years ago. It must still be there."

"I'll check," I said. "Should be easy enough. Little Italy's only two blocks now, anyway."

I drove these well-kept roads, riding the brake so as not to rear-end cars in front turning in to strip malls. We talked more about New York, how he missed it, how he never wanted to leave. I realized there were no people out walking, even if it was a glorious, crisp day. I told my father that people, people in my industry, were starting to move to Brooklyn.

"Really? Isn't that something?" he said, and laughed. "You'll have to tell your mother that—she won't believe it. Giuliani is really clean-ing up the city. And I bet they don't even give him credit for it."

"No," I said. "They call him a fascist."

My father laughed. "Is that the best they can come up with?" he said. "He was never my favorite person in the world, but that really devalues the word."

"But even if he's started to clean things up," I said, "we won't be able to afford it. If we couldn't afford it then, we won't be able to afford it now, or later."

"Yeah," he said, quietly. I wasn't sure if he heard me. He often simply said "yeah" when he didn't hear me.

I felt eyes on me, eyes in bigger cars, in SUVs, in pickup trucks, looking down at the Geo-Metro and at me and my father. I was wear-ing a Texas A&M baseball cap that a college friend once bought me when he knew my nickname was once "Aggie." When these eyes were on me, I heard, *Y'all don't look like Texas A&M. Y'all look like Yankees.*

Then I turned into a mini-mall and front-ended a wall in the parking lot while I parked. *Shit!* I wasn't driving well; this was awkward.

My father ran inside to a wine store, loaded up on a few bottles— "might as well, since you have the car"—and said we should go to the storage space, to look at his books, to see if I wanted any. *They could be useful in your line of work.* Besides, he hadn't seen those books himself since they moved here. He missed them.

I told him I had no idea how to get there, to get anywhere in this place, that I still felt uncomfortable, even a little panicked, behind the wheel right now.

"Don't worry," he said, "I'll lead the way. And we have this map right here."

Still, we got lost. We ended up in a dark alley or as dark as alleys can get in the New South—*South to a Very New Place*, I thought— and I banged on the steering wheel and yelled at him to read the goddamn map that was right in front of him. "What the hell, Daddy? Jesus Christ!"

He let it go.

And we kept driving. Soon he was navigating, by instinct, as he had before, in places sometimes unfamiliar, in situations often unknown, always with me and for me: Make a right here, he said, now a left; careful that's a one-way street; see if you can't make a U-turn, no one's around; don't forget to signal. At a red light, I saw a bus. Only black people were aboard, but I knew that.

"How do you like the buses down here?" I asked.

"They're very good," he said. "Neat and clean, not like up North. I just wish they ran more frequently. I rely on them a lot."

Then he began directing again: Make a left at this corner; your turn was a little too wide; let this guy pass; slow down, what's the rush?; there's a stop sign; you're going to want to bear to your right now; yeah, you have plenty of room; why not change lanes here?; it's getting dark, better put on your headlights; do you know where the wipers are, just in case?; see the yield sign?; easy, they have the right of way; you're doing fine.

I relaxed, at another red light. And I realized this: My father was teaching me how to drive. "Now," he said, "tell me about your trip. Tell me all about Rome."

ACKNOWLEDGMENTS

My deepest gratitude to Jeanette Perez, a fine editor who handled this material—my life, and the lives of my parents—with great care and sensitivity. A sincere thank-you to my agent, Jennifer Gates, who believed in this project when few others did. Special thanks to Miles Doyle, who understood what I was trying to do from the start. Thank you to my sister, for her ongoing encouragement. And thank you to David Hirshey, in central midfield, for having faith in me.

Thank you also to Chris Raymond, Gueorgui Milkov, Jay Stowe, Erika Mansourian, Mark Warren, David M. Friedman, Domenico Sicilia, Brian Lee, and Jill Schwartzman. And thank you to Lila Cecil and Joy Parisi at Paragraph, their wonderful workspace.

At HarperCollins, thank you to Christine Van Bree, Emily Taff, Rachel Elinsky, and David Koral.

For photo assistance, thank you to Miranda Schwartz, Susan Kriete, and Itty Mathew at the New-York Historical Society; Laura Tosi at the Bronx Historical Society; Michael Massmann at Redux Pictures; Katrina Doerner; Michael Shulman at Magnum Photos; and Bruce Davidson.

With great love and admiration, thank you to Andrea Gohl. And lastly, as ever, to my parents, their stories, their memories, their words and deeds. Thanks again, for everything.

Selected Bibliography

Books:

Caro, Robert A. *The Power Broker*. New York: Alfred A Knopf, 1974.

Freeman, Joshua B. *Working-Class New York: Life and Labor Since World War II*. New York: The New Press, 2000.

Jackson, Kenneth T. *The Encyclopedia of New York City*. Yale University Press, 1995.

Meyer, Gerald. *Vito Marcantonio: Radical Politician, 1902–1954*. New York: State University of New York Press, 1989.

Mitchell, Joseph. *Up in the Old Hotel*. New York: Pantheon Books, 1992.

Orsi, Robert Anthony. *The Madonna of 115th Street: Faith and Community in Italian Harlem, 1880–1950*. New Haven and London: Yale University Press, 1985.

Plunz, Richard. *A History of Housing in New York City*. New York: Columbia University Press, 1990.

Other:

Schuman, Tony. Paper: "Labor and Housing in New York City: Architect Herman Jessor and the Co-operative Housing Movement."

The Brooklyn Historical Society, Exhibit, "Up In Flames."